KV-638-781

# The Falklands War

## Britain Versus the Past
## in the South Atlantic

*by* DANIEL K. GIBRAN

McFarland & Company, Inc., Publishers
*Jefferson, North Carolina, and London*

EDINBURGH UNIVERSITY LIBRARY

WITHDRAWN

COAUTHORED BY DANIEL K. GIBRAN

*The Exclusion of Black Soldiers from the Medal of Honor in World War II* (McFarland, 1997), with Elliott V. Converse, John A. Cash, Robert K. Griffith and Richard H. Kohn

British Library Cataloguing-in-Publication data are available

Library of Congress Cataloguing-in-Publication Data

Gibran, Daniel K., 1950–
    The Falklands War : Britain versus the past in the South Atlantic
/ by Daniel K. Gibran.
        p.    cm.
    Includes bibliographical references and index.
    ISBN 0-7864-0406-X (library binding : 50# alkaline paper) ∞
    1. Falkland Islands War, 1982.    2. Great Britain—Military policy.
I. Title.
F3031.5.G53   1998
997'.11024—dc21                                                        97-42193
                                                                        CIP

©1998 Daniel K. Gibran. All rights reserved

*No part of this book, specifically including the index, may be reproduced or transmitted in any form or by any means, electronic or mechanical, including photocopying or recording, or by any information storage and retrieval system, without permission in writing from the publisher.*

Manufactured in the United States of America

*McFarland & Company, Inc., Publishers*
  *Box 611, Jefferson, North Carolina 28640*

The Falklands War

To the glory of God and to my wife Joan
and our two daughters, Marianne and Nicole

# Table of Contents

# Preface

When Argentina invaded the Falkland Islands in April 1982, the South Atlantic was instantly transformed into a grand military stage that riveted the world's attention for the next seventy-four days. It was an unexpected limited war, fought for limited objectives with limited means in a remote corner of the globe. Yet much depended upon its outcome. At the end of the fighting in June, the Argentine military junta was completely disgraced, setting the stage for a return to democracy in a country long bowed by military dictatorship and oppression. For British prime minister Margaret Thatcher, victory in the Falklands vindicated the decision to resist Argentine aggression; represented a triumph of "democratic principles"; and guaranteed another term in office. For the British government, victory resulted in international respect and a reputation for standing tough against dictators. For the British people, victory inspired a wild euphoria and the conviction, so dear to a seafaring people, that Britannia still ruled the waves.

The Falklands War also had an impact on British defense policy and gave greater prominence to "out-of-area" conflict arenas. Prior to April 1982, allocations for out-of-area operations represented only a minuscule part of the defense budget. The defense of the homeland, of NATO waters and territory, constituted the major thrust of British defense dispositions. The war's impact on British defense policy can be measured by the many changes that took place afterwards against a background of economic constraints. In short, the Falklands War challenged the conceptual orthodoxy which attributes the reduction of Britain's defense dispositions entirely to economic factors.

Studies on British defense policy and on the Falklands War abound. They range widely in academic substance and style and cover topics from defense economics, history, and strategy to diplomacy, military operations, and politicostrategic lessons. But while most of these tomes discuss specific

1

aspects either of the conflict or of British defense policy, none juxtaposes the two in an interesting yet comprehensive way that constitutes a formidable challenge to postwar defense orthodoxy. Moreover, published works on the Falklands War are deficient in their treatment of British motivations to retake the islands, do not provide a careful, detailed, and judicious examination of the disputants' claims to sovereignty, and fail to offer a balanced analysis of the historical evidence.

This book attempts to bring balance to the contentious debate confronting postwar British defense policy. It challenges the common wisdom, asserting that in the formulation of postwar British defense policy, strategic developments in the international environment are at least as important as domestic economic considerations—perhaps more so. This work also provides a comprehensive examination of the motivations behind the government's decision to fight for lost territory. This examination takes place in the context of strategic realism and foreign policy considerations of pride, principles, prestige, and national honor.

The research for this book was completed a few years ago when I was a doctoral student at the University of Aberdeen in Scotland. Most of the primary and nearly all the secondary sources were found in the university's library, where the able staff frequently came to my rescue. As the research progressed, I had the good fortune to meet and interview a number of well-placed government officials whose insights and recollections proved extremely useful. Many took an interest in my research, and some even expressed delight in seeing a researcher from a former British colony attempting to come to grips with British defense policy—a preserve of the conservatives and upper class.

But I first became interested in the Falklands conflict during my year at the Institute of International Relations of the University of the West Indies in Trinidad. I was fascinated by this little war because I had an interest in warfare going back to my days in the British and Guyana military establishments. The British army at war meant to me a kind of personal involvement, distant but not completely detached. The idea of analyzing the Falklands War in the context of British defense policy never surfaced, however, until my first year at Aberdeen. My thesis adviser, Professor James Wyllie, suggested that such an analysis might pose a challenge to the conceptual framework of British defense. He turned out to be right. Jim was helpful in many ways, encouraging my approach to analysis and praising my style of writing.

I must pause here to thank certain other individuals who have aided me in the process of researching and writing this book. Lords Carver and

Lewin have been most generous with their time. Both provided me with many useful insights into the intricacies of British defense policy and of the Falklands War. It was Lord Lewin who first shed considerable light on a very critical aspect of the government's decision making as it relates to the time frame for war. While most researchers contend that the British decision to wage war in the South Atlantic was taken incrementally, Lord Lewin made it abundantly clear to this researcher that such was not the case.

Brenda Cool typed the entire manuscript with patience and skill. To her I owe a great debt of gratitude. I thank Professor Richard Kohn of UNC-Chapel Hill for his encouragement and friendship. My wife, Joan, and our two daughters, Marianne and Nicole, cheerfully endured long hours of my absence from home and were always encouraging. I thank them for their help in making their Dad's dream—his first solo book—a reality.

# Introduction

The Falklands War raises a number of compelling issues in both the theory and the practice of international relations. Some of these issues involve territorial conflicts, democracy versus totalitarian dictatorship, miscalculation and misperception, the role of cultural differences and historico-legal perspectives, and the hypothesis that statesmen will launch a war in order to distract the public from domestic problems.

Conflicts over territory are endemic in relations among states. But while they are not a permanent state of affairs and do not always lead to war, they nevertheless raise serious concerns about future relations and state-to-state military engagements. And in the Falklands War, the ownership of territory was indeed a topic of hot dispute between Britain and Argentina.

It is now a commonly held belief that democracies do not go to war with each other. The history of post–World War II conflicts suggests that democracies tend to rely on instruments other than military force to settle their conflicts. At the time of the Falklands War, Argentina was a military dictatorship. Indeed, the terms *fascist* and *totalitarian* were part of the language hurled at the military junta. This conception of Argentina as a totalitarian state made it easier for Britain, a strong democracy, to stand up to aggression even if it meant going to war.

Misperception and miscalculation of intentions also propelled the countries into war. That both belligerents misperceived each other's intentions is a fact worth noting. The Argentine junta did not believe that Britain, which was led by a woman prime minister and was experiencing severe domestic economic pressures, would resort to war in a theater eight thousand miles away. Britain, on the other hand, did not believe that the junta would forcefully grab territory, simply because it had not attempted this before. The two countries' miscalculations, based on a lack of empathy

5

for each other's interests, blinded policymakers to the pressures and constraints that shaped one another's decisions. This mutual miscalculation escalated until war was virtually unavoidable.

Apart from these important issues, the Falklands War was also noted for some peculiar characteristics. It came after a prolonged period of contentious, and sometimes twisted, legal and political posturing that emanated from a history shrouded in some mystery. It was a classic limited war in every sense of the term. And the British decision to fight for a piece of distant disputed real estate had more to do with strong feelings of national honor and pride than with budgetary constraints or domestic economic pressures.

The British actions in the Falklands War illustrated the importance of strategic realism—a posture dictated by vital interests. The projection and use of the instruments of national power for the defense of perceived national interest and the preservation of national pride, prestige, and honor underscored the fact that "high politics"—a demonstrated concern for political and strategic gains—still governs the world of global relations. But the pursuit of high politics is not an end in itself. It is merely one aspect, albeit a very important one, of a state's behavior. High politics mirrors the anarchical state of the international political system in the sense that there is no higher government endowed with supranational powers to maintain law and order. Clearly, states will continue to prosecute their own interests in their relations with other states. The British response, it would seem, demonstrated the role of defense policy in high politics—a posture that represents a "synergism of policies and programs designed to cope with not only outbreaks of hostility but to reinforce the process of peace."[1]

To understand British motivations for recapturing the Falkland Islands and to understand the effects of strategic realism on the formulation of British defense policy, one must enter the realm of theory. Theory is not opposed to reality. The two cannot be separated. Every statement that attempts to describe or explain anything relating to British motivations or defense policy, or in the world society as a whole, is a theoretical statement. It would be highly superficial to discuss issues of motivation and defense policy or other aspects of international relations solely on the basis of "facts." Facts are abstract. Any set of facts selected for analysis must have significance in a certain argument. In other words, they must be chosen from a much bigger menu of available facts because they are important. And their importance is measured by how well they fit a concept; how well the concept fits a theory; and how well the theory fits an overarching view of the world. Thus the view of the world as seen through realist spectacles provides the theoretical setting for this undertaking. And for the realist, the central problem of international politics is war and the use of force.

The picture of the world provided by the realist framework, though far from wholly adequate, offers a powerful synthesis of the behavior of states. This large idea has helped to shape "the explanations of international relations offered by the scholar, guides the decision-makers who conduct the policies, and prescribes the blueprint for each of the periodic attempts to reform the system of world politics."[2] Realism and realist ideas were best expressed, promulgated, and synthesized by Hans Morgenthau in his monumental *Politics Among Nations* (1948). The theoretical and comprehensive nature of this work made it the exemplar for realist thinkers. "Morgenthau's work," according to John Vasquez, a leading specialist in international relations theory, "was the single most important vehicle for establishing the dominance of the realist paradigm within the field."[3]

In *Politics Among Nations*, Morgenthau not only provided an account for the anomaly of World War II, but he also attempted to delineate those laws of behavior that appear to govern interactions among independent sovereign states. Further, he asserted that all politics is a struggle for power; that states strive continuously to protect their perceived national interests; and that the power of one or more states can be effectively limited by the power of another. His delineation provided a view of the world for the international relations scholar and practitioner. That view has gained widespread acceptance, and although its universal dominance has declined, it continues to provide a framework for the analysis of conflicts and state behavior. This book draws heavily on that perspective.

When the British decided to recapture the Falkland Islands after their forceful seizure by Argentine troops on 2 April 1982, the decision appeared at the time to be based on several considerations. From a realist perspective, that decision clearly underscored the security objective of foreign policy. And the pursuit of that objective revealed in no uncertain way that domestic economic constraints could be pushed aside for the higher political considerations of perceived national interests. Thus the question of affordability in defense policymaking is a relative one. A state, it seems, can always find or mobilize the resources it needs in order to protect its interests. The Falklands War unambiguously illustrated that realist propensity in state behavior. The war also demonstrated, as will be discussed in this book, that Britain fought for considerations of national pride and prestige which the government justified and perceived to be vital.

No one denies the fact that in a democracy the resources allocated for defense are normally constrained. The competing demands for resources from other sectors of the economy continuously restrict public spending. But for the defense of the realm and considerations of national security, the amount of the allocation is not determined purely by domestic economic considerations. Other factors, notably strategic developments and the nature of external threats, will ultimately determine the level of appropriations that will be allocated to the defense effort. Economic considerations do indeed arise and, in fact, do impose some kind of limit on the resources that are available for defense. This is particularly the case in a pluralist Western democracy, where a state would not want to be militarily stronger than its basic economy would allow. There has to be a sensible balance that provides a defense capability commensurate with the tasks given to the country's armed forces.

The analysis advanced in this book does not deny the constraining effects of economic factors on the formulation of British defense policy. Rather, it challenges the idea that those factors are, and have been, the predominant influence on British defense policy. Overemphasis on that line of argument for the past three decades has unbalanced the intellectual debate and distorted the larger picture of British defense policy. Defense capability is an instrument of national power and must be kept in rough parity with the political and security dictates of the international environment. In short, the development of defense capabilities must go hand in hand with both economic and politicostrategic considerations.

Apart from this thesis, which is the thrust of this book, I shall also examine some of the significant motivations behind the British decision to recapture the Falkland Islands. These motivations not only serve to illuminate an important aspect of decision making, but also strengthen the case for the politicostrategic arguments. The hypotheses examined in this analysis reflect the diversity of ideas found in the general literature on the Falklands War.

To accomplish the twofold goal of this book—that is, to examine the motivations and to propose and defend my major thesis—I will attempt to answer the following questions:

1. Who owns the Falkland Islands and why is the issue of sovereignty so contentious?
2. Why did Argentina invade and seize British territory? What were the deep-seated and "strike-out" conditions that impelled the junta to use military force?
3. What were the real motivations behind the British decision to recapture the Islands, and when and how was that decision taken?

4. What military, technological, and strategic lessons can be learned from the war?
5. Did the Falklands War bring about a shift in British defense policy?
6. If so, what was the extent and significance of that shift, and how did it shape the future of British defense policy?
7. As a significant case, did the war effectively demonstrate the impact of politicostrategic considerations in the formulation of British defense policy?

Chapter One provides background information. It examines each nation's claim to sovereignty as well as Britain's relationship with the Falklands prior to their forceful seizure by Argentina on 2 April 1982. It is readily apparent that neither Britain nor Argentina can make an indisputable case for sovereignty; both sides' claims rely in part on ill-formed arguments. This book points out, however, that despite some strong reasoning from the Argentine side, the British claim, resting on extinctive prescription, is on balance more solid and persuasive. The distinction between acquisitive and extinctive prescription is a crucial one and will be given adequate treatment in this chapter. Although both forms of prescription entail the possession of territory over a long, continuous period, only through extinctive prescription could Britain bolster its case. In the end, though, the entire conflict between the two belligerents in early 1982 was reduced to issues of will and power. Julius Goebel, the American author of the standard work *The Struggle for the Falkland Islands* (1929), made the salient observation that "there is a certain futility in interposing the lean and ascetic visage of the law in a situation which, first and last, is merely a question of power."[4]

While Britain had both the will and the power to seize the Falkland Islands in 1833, its determination to regain them in 1982 cannot be attributed to these two factors alone. The issues facing Downing Street in 1982 were too complex to allow such a simple explanation. Thus Chapter One also examines the critical issue of Britain's interest in the southwest Atlantic region prior to April 1982. Britain's overall behavior in that subregion, brought about largely by a diminution of its strategic interest, created a certain perception among Argentine leaders which emboldened their adventurous policies. It is widely accepted that British policies and pronouncements encouraged Argentina to execute its invasion plans. The British Defence Review of 1981, the proposed withdrawal of the ice-patrol ship HMS *Endurance*, a new Nationality Act that denied British citizenship to the Falkland Islanders, and the intended closing of the British Antarctic

Survey base (the only British presence on the island of South Georgia), all suggested to the Argentines that Britain was either losing interest in the region or compelled to leave the area.

Chapter Two broadens the analysis by weaving into the tapestry a few strands that explain Argentina's behavior. The motivations behind the junta's decision to seize the Falklands by military force are not as clearcut as they might seem. Among the variables one must examine are systemic variables relating to great power status, United States support, strategic gains, and a multitude of domestic economic, political, and social factors that made for an explosive situation. It will be argued that this combination of domestic factors provided the "strike-out" conditions for the unpopular military dictatorship to divert attention by launching the invasion. Chapter Two also examines the British military response and the legal dimensions of the use of force in the Falklands War. Underscoring both these subtopics is the view that Britain was acting in legitimate self-defense. The rapid assembly and dispatch of the Task Force attested to not only the depth of British logistical expertise, but as Lord Lewin, admiral of the fleet and chairman of the defense staff, put it, to the strength of the British intention "to carry out the objectives set out in U.N. Resolution 502," which called for the immediate withdrawal of Argentine troops from the Islands.[5]

As Chapter Two points out, Britain's use of force suggested an awareness of proportion. The military undertaking was guided by prudence, and the objective of restoring British rule over the Islands was clear from the inception of Operation Corporate. Although the sinking of the Argentine cruiser *General Belgrano* would seem to suggest that proportion was tossed out of the window, closer examination reveals otherwise. British naval commanders considered the *Belgrano* a threat to the Task Force. Apart from this military reasoning, there was also a political payoff. The sinking of the *Belgrano* and its effects locked both governments into an escalating but controlled spiral of force. The resulting situation dovetailed with the machinations of the Thatcher government. It was clearly not "an action intrinsically cruel because it was so unnecessary."[6] Rather it was, according to Lord Lewin, "militarily and politically expedient to neutralize this menacing threat."[7] And it turned out that by taking this action, the British forces were able to restrict further movements of the Argentine fleet. In short, the sinking of the *Belgrano* effectively bottled up the Argentine navy in port.

Chapter Three examines in some detail several hypotheses that have been offered concerning British motivations for recapturing the Falkland Islands. It will be shown, however, that only a few of the hypotheses throw sufficient light on British motivations. Of these few, the ones pertaining to national honor and the defense of democratic principles are especially significant and provide a solid foundation on which to base our conclusions. Lord Michael Carver summarized it well when he said to this author, "It was the pressure of public opinion and the insult to British pride that lay behind the government's decision to retake the Islands."[8]

Chapter Four examines the impact of the Falklands War on British defense policy. While no major shifts occurred, the war did bring about a number of small but significant changes. In fact, the period immediately following the Falklands War was a dress rehearsal of sorts for the changes that would take place in British defense policy in the 1990s. The war also demonstrated the speed with which constraints can be removed and heightened the demands for greater strategic mobility and a renewed awareness in out-of-area operations. In short, the Falklands War had a significant effect on British defense policy by underscoring the importance of external developments and political realism. And while it is true that British defense policy has been influenced by economic considerations, it is equally true that the Falklands conflict was pursued despite such constraints.

Finally, Chapter Five examines four significant issues relating to the Falklands War and Britain's involvement. These all have an important relation to the analyses presented in this book. They are, first, the political nature of the Falklands question in Britain; second, the time frame of the British decision to recapture the Islands; third, the recalcitrant issue of economic constraints on the formulation of British defense policy; and fourth, the importance of strategic and political realism in British defense policy-making after the Falklands War. It ends with a short assessment of this work.

This book offers a new contribution to the literature of the Falklands War by providing a synthesis of many disparate elements and contentious issues. It strengthens the case for external developments and their impacts on the formulation of British defense policy, thereby bringing balance to the intellectual debate. In short, it presents a comprehensive treatment of some of the major issues flowing from this war hitherto neglected or not adequately covered in the literature currently available.

# One

# Background to the Falklands War

Geography, economics, history and international law assume unique salience in any analysis of the Falklands War of 1982. The application of legal principles to the thorny and contentious issue of sovereignty demands an understanding of certain relevant geographical and historical facts. Moreover, this type of background information provides a solid epistemological base for plausible conjectures and theoretical conclusions that appear to be both reasonable and well grounded. On the other hand, the historic claims to sovereignty by the two disputants (Britain and Argentina) must be examined in the proper context in order to make efficacious the application of appropriate legal norms. The incorporation of legal arguments serves to elucidate obscure issues and at the same time to buttress, in one way or the other, the respective claims. An exclusion of such arguments from any meaningful analysis is, according to one legal analyst, "contradicted by the attitudes of the disputant States, of the third States, and of international organizations, all of whom measured the disputed conduct by standards of international law."[1]

The question of sovereignty lies at the very heart of the Falklands dispute. In addition to being a highly charged and divisive issue, it is also one that is fraught with obfuscation. In other words, neither the British nor the Argentine claim to sovereignty over the Falkland Islands is cut and dried; conclusions cannot be easily distilled from the relevant substance of international law. Rather, both claims seem to abound in confused historical interpretations, and the two respective accounts appear contradictory in several respects. It is in this context that a fairly elaborate background account is set forth in this chapter. This task is undertaken with a view to synthesize the different accounts so that a more meaningful application of the law can be effected. It also provides a laboratory for the testing of many hypothetical questions that emanate from the search and for the examination within this context of the wider implications flowing from the sovereignty issue.

In the section that follows, an attempt is made to explore some pertinent geographical data. The importance of this type of information cannot be overemphasized. Its relevance becomes apparent when we examine some aspects of the wider issues that impacted on the British decision to retake the Falkland Islands in 1982. (These issues will be taken up in Chapter Three.) Historical information, as it relates to discovery and settlement, will be the theme following the section on geography. This will then be followed by a lengthy examination and analysis of the legal issues involved and the relative strengths of the two claims. Finally, I shall examine Britain's relationship to the Falklands prior to 2 April 1982 before making a few concluding remarks.

# The Islands and Their People

## Geography

A distance in excess of 7,500 miles separates Britain from the Falkland Islands. Their exact location is between latitudes 51 and 53 degrees south and longitudes 59 and 62 degrees west in the South Atlantic Ocean. The archipelago is separated from Río Gallegos, Argentina, the nearest point on the South American mainland, by approximately 300 miles of open sea. It consists of two large islands, East and West Falklands, and about two hundred smaller islands and islets. Together they aggregate an area of roughly 4,700 square miles.[2] This area can be broken down as follows:

| | |
|---|---|
| East Falkland | 2,500 sq. miles |
| Adjacent small islands | 110 sq. miles |
| West Falkland | 1,750 sq. miles |
| Adjacent small islands | 340 sq. miles |

In total area the Falklands are about equal in size to Wales and somewhat smaller than the state of Connecticut, but they are significantly larger than famous islands such as Cyprus, Jamaica, and Puerto Rico.

The two main islands run from the northeast to the southwest and are separated by the Strait of San Carlos or Falkland Sound (from which the islands derived their name).[3] This waterway played a crucial role in the British landing operations of troops and war materiel during the 1982 war. In this channel, which is 50 miles long and 10 miles wide, there are several islands. Three in particular, Borbon, Vigia, and Trinidad, together with the coast of West Falkland, form the early historical settlement of Port Edgmont, where the British first settled in 1765.

As to the Falkland Islands Dependencies, "which were first brought under the administration of the Governor of Stanley, the capital, in 1908, … these comprise South Georgia, the South Sandwich Islands, the South Orkneys, the South Shetlands, the Graham Island Peninsula, and a certain number of barren Antarctic islands."[4] The British Antarctic Territory established in 1962 constitutes the last four island groups.

Both East and West Falkland Islands are noted for their extremely irregular coastlines, and this feature in turn has led to the formation of many good landing sites and potential harbors. The land surface on both islands is generally hilly, with the highest point reaching 2,312 feet (Mt. Usborne on East Falkland). "The Hornby Mountains on West Falkland run parallel to the Falkland Sound with Mount Moody, at 1,816 feet, while Mount Maria reaches 2,158 feet. Although Mount Usborne on the East is the highest peak in the archipelago, generally speaking West Falkland is more impressive in its appearance."[5] Much of the upland is generally bare of vegetation and consists of eroded peat, spree, and stones. Because of the harsh nature of the climate, there are few trees, and in the lower areas the natural vegetation is of a grassland type, with some species of heath and dwarf shrubs. Both islands abound with streams and small rivers. Ponds or shallow lakes are numerous, largely because of the generally impervious nature of the soils and peaty areas of the lower regions.

Geologically, the islands are composed almost entirely of Paleozoic and Mesozoic sedimentary rocks. Ian Strange, a geographer who lived in the Falklands for many years, made an interesting point when he stated that there is a very strong stratigraphical similarity between the islands and South Africa and that the fossil fauna and flora between the two regions also show a striking similarity. He concluded, "These close relationships add evidence to the suggestion that the group may have moved from the vicinity of south-east Africa and that the rocks now forming these islands represent the missing section of the Karroo basin of Natal and eastern Cape Province."[6]

Although not a definitive statement of facts, the above opinion does harmonize with an observation made by an Argentine patriot who noted

15

the "unique features" of the islands, which are not too dissimilar to those of Patagonia.[7] The Argentine claim that the Falklands are on Argentina's continental shelf and part of the natural land formation of Patagonia cannot be substantiated by geographic evidence. A number of geologic investigations conducted over a twenty-year period revealed that the islands have no mineral wealth. Low-grade peat serves as the only local source of fuel. The impervious nature of the quartzite and sandstone soils limits drainage, and most of the rocks lack important minerals to sustain plant growth. The absence of limestone is partly responsible for the acid content of the soil.

Climatically, the Falkland Islands are characterized by narrow temperature ranges, strong gale-force winds, and day-to-day variability in weather conditions. The only long-term climate records available are the records of observations made at Stanley, the capital. There appears to be little precise information on how weather and climate vary through the archipelago as a whole.[8]

The Falkland Islands' location on the northern edge of the depression belt which runs through the Drake Passage has to a considerable extent determined the variation in weather conditions they experience. This variation is caused by the air masses and fronts which pass across the Drake Passage, thus producing a cool oceanic climate for the Falklands. At Stanley the air temperature has never been known to exceed 21.1°C or to fall below minus 11.1°C. The mean monthly temperature varies between 9°C in January/February and minus 1°C in July. Rainfall at Stanley averages 25 inches per annum, spread fairly evenly throughout the year, with an average of 16–20 days per month on which precipitation occurs. No month is entirely frost-free. Snow falls on about fifty days during any one year, and no month escapes from the blast of snow showers, however light. The prevailing winds are westerly, averaging speeds of about 17 miles per hour. "Although storms are recorded several times each month, gales with winds in excess of 55–63 mph (a whole gale) are almost unknown. Calm conditions are more frequent than storms."[9]

Ian Strange observes that the mean winter temperatures are similar to those in Great Britain but that the summer mean is more in keeping with that of Scotland. The total sunshine recorded is about the same as in many parts of England, and the mean annual rainfall recorded at Stanley compares with the center and east of England.[10]

## Climatic Averages for Stanley[11]

| | |
|---|---|
| Mean annual windspeed | 17 mph |
| Mean annual rainfall | 25 inches |
| Mean annual temperature | 5.50°C |

### Average Monthly Rainfall

| | |
|---|---|
| January | 2.8 inches |
| April | 2.4 inches |
| July | 2.2 inches |

It is very heartening to note that atmospheric pollution is nonexistent in and around the Falkland Islands.

## Population

During the past one hundred years, the inhabitants of both islands have been, and still are, almost entirely of British origin. No indigenous population of *Homo sapiens* existed prior to the advent of Europeans. Hence the present population, although mostly island-born, are considered "settlers."

The first settlers, some of whose descendants still live on the Falkland Islands, began to arrive during the uneasy years which followed the establishment of the British colony in January 1833. Population figures have been recorded on a fairly regular basis. In 1851 the population was around 287; it reached a peak of 2,392 in 1931 and has declined since that year. The following table illustrates the population fluctuations:

### The Falklands Population in the Census Years 1851–1980

| Year | Population | Year | Population |
|---|---|---|---|
| 1851 | 287 | 1921 | 2,094 |
| 1861 | 541 | 1931 | 2,392 |
| 1871 | 811 | 1946 | 2,239 |
| 1881 | 1,510 | 1953 | 2,230 |
| 1891 | 1,789 | 1962 | 2,172 |
| 1901 | 2,043 | 1972 | 1,957 |
| 1911 | 2,272 | 1980 | 1,813* |

*Source: Falkland Islands Government, Report of the Census, 1980.*

*This figure excludes 42 Royal Marines at Moody Brook Barracks and the crews and passengers of the two visiting ships in Stanley Harbor on census day.

The extent to which persons of other nationalities were free to settle in the newly occupied British colony, or did settle there, is not entirely clear. It appears to be the case that no original settler of Spanish or Argentine stock remained on the islands after the upheavals of 1833.[12] Argentina maintains to this day that when the British seized the islands in 1833, many Argentine settlers were living on the islands and were forced to leave in the aftermath of the British seizure.[13] One of these exiled settlers was Antonio Rivero, who is now a national hero of Argentina. In the first forty years following the British occupation of the islands in 1833, naturalization ordinances were passed in the colony. Many of those individuals to whom the grant was made were originally from various places in Europe, North and Central America; one or two were from Argentina. On this issue of ethnic composition, Hazel Fox's conclusion is of some significance. She asserts that "it is possible, therefore, that in the early days the Colony was less overwhelmingly composed of British stock than it has now become."[14]

The 1980 census showed a population of 1,813, and of this number 75 percent, or 1,360, were born on the Falkland Islands and 302 in Britain. In that same year also, there were 30 Argentine nationals on the islands. They were engaged in aerodrome activities—operating the fuel depot and managing air services. Further, the 1980 population figures represent a 25 percent decline from the high reached in 1931. According to one report, "this decline is due mainly to young people leaving the islands in search of jobs and a more modern lifestyle. This is especially true of the female population, many of whom marry expatriate workers and leave with them when their contracts expire."[15]

Stanley, located on East Falkland, has a population of 1,050 (1980 census) which is nearly 60 percent of the overall population of the island. The rest of the population live in areas referred to as "camps" (from the Spanish word *campo*, meaning countryside). There are thirty five such "camps," or rural settlements, with the largest located at Goose Green, where the first battle was fought in the 1982 conflict. Goose Green has a population of just over 90 inhabitants.

It is of great interest to note that almost all of the Falklanders are of Anglo-Saxon origin. One writer summarized it well when he said that "in beliefs, language, habits and appearances, they are British."[16] The remark has often been made that Falkland Islanders, or Kelpers, as they are commonly called, are more British than the British. It is not an ill-founded remark, given their history and demonstrated affinity to Britain over the years.

## The Economy

The natural vegetation, which is mainly grassland, has to a large extent determined the economic activities of the Falkland Islands. Following the first settlement by the French in 1764, cattle ran wild in East Falkland. By 1840 their numbers had proliferated to about 100,000 and appeared to be increasing rapidly despite large numbers being slaughtered annually. During the early years of the British colony (ca. 1850), the export of hides represented the principal economic endeavor.[17] Within a span of ten years, sheep began to replace wild cattle, which were being systematically slaughtered, until they had been virtually exterminated by 1880. From 1870 onwards, sheep farming developed rapidly and has remained one of the major sources of income and occupation for the Falkland Islanders. It was estimated that by 1899, there were more than 750,000 sheep in the Falklands. Today sheep outnumber people by about 300 to one, and hence mutton forms a large part of the local diet. During the 74-day war in 1982, hundreds of sheep were slaughtered indiscriminately. The early postwar period revealed a new problem—scores of dead and badly mutilated sheep that were innocent victims of land mines.

Until 1982 the economy of the Falkland Islands was totally dominated by the production of wool for export. Falklands' wool is noted for its fine quality; it is soft and springy and has tensile strength. It is quite often referred to as "the high-quality Falklands wool." Serious problems plagued the industry, however, and eroded output. The farming technique employed was based on extensive grazing, which meant that enormously large tracts of land were required to sustain just a few thousand sheep. An immediate solution to this problem would have been to improve soil quality and grass-planting techniques. Another problem that confronted this industry had to do with the nature of the product itself. It was and still is a raw material and therefore subject to price fluctuations on the international commodities market. The economic uncertainty involved in wool production for the export market is clearly illustrated by the wide band of price variations that Falkland farmers received for their "clip" over the period 1972–80:

### Reported Wool Selling Price, Port San Carlos
*(In Pence per Kg.)*

| 1972 | 1973 | 1974 | 1975 | 1976 | 1977 | 1978 | 1979 | 1980 |
|------|------|------|------|------|------|------|------|------|
| 57 | 62 | 117 | 56 | 98 | 127 | 115 | 124 | 114 |

*Source: Port San Carlos Ltd., Annual Company Reports.*

The uncertainty hanging over export prices, combined with steadily increasing production costs, did serve to deter large-scale investments in this economic activity, but this was clearly not the whole story. In such an economic climate, the inevitable result was bound to be a decline in productivity. During the 1960s and early 1970s, the total wool clip declined steadily. One report noted: "It revived somewhat in the mid-seventies before starting to fall once again. The total clip in the 1980/81 season amounted to 4.66 million pounds of wool. However, to obtain that quantity of wool, 593,889 sheep had to be shorn. In the 1963/64 season, 4.81 million pounds of wool were obtained from shearing 573,897 sheep."[18] This difference in the requirement of almost 20,000 more sheep to meet the 1963-64 production target clearly pointed to the decline in pasture quality.

The monocultural nature of the Falklands economy up to 1982 can be gleaned from the export statistics. Wool was king in the Falklands, as was sugar in many of the former British colonies, especially those in the Caribbean. In the ten-year period from 1965 to 1974, unprocessed wool accounted for almost 99 percent of total exports in each of those years.[19] The exports of other products, mainly hides and skins, were also susceptible to variation in market prices, but their overall impact on the Falklands' economy and balance of payments appeared negligible. The following table shows the Islands' current account for the fiscal year 1980. Trading was, and still is, carried out almost exclusively with the United Kingdom.

### U.K. Trade with the Falkland Islands, 1980

| | Imports from F.I. Value (thousands of pounds) | % | Exports to F.I. Value (thousands of pounds) | % |
|---|---|---|---|---|
| Food and Live Animals | 5 | 0.2 | 258 | 12.4 |
| Beverages and Tobacco | 0 | 0.0 | 206 | 9.9 |
| Raw Materials | 2,787 | 97.9 | 36 | 1.7 |
| Minerals, Fuels, & Lubricants | 0 | 0.0 | 30 | 1.4 |
| Animal and Vegetable Oil | 0 | 0.0 | 5 | 0.2 |
| Chemicals, etc. | 0 | 0.0 | 75 | 3.6 |
| Manufactured Goods | 21 | 0.7 | 275 | 13.2 |
| Machinery and Transport | 10 | 0.4 | 534 | 25.7 |
| Miscellaneous Manufactures | 7 | 0.2 | 215 | 10.3 |
| Other Goods | 17 | 0.6 | 448 | 21.5 |
| TOTAL | 2,847 | 100 | 2,082 | 100 |

*Source: Overseas Trade Statistics of the U.K., 1980, Tables II and V.*

In spite of the fact that the Islands' external balance sheet did show a surplus in 1980 and had done so for several years, this surplus does not accurately portray the overall economy. Decapitalization was a distinct feature of the economy, and this outflow of profits strongly militated against attempts at both diversification and qualitative infrastructural improvements. The regular one-way flow or hemorrhaging of surplus meant that capital was not being accumulated locally. The majority of the profits from the sale of the wool clip accrued to absentee landlords, who own most of the farms on the Islands. These profits were never plowed back into the local economy. Absentee landlordism and the realities of under-investment have led to a decline in the overall economic growth of the Islands. The U.K. center was and still is the main beneficiary of this vicious circle of impoverishment of the periphery. In an article titled "The Future of the Falkland Islands," Richard Johnson indicated the size of the flow when he pointed out that "over the last 25 years roughly 10–12 m. [pounds sterling] in constant 1974 prices of company funds have flowed out of the Islands to the U.K. It is also estimated that over the same period the U.K. Exchequer has benefited by way of corporation and dividends tax to the tune of some £4m."[20] His conclusion is also highly significant: "It is readily apparent that the Islands have suffered from a considerable net out flow of resources, and that historically the U.K. taxpayer has been a financial beneficiary rather than a supporter of the Falklands."

And the Shackleton Committee Report emphasized that an economic transformation of the Islands would be not only a matter of external assistance, but rather there was also a "need for local commitment" in the form of action to reverse the flow of funds from the Falklands and to promote reinvestment of profits locally.[21] This very conclusion was reached in a 14 September 1982 update of that report, which Prime Minister Thatcher called for in May of the same year. We now turn our attention to an area of great controversy—the historical aspect of the sovereignty issue—which will be examined from both the Argentinian and British perspectives.

# Historical Background:
# Discovery and Settlement, 1492–1833

History is more than the accumulation and presentation of facts. Inasmuch as it is a subject rooted in the past, it is "indispensable to an appreciation of present and even future developments, thereby confirming the subject's relevance and utility."[22] Insofar as the Falklands dispute is concerned, history is highly relevant because it provides the building blocks for any in-depth analysis that seeks a wider and deeper understanding of the conflict, particularly the question of sovereignty. In this section, an attempt will be made to present the two historical accounts followed by an assessment. These accounts relate first to discovery, then to settlement and possession.

## Period of Discovery: 1492–1763

According to the Argentine version, the Malvinas (Falkland Islands) were first discovered by Spanish sailors during the first half of the sixteenth century.[23] The islands appear on early sixteenth-century Spanish maps and planispheres. The first map was that of Pedro Reineel in 1523, who marked an archipelago at 53°51' latitude south. This marking also appeared later in the works of the chief cartographer of Charles V of Spain. Discovery of the islands is credited to Esteban Gomez, a Portuguese sailor in Magellan's expedition of 1520. Two Spanish navigators, Simon de Alcabaza and Alonso de Camargo, also sailed in the area in 1534 and 1540, respectively.[24] In 1600 the Dutchman Sebald van de Weert navigated in his ship, the *Geloof,* through the Straits of Magellan and into the Atlantic Ocean where he "discovered" the islands.

There is another view of discovery, however, which has been put forward by both Argentine historians and Julius Goebel.[25] These writers have asserted that the Malvinas Islands were discovered on 4 February 1540 by the ship *Incognita*, which was part of Bishop Plasencia's expedition. Destefani, a former head of the Department of Naval Historical Studies of the Argentine navy, summarized his country's view thus: "Sebald de Weert is generally accepted as the discoverer of the Malvinas and the Spanish ship 'Incognita,' which had done so before, had carried out the pre-discovery."[26]

An assessment of the Argentine version reveals the following:

1. The cartographic placing of an archipelago at 53°51' south latitude in early Spanish maps would seem to fit today's more accurate location of the islands. Navigational accuracy in charting hitherto unexplored areas of the world in the fifteenth and sixteenth centuries is very dubious, however, and should not be taken as conclusive.
2. The prevalent Argentine view of the period—that Esteban Gomez was the first discoverer of the Malvinas Islands in 1520—is hotly contested even by some Argentinians. Hector Ratto, a prominent

22

Argentine naval historian, strongly disagrees with the view that Gomez's ship, the *San Antonio*, discovered the Malvinas upon leaving the Straits of Magellan on its way to Spain. The historical accounts suggest otherwise. Gomez left the Straits with his ship on 1 November 1520, and upon his arrival in Spain, he was brought before an inquiry on 6 May 1521. Documents on the hearings reveal that he did not set sail for the Cape but for the Guineas on the African coast on a direct route to Spain. Thus he did not pass even close to the Malvinas Islands. Neither was anything said about the discovery of the islands in testimony given by 53 members of his crew during the hearings.[27]

3. The discovery, or better yet, the "rediscovery," of the islands in 1600 by Sebald van de Weert is generally accepted by both Argentinian and British historians.

4. The general point in this assessment is that no absolute certainty exists in the Argentinian version insofar as discovery is concerned.

According to the British version, the Falkland Islands were first sighted in 1592 by a British sea captain, John Davies, from the ship *Desire*. In 1594, Sir Richard Hawkins sailed along the northern coast of the islands.[28] In 1598, Sebald van de Weert "is credited with having charted three islands in the Falklands group, which van Weert named the Sebaldes."[29] Ninety-two years later in January 1690, Captain John Strong of the Royal Navy made the first known landing on the previously uninhabited islands. He named the sound or channel between the eastern and western islands, Falkland, in honor of the third Viscount Falkland, Anthony Cary, who was at that time a commissioner and was later the first lord of the Admiralty. "On that occasion Captain Strong did little more than make a survey and then departed."[30] Nothing of significance materialized as a consequence of this landing, and not much happened until 1764.

We can assess the British version as follows:

1. Almost all of the British accounts have asserted with some degree of finality that in 1592 John Davies was the first to sight the Falkland Islands. He may indisputably have been the first Englishman to have done so. On the other hand, Goebel, among others, does not share this view, offering the following reasons:

   a. The account of Davies' voyage and discovery was published by John Jane, one of Davies' crew, in 1600, eight years later. It is ironic that in that very year on 4 July, the Dutchman Sebald

23

       van de Weert had returned to Holland and had made public his discovery of the archipelago.

   b. Davies was a deserter who had to "discover" something in order to improve his personal situation upon returning to England.

   c. Davies' siting of the islands is inexact, even for that period. It is also remarkable that a great explorer like John Davies did not even offer any description of the islands.

The above observations inevitably cast serious doubts on the British claim that John Davies was the discoverer of the Falklands. And even if this version is accepted, then what of the ship *Incognita*?

2. The Hawkins discovery has received much attention from both Argentine and British historians. Most seem to emphasize the differences between the description and reality of the islands and the discrepancies relating to "latitude" position, stated as being approximately 48° south. Despite these inconsistencies, the Hawkins account still appears highly probable.

3. No one disputes the fact that Captain John Strong landed on the islands in January 1690.

The nagging question of discovery is at best shrouded in mystery. Most of the tales, claims, and counterclaims seem to lie in the realms of legend and folklore. Professor J. C. Metford's comment aptly summarizes the situation: "An accurate answer to the question, who first sighted the Falklands? is unlikely ever to be forthcoming."[31] Thus the discovery of the islands was in itself a point of contention between Argentina and Britain, and the debate did become all the more futile because of the sketchy and oftentimes nebulous nature of the available data on early voyages to the South Atlantic. It should also be noted in this regard that prior discovery of territory does not give rise to automatic title of ownership under international law.

## Settlement and Possession: 1764–1833

Both Argentina and Britain acknowledge that the first settlers on the Falkland Islands were the French. One source succinctly stated, "Although there is disagreement on the issue of who discovered the Islands, there appears to be no question as to which country first settled them."[32]

In March 1764, Antoine Louis de Bougainville, a French navigator, established a small settlement called Port Louis on East Falkland. He had fought with Montcalm at Quebec in 1759 and was then given leave by a minister of Louis XV, the duc de Choiseul, to establish a colony of immigrants from Acadia (Nova Scotia) and St. Malo on East Falkland. The rationale for this policy was quite evident. A French presence in the South Atlantic would serve to buttress and consolidate French exploits in the Pacific, especially at a time when France's loss of Canada to the British in the Seven Years War (1756–63), was still being keenly felt.

Bougainville laid the foundations for a French colony on the Falkland Islands. Soon after his arrival, he claimed possession of all the islands in the name of Louis XV. News of French activities in the South Atlantic were met by a strong chorus of protest from Spain. These protests were based on such grounds as proximity to other settlements, Spanish insistence on discovery, and on the 1494 Treaty of Tordesillas, which divided the New World between the two Catholic powers of Spain and Portugal. The dividing line ran from the North Pole to the South Pole, 370 leagues to the west of Cape Verde; the area to the east of the line was to belong to Portugal, that to the west to Spain.

The French withdrew their settlement in 1767, receiving the substantial sum of twenty-four thousand pounds sterling by way of compensation. On 1 April 1767, Spain took formal possession of the Falkland Islands and established a new colony almost immediately after the French withdrawal. But unknown to the French and not aware of any other settlement on the islands, the British had begun to establish a colony on West Falkland in 1765. This occurred at the time when the French and Spanish were sorting out their claims and other problems relating to the French settlement on East Falkland. On 23 January 1765, Commodore John Byron, the poet's grandfather, arrived on the islands and claimed them for King George III. He based his claims on British prior discovery. A settlement was not established, however, until 8 January 1766.[33]

When he arrived on West Falkland in January 1765, Byron undertook some preliminary survey work and then departed. A second British expedition arrived a year later in January 1766 under the command of John McBride, commander of HMS *Jason*. The British settlement at Port Edgmont on West Falkland began in earnest from this date, nearly two years after the French had landed and fourteen months before the Spanish took "formal" possession of the islands.

The British settlement, like that of the French, was short-lived. The Spanish authorities in Buenos Aires, having been made aware of the British settlement, began issuing warnings to the British to leave the islands, which were considered Spanish territory. British noncompliance was met by Spanish force. Some 1,400 Spanish soldiers in five ships were dispatched from the Argentine mainland to drive out the British from West Falkland. They met very little resistance. The British settlement was outnumbered, and the Spanish finally entered Port Edgmont on 10 June 1770.

News of this forcible eviction created much commotion in Britain. The British government was outraged at what it considered to be a despicable act, and the incident nearly led to an outbreak of war against Spain. Some amount of rationality prevailed, however, and after a series of intense negotiations between the two maritime powers, they reached agreement on the restitution of the former settlement to the British—"to restore the status quo and hand back Port Edgmont to British control."[34] This agreement took place on 15 September 1771, six months after the Port Edgmont eviction. The short time frame is significant. Spain's military actions at Port Edgmont aroused fears of war on the Continent, and in the context of Britain's overwhelming military superiority, the Spanish were more than willing to seek an early and amicable solution with their "injured" counterpart. A caveat is in order here: the later raging controversy over sovereignty of the Falklands stemmed to a large extent from the confusion surrounding the terms of the agreement entered into between Britain and Spain in 1771. Argentina claimed that a secret deal was struck between the two parties, based on the understanding that Britain would evacuate the Falkland Islands and give up its claims to them at a later date (presumably to save face), but more importantly, that Spanish sovereignty over the Falklands would remain intact. Most British authorities forthrightly denied the existence of any such secret deals between His Majesty's government and Spain.

The colony at Port Edgmont was eventually closed down in 1774. The British withdrawal was voluntary, partly because of new strategic priorities and economic considerations. Meanwhile, the Spanish colony on East Falkland continued to exist and, from 1776 until 1811, it was governed as part of the vice-royalty of Buenos Aires. After the British evacuated Port Edgmont, their connection with the Falklands was severed for almost sixty years. At the time of withdrawal though, Lt. Samuel Clayton, who supervised the dismantling of the settlement, left behind a plaque with the following inscription:

> Be it known to all nations that the Falkland Islands, with this fort, the storehouses, wharfs, harbours, bays, and creeks thereunto belonging are the sole right and property of His Most Sacred Majesty George the Third, King

of Great Britain, France and Ireland, Defender of the Faith, etc. In witness whereof this plaque is set up, and His Britannic Majesty's colours left flying as a mark of possession. By S. W. Clayton, Commanding Officer at Falkland Islands. AD 1774.[35]

From 1774 to 1810, Spain, through its vice-royalty in Buenos Aires, was the sole administrator of the Falkland Islands. During these thirty-six years, the colony never amounted to much. "In the mid–1780s the population numbered about 80, and the viceroy in Buenos Aires was so unimpressed that he vainly suggested to the Crown that the less thriving colony be abandoned."[36] Spanish activities were concentrated around the old settlement, which was used mainly as a prison camp. West Falkland was left alone in ruins.

A significant turn of events materialized in 1811. When Spain was threatened by Napoleon and the British attacked Buenos Aires in 1806, the Spanish governor in Puerto Soledad (Port Louis) decided to flee from the Malvinas. What was left of the Spanish garrison was withdrawn in 1811.[37] This withdrawal was authorized by the governor of Montevideo, thus leaving the Falklands practically uninhabited except for a few gauchos and fishermen who had to look after themselves.[38] One British source contends that the Spanish withdrawal took place in 1806.[28] Most historians, however, stick to 1811 as the year of the Spanish evacuation from the Falkland Islands.

On 9 July 1816, the United Provinces of Rio de la Plata declared their independence from Spain. The central government located in Buenos Aires (Argentina was still a loose federation of provinces) made it known that the new federation had taken over Spain's rights to the islands in the South Atlantic, which included the Malvinas. In prosecuting this declaration of intent, the new federal administration dispatched an expeditionary force in the frigate *Heroina* under the command of Colonel Daniel Jewitt to the Falklands on 6 November 1820. Three days after landing at Port Louis, he took possession of the Falkland Islands in the name of the government of the United Provinces of Rio de la Plata. Jewitt also ordered the masters of the more than 50 ships that he found there to quit their fishing activities and leave the area.

Three years later in 1823, Buenos Aires appointed Don Pablo Areguati as governor of the islands and also granted fishery and livestock concessions to Jorge Pacheco and Louis Vernet. The latter, although an Argentine citizen, was a merchant of French extraction from Hamburg. He established a settlement on the Falkland Islands in 1826 and in 1829 "was appointed governor of the new military district of Las Malvinas, an

Argentine demonstration of authority which resulted in a diplomatic protest from Great Britain."[40]

Louis Vernet undertook his activities with much enthusiasm. Between 1826 and 1831, he established 90 settlers of various nationalities: Dutch, British, German, Spanish, Portuguese, French, and South American Indian. Further, he took steps to prevent the continuation of fishing activities by foreign vessels around the Falkland waters. In his view, "a major thorn was the foreign whalers and sealers, who had become accustomed to fishing the area during the decade in which no country had control."[41] There was a wider implication that flowed from Vernet's action. Through his endeavors, the regime in Buenos Aires claimed that its rights to regulate fishing and seal hunting in and around the Falkland waters had been inherited from Spain through the principle of *uti possidetis*. The regime also asserted its rights to sovereignty over the islands and took practical steps to enforce those territorial rights.

Vernet's go-ahead spirit backfired in 1831 when he seized three United States sealing vessels which had refused to respect his exclusive fishing rights. In essence, these vessels had violated the United Provinces' territorial waters by fishing in and around the Malvinas waters. The Americans, however, did not see their action as a violation of Argentine sovereignty. Vernet took one of the vessels, including its crew, to Buenos Aires for indictment and enforcement measures. The owner of the seized vessel demanded compensation from the Argentine state, and the United States Consul in Buenos Aires, George Slacum, demanded that Vernet should be taken to court and tried for piracy. The Argentine authorities refused to comply with the American demand. Their refusal was subsequently met with swift American reaction. Professor Northedge, in a well-written piece on the incident, mused, "In the gun-boat tradition familiar to nineteenth-century European history, the U.S. ship *Lexington* was sent to show the flag in the River Plate."[42]

In December 1831, three days after Christmas, Captain Silas Duncan of the *Lexington* exacted revenge by sacking the Argentine settlement of Puerto Soledad on East Falkland.

Duncan's actions had far-reaching implications, particularly on the sovereignty question to be discussed later. He plundered the settlement, completely destroying buildings and ammunition dumps in the process, and then declared the Falklands "free of all governments." Duncan's destruction of years of work undertaken by Vernet and his men in the settlement was a great blow to Vernet. Absent from the colony at the time, he never returned to the Falklands. "Later, he attempted to obtain compensation from the British Government for stock and produce he had left behind and which had subsequently come under British care in 1833. Of the £14,295 claimed, he was eventually awarded £2,400, twenty-six years after leaving the Malvinas."[43] Vernet also filed claims against the U.S. government for damages but was never awarded any compensation.

Following Duncan's destruction of the Argentine settlement in December 1831, the United Provinces government in September 1832 appointed Juan Mestivier as governor (to replace Vernet). Mestivier arrived at Port Soledad sometime later that year and took charge of the settlement, which lay in ruins. His tenure in office was short-lived. A mutiny broke out in the colony, and he was killed in the ensuing gunfight.

At this juncture, a point of discrepancy appears in the historical narrative. The British account maintains that after the American attack and subsequent destruction of the settlement, the Falkland Islands had "no visible authority" from December 1831 until the time the British arrived there on 3 January 1833. The above account of Mestivier's appointment as governor in 1832 is completely ignored in the British perspective. Most accounts support the Argentine view that Mestivier, along with others onboard the *Sarandi*, arrived at Port Soledad in September 1832. Mestivier's sojourn, though brief, indicates that the Falklands were not *res nullius* and that Argentina had no intention of abandoning the territory, as the British claimed.

When the British ship *Clio* arrived at Port Edgmont on West Falkland on 20 December 1832, its commander immediately took possession of the island. Fourteen days later the *Clio* appeared at Port Soledad on East Falkland. Against a background characterized by confusion and chaos, Captain J. J. Onslow, the ship's commander, entered Port Soledad, where a mutiny had taken place earlier in which the governor had been killed. It was reported that Onslow pulled down the Argentine flag and hoisted the Union Jack, which has been flying ever since, except during the short-lived Argentine occupation of April–June 1982. Captain Onslow justified his actions by maintaining that the Falklands were *res nullius*, belonging to no one, and therefore open to occupation by the British. In other words, the islands were up for grabs.

It appears that Captain Onslow's interpretation of what he saw and subsequently did was highly misleading. As it happened, he found a visible Argentine presence of around fifty men under the command of Jose Maria Pinedo, the deputy governor, on the island. Pinedo and his men, plus a few Argentine civilians, mainly prison warders and internees from the penal colony, were rounded up and sent packing. The Argentine schooner

*Sarandi* finally arrived at Buenos Aires around 12 January 1833, whereupon Pinedo was seized and then court-martialed for failing to put up a fight against the British. His small garrison at Port Soledad had been overwhelmed by the sheer numbers of British might. A second British ship, the *Tyne*, had reinforced the *Clio* on 3 January 1833.

Here ends the short history of the Falkland Islands as it relates to discovery, settlement, and possession. The year 1833 was the turning point in that history, which up until that time had been characterized by some degree of confusion. From that year onwards, British rule was gradually consolidated, and a period of peaceful settlement commenced, but under continuous protest from Argentina. Against this relevant geographical and historical background, we now turn to an examination of the legal ramifications pertaining to the contentious issue of sovereignty—who owns the Falkland Islands or Islas Malvinas.

## Legal Standing of Conflicting Claims to Sovereignty

Sovereignty is a fundamental principle in customary international law, but the concept is fraught with ambiguities. Sovereignty issues are all the more difficult to unravel because of the level of escalating emotional rhetoric usually associated with them. Stripped of these appendages, sovereignty has been defined as "the right to exercise state functions over territory to the exclusion of any other state."[44] Judge Huber in the *Isle of Palmas* case made a succinct distinction between the two uses of the term: "sovereignty in relation to a portion of the globe as the legal condition necessary for the inclusion of such portion in territory of any particular State," "sovereignty in relations between States" which "signifies independence. Independence in regard to a portion of the globe is the right to exercise therein, to the exclusion of any other State, the functions of a State."

Following similar lines of reasoning, two commentators put forward their views of sovereignty thus:

1. The freedom of a State from outside control in the conduct of its internal and external affairs
2. The supreme power of the State over its territory and inhabitants, and independence from any external authority.[45]

In spite of the seemingly precise meaning which the term gives rise to, sovereignty has not been altogether viewed as a precise term in international relations. One writer of a modern law text refers to sovereignty as a "term of art rather than a legal expression capable of precise definition."[46] As a "term of art" used for convenience, its absolutism has persisted as a dangerous bone of contention in the affairs of nations. Further, the term has been conveniently invoked to galvanize support for the "national interest," however loosely defined. And reliance on this idea of sovereignty as a nonbreakable concept has been used as a political instrument in the harangues of many leaders because of the emotionalism it stirs. But the quintessential point as advanced by one writer is that "sovereignty ... essentially relates to territory, not to people."[47] Britain's controversial behavior with regards to the Ilois people on the island of Diego Garcia in the Indian Ocean demonstrated a scant regard for the welfare of the 1,800 inhabitants, but strongly underscored the quintessence of the above view. In this assertion of sovereignty, the essence was territory, not people. Could the same be said of the Falklands? We shall return to this issue in Chapter Three when we examine the concept of self-determination in some detail.

What then of sovereignty with respect to the disputants' claims to the Falkland Islands? It was the key word underlying the dispute between Britain and Argentina. Francis Pym, the foreign secretary during the 1982 war, referred to it as being "at the heart of the issue and dispute."[48] And Peter Beck, that prolific historian on the Falklands/Antarctica region, asserted that "the sovereignty issue remains the key point of disagreement, for the opposing points of view adopted in London and Buenos Aires on this question explain both the 1982 War and the persistence of the dispute."[49] Although the sovereignty issue did not represent the totality of the dispute, it clearly determined its language, form, and posture.

Before embarking on an examination of the two respective claims, we pause to consider briefly the different modes of territorial acquisition as distilled from international legal practice. Hackworth's *Digest of International Law* discusses twelve modes of acquiring or losing territory that have generally been accepted in international law. These are discovery, occupation, accretion, conquest, erosion, avalsion, cession, prescription, abandonment, revolution, succession, and annexation. Not all twelve modes share, however, the same degree of importance or carry the same weight among international jurists. Consensus seems to revolve around only five of these traditional modes—cession, occupation, accretion, subjugation, and prescription.[50] Surprisingly, discovery is not one of them.

*Cession* is title derived from another state by the transfer of sovereignty of territory by the owner of the state to another state. Cession also requires possession or occupation by the new owner in a demonstrable way.

International law prescribes no set format for cession to occur. The essential point under this mode is that the transfer must take place with the full consent of the governments concerned.

*Occupation* is the act of appropriation of territory which is not at the time under the sovereignty of another state. Two conditions or requirements must be met for a country to acquire sovereignty by occupation. The territory in question must be *res nullius*, that is, must belong to no one; the occupation must also be "effective." Effective occupation "requires both possession and administration."[51]

*Accretion* is the term given to a physical increase in the existing land mass caused by new geological changes. An example would be the formation of a new island in a river. This form of territorial acquisition is not relevant to our present area of interest and thus will not be explored further.

*Subjugation* is "conquest which has been firmly established and is followed by formal annexation constitutes acquisition of title by subjugation."[52] One prominent jurist advances the point that prior to the introduction of the Covenant of the League of Nations, subjugation was a widely recognized form of acquisition of territory.[53] In order for subjugation to take effect, there must be an end to the state of war, either by a formal peace treaty or by the simple cessation of hostilities. Annexation that takes place during a war does not constitute a firmly established conquest, which is a necessary prerequisite for acquisition of title through subjugation.

*Prescription* is a form of acquisition that entails the possession of territory over a long, continuous period resulting in the possessor having title to the said territory. Certain important caveats must be established, however, when a state is claiming territory under this mode. First, the territory in question must be *res nullius* and must be "obtained either unlawfully or in circumstances wherein the legality of acquisition cannot be demonstrated."[54] Second, the possession must be made public, that is to say, there must be widespread awareness, and possession should be peaceful and uninterrupted. Third, and more important, the time period should be sufficiently long to allow either *acquisitive* or *extinctive* prescription to be effective and must rest upon "the implied consent of the former sovereign to the new state of affairs. This means that protests by the dispossessed sovereign may completely block any prescriptive claim."[44] Acquiescence, therefore, is essential in a prescriptive claim.

We now turn to an examination of the disputants' claims, beginning first with Argentina. In the analysis that follows, principles of relevant leading cases will be abstracted and dovetailed into the arguments.

# Bases of Argentine Claims

Over the years, Argentina has maintained that its claims to sovereignty over the Falkland/Malvinas Islands derive from prior discovery, the Treaty of Tordessillas (1497) between Spain and Portugal, effective occupation, the illegal nature of its expulsion by the British in 1833, and the principle of territorial integrity. Let us now consider these claims in order to establish their strengths, weaknesses, and relevance.

## Discovery

Argentina claimed sovereignty over the Falklands as a result of the discovery of those islands by Spain. Since Argentina maintained that it had acquired Spanish rights by being a former colony of Spain, the right of Spanish discovery was Argentina's by inheritance. Although the available data on discovery is at present imprecise, scanty, and sometimes conjured up, the legal implications relating to this mode of territorial acquisition take precedence and are clearly delineated in the *Isle of Palmas* case.

Very succinctly, *Palmas* involved a dispute between the Netherlands and the United States of America over an island located between the Philippines, at that time part of the U.S. territory, and the Netherland Indies. It was and still is a landmark case in the law relating to territorial acquisition and one that has quite often been quoted or referred to. In granting sovereignty to the Netherlands, the Swiss arbitrator, Max Huber, held that discovery without further action on the part of the state claiming title through this mode vests no more than an inchoate title. In applying this line of legal reasoning to the Falklands' case, it is clear that Argentina's inchoate title could have been developed with the passage of time into a definitive title had the British occupation not taken place. Mere discovery of territory is not enough for the derivation of definitive title. Discovery must be followed by the accomplishment of further acts within a reasonable time. In short, "discovery does not give rise to an exclusive right to occupy" unless that right is fully exercised.[56]

The historical account clearly revealed that Spanish occupation of the Falklands occurred decades after discovery, and even when it did take place, it was not "effective." Argentina would be in a position to claim definitive title if it could demonstrate indisputable control over those islands after discovery. The conclusion, therefore, is that discovery was not sufficient to

33

support Argentina's claim to sovereignty over the Malvinas and would obviously be a very weak argument in front of a court or an arbitrator.

## Occupation

Argentina also claimed sovereignty based on both Spanish and Argentine occupation of the Falklands. From the historical account, one gleans the following: First, that Spain had a settlement on East Falkland during the period 1767 to 1811; second, that Argentina had settlements during the periods 1823–31 and September 1832 to January 1833; and third, that Argentina formally took possession of the Falklands in 1820 and argued that the periods of settlement indicated above strongly supported its claims to sovereignty.

It was noted earlier that for occupation to vest title, two conditions must be met, *res nullius* and effectiveness. The latter criterion was clearly spelled out in the now famed *Isle of Palmas* case. The arbitrator in that case indicated that "the country occupying the territory must be able to perform the rights and duties that are required of a sovereign in relation to its territory for the occupation to be effective."[57] This line of reasoning was well supported in the Eastern Greenland case. The International Court of Justice in its ruling upheld the view relating to an "actual exercise or display of authority."[58] In essence, administration and possession must flow from "effective" occupation in order for this mode to vest title and at the same time be legally valid.

In the context of this claim, several writers of British persuasion have advanced the view that Argentina's occupation was not "effective." In other words, they asserted that Argentina had not effectively occupied the Falkland Islands. In light of the historical account, this argument is not a valid one. For a period encompassing almost sixty years (1774–1833), the Falklands were administered from Buenos Aires. Although their settlement was confined to East Falkland, attempts were made to display Argentine assertion of authority over the entire area. Moreover, Argentina was the sole occupier of the Falkland Islands, and its continued assertion of authority in and around the Falkland waters invoked no protest from Britain or any other European power. According to Rubin, "no British protest over the continued Spanish colony between then [1774] and 1811 seems to have occurred."[59]

When the Argentine occupation on East Falkland came to a temporary end in 1811, this act did not constitute an intention to abandon the

Falklands or signal an attempt to renounce its claims. Indeed, "the hiatus of 1811–23 is legally irrelevant and does not return the Falkland/Malvinas Islands to the status of *res nullius*."[60] The legal basis for this line of reasoning is distilled from the Clipperton Island arbitration between Mexico and France. The arbitrator, King Victor Emmanuel III of Italy, espoused the view that Mexico (the losing claimant) had established no manifestation of sovereignty over the island prior to a French proclamation and visit of 1858.[61] Moreover, the award noted that the French failure to exercise authority in Clipperton Island between 1858 and 1897, when both France and Mexico landed there, did not return the island to the legal status of *res nullius* because France demonstrated no intention of abandoning its claim. Rubin made an important point when he compared this case with that of the Falkland/Malvinas. He concluded: "Given the political and economic vicissitudes of France between 1858 and 1897, this is understandable; so is the equivalent Buenos Aires silence of 1811–23. This situation is distinguishable from the British loss after 1774, because Great Britain's intention to abandon its claim can be derived from its silence in the face of adverse Spanish continuous and peaceful administration."[62]

In sum, the display of Spanish and Argentine authority over the Falkland Islands in the context of British acquiescence would seem to support the "occupation" mode claimed by Argentina. The efficacy of their occupation, though somewhat questionable, should not be dismissed outright. American activities in the South Atlantic were met with stiff Argentine resistance, although the intended outcome did not materialize in Argentina's favor. Moreover, to assert, as the British do, that by 1833 Argentina's occupation did not give rise to definitive title would also be highly questionable. What is unambiguous on this issue is the fact that the law is not very helpful, and therefore a legal opinion cannot be easily distilled from the relevant cases.

## Prescription

The evidence on which Argentina relied to show occupation could also be used when applying the mode of prescription as a basis for its claim to sovereignty. The two forms of prescription, acquisitive and extinctive, must be applied separately. In applying acquisitive prescription, one must be able to demonstrate that Argentina had absolute possession of the Falklands between 1767 and 1833. The historical record indicates otherwise. The British ten-year occupation of West Falkland not only interrupted

Argentina's period of settlement but posed a serious challenge to its claims of absolute possession over the entire geographic area.

Insofar as extinctive prescription is concerned, this mode would definitely be more supportive of the British claim because Argentina's occupation was not "wrongful." This is a necessary condition in the application of extinctive prescription. There is no evidence or support for the view that Argentina's possession of East Falkland between 1767 and 1833 was wrongful. What was and remains questionable is its claim to "open and notorious" possession. If it could be demonstrated that Argentina's possession was not ineffective and unsuccessful between that period, but was open and notorious, as the law requires, then its acquisitive prescription would be sufficient to give rise to title. Such demonstration has not been forthcoming, however, and cannot be gleaned from the historical record.

## *Abandonment*

The Argentine claim of British abandonment of the Falkland Islands in 1774 appears to be a valid one. This line of argument found expression in a speech made by Dr. Jose Ruda, the Argentine delegate to the United Nations Special Committee on the Situation with regard to the Implementation of the Granting of Independence to Colonial Countries and Peoples in 1964. Ambassador Ruda maintained that Britain's diplomatic silence from 1774 to 1833 had confirmed Spain's rights and that the Argentine state in 1810 had succeeded in those rights.[63] This extended period of British diplomatic silence combined with their voluntary withdrawal seems to have been sufficient to relinquish their claims to the Falklands. Abandonment requires that a country must show an intention to actually abandon the territory.

According to one British historian on the Falklands issue, J. C. Metford, the Spanish departure from the Falkland Islands in 1811 and the American destruction of Vernet's settlement in 1831 left the Falklands *res nullius*.[64] This same historian, however, went on in no uncertain terms to place great symbolic virtue in the British plaque as "reiterating British rights." There was no mention of the British abandonment of the Falklands in 1774. In other words, a piece of metal hanging on a dry stick was sufficient to preserve Britain's symbolic claim for almost sixty years. Metford's classification of the facts, imputing to Buenos Aires an intention to abandon the Falkland Islands, seems almost capricious. Rubin, an American legal expert, raised a fundamental question in the debate: "Can it be seriously argued that the symbolic plaque left in 1774 was sufficient to preserve a British claim to the islands allegedly abandoned voluntarily, while active Argentine protest was not effective to preserve a claim to islands evacuated under threat of force?"[65]

If anyone abandoned the Falklands, it was unquestionably the British when they voluntarily did so in 1774. The mode of abandonment does support Argentina's claim to sovereignty over the Falkland Islands. This conclusion was not readily accepted, however, by most writers who were sympathetic to the British case. Their counterargument revolved around the "efficacy" of the plaque left by Lt. Clayton at the time of withdrawal. That plaque was subsequently destroyed in 1781, but more importantly, British silence between 1774 and 1811 and again between 1823 and 1832 "in the face of open Buenos Aires assertions to sovereignty" was both a necessary and sufficient condition that signaled their intention to abandon the Falkland Islands.[66] The plaque argument is legally weak and rationally unsound. The current official British position takes no notice of it.

## Succession

Several distinguished Argentinian scholars have repeatedly advanced the "succession" argument in combination with the practice of *uti possidetis juris* as a basis for Argentina's claim to sovereignty over the Falkland Islands. Moreno Quintana offers the view that "the Malvinas were an integral part of the Spanish dominion in America, which was then transmitted by the right of succession to the legitimate heir, Argentina."[67] Martínez Moreno advances a not too dissimilar view: "As Spain was the owner of the Islands, when the independence of our nation was achieved, they passed into the national dominion by succession, and legitimate Spanish possessions and those of Argentina became united both in reality and legally."[68]

To be able to apply the law relating to succession, it is absolutely necessary to have an understanding of the principle of *uti possidetis juris.* The "as you possess, so may you possess" principle was a Latin American doctrine devised in order to settle the colonial boundary problem legally and peacefully. According to this doctrine, the new Latin American states would have a territorial expanse which corresponded to the administrative division of the Spanish colonial empire. Further, this doctrine remained a guiding principle among all the Hispanic-American states since 1810. "By virtue of this principle, the states in question gave reciprocal guarantees concerning territorial status."[69] Thus the principle of *uti possidetis juris* represented a right to succession of territory. It means therefore that Argentina's claim to Spanish succession based on this principle would only make sense if Spain was in fact the undisputed possessor or owner of the Falkland Islands. Spain cannot cede possession of a territory in question if it has no legitimate possession of the said territory.

At the time of Argentina's independence in 1816, it was highly questionable whether Spain had title to the Malvinas. If Spain did have title, then the *uti possidetis* principle could be applied. On the other hand, if Spain's title was questionable, then that of Argentina's, under the succession mode, would also be questionable. Rubin, in a well-balanced appraisal, summarizes the *uti possidetis* principle thus: "The key transaction purporting to fix rights in the Falklands/Malvinas Islands during this period involved treaties between Spain and England in 1667 and 1670. But there seems to be no credible evidence that either had actual possession of the islands before, during, or immediately after that time."[70] Therefore it would appear that the Malvinas, according to the *uti possidetis juris* principle, did not form part of the vice-royalty of the River Plate in 1816.

## Contiguity/Continuity

Argentina's reliance on the "theory of continuity" as a basis for its claim to the Malvinas has found expression in practically all of its posturing. Bologna strongly emphasizes this mode of territorial acquisition and asserts that "it [was] of vital importance."[71] In several of the arguments relating to this mode, two fundamental points appear to have been omitted. The first relates to the distinction between contiguity and continuity. Contiguity applies exclusively to islands, while continuity is applicable to territory not separated by water. Thus the continuity argument would be a misapplication in the Falklands' case. Contiguity on the other hand, would be more relevant and hence meaningful.

The second fundamental point relates to the question of legal application. The Argentine arguments relating to geographical contiguity lack legal relevance in today's situation. Contiguity aspects can influence a legal settlement in the case of uninhabited islands or continental shelf issues, but the practice of states has not sanctioned a more general principle.[72] And as stated in the Palmas case, Judge Huber made a decisive point about contiguity when he said: "It is impossible to show the existence of a rule of positive international law to the effect that islands situated outside territorial waters should belong to a state from the mere fact that its territory forms the terra firma."[73] Argentina's contiguity thesis based on the geographic fact that it is the most proximate state to the Falklands was clearly not a valid one. Should the argument of contiguity be a legally valid and acceptable practice in international law, then the island of Trinidad in the Caribbean Sea would naturally belong to Venezuela and the Jersey Islands to France. The problems and frictions that would arise among states were this to be the case would be staggering.

Both the geological and geographic arguments, subsumed under the rubric of "contiguity," have been vehemently opposed by Great Britain. The fact that contiguity as a mode of territorial acquisition has not been generally recognized in international law did not help Argentina's claim. Argentina's continued reliance on this mode neither buttressed its claims nor served to strengthen its case.

# Bases of British Claims

## Discovery

Britain, like Argentina, argued that the mode of discovery supported its claim to sovereignty over the islands.[74] The basis of this mode stemmed from the ubiquitous British assertion that Captain John Davies first sighted the Falkland Islands in 1592. The strong reliance placed on discovery by British writers and politicians was typically exemplified in a farcical piece by Byron Farwell at the end of the war in 1982: "To begin at the beginning: the Falkland Islands were first seen by British navigator John Davies in 1592."[75]

The problems relating to discovery have already been noted. It cannot be conclusively demonstrated or established from the historical records exactly who first discovered the Falkland Islands and from which European country they came. Attempts to assert otherwise fall into the realm of wishful thinking. We know for a certainty that the early history of the Falklands is patchy and nebulous and cannot be relied upon as authentic. In spite of these recalcitrant problems, however, two points can be distilled from the British arguments. If we agree that Britain first discovered the Falklands, this would, under the *Palmas* case, establish at best only an inchoate title. And an inchoate title is not sufficient to vest sovereignty. This point is significant because Britain's inchoate title did not develop into a definitive title because of historical circumstances. The second point relates to the shift in British official posture: discovery is not relied upon—the emphasis is on prescription.

In sum, Britain's claim to sovereignty based on discovery was much weaker than Argentina's. Both disputants' claims, based on this mode, were not sufficient and compelling enough to vest definitive title. The point is worth repeating that mere discovery of territory does not automatically give rise to title or ownership under international law.

## Occupation

Over the years Britain has also relied on the mode of occupation to boost its claim to sovereignty over the Falklands. For title to flow from occupation, however, a fundamental principle based on the existence of an unambiguous situation must be observed: the territory must be *res nullius* or belonging to no one at the time. When the British first established a settlement on West Falkland in 1766, the Falklands were not res nullius because the French had already established a settlement on East Falkland two years earlier. Moreover, the Spanish were also vigorously asserting their claims. Britain's ten-year occupation of West Falkland was not on territory regarded as "belonging to no one," and moreover, the occupation could not in any way be regarded as being "effective." British activities were confined to the immediate environs of Port Edgmont, and no display of authority comparable to Spain's was demonstrated.

When Britain reasserted its claims to the Falkland Islands in 1833, the territory was occupied and clearly not *res nullius*. The Argentine settlement was forcefully brought to an end by British evictors. Effectiveness of occupation between 1774, the year the British withdrew, and 1833, the year they returned, was nonexistent. During these fifty-nine years, there was clearly no evidence to support an actual exercise or display of authority by the British. The plaque argument has already been put to rest.

Finally, if we were to assume that Britain's occupation since 1833 had been effective, then for this mode to vest title the first requirement, which prescribed that the territory be *res nullius*, would have to be validated. Such validation would be contrary to the "accepted" historical data, particularly from 1833 onwards. Thus Britain's "argument is still defective inasmuch as it fails to meet the first requirement, that the territory be *res nullius* at the time of discovery."[76]

## Prescription

Over the years a significant shift in British official posture on the issue of sovereignty over the Falklands has taken place. More than ever before, Britain is relying on the mode of prescription to support its claim to sovereignty. The 1982 war underscored this shift and added a new dimension to the negotiation processes between the two disputants. One columnist from the *Times* highlighted this shift when he said, "The British claim is based principally on the fact that its citizens have occupied the islands continuously for the last 149 years."[77]

British continuous occupation of the Falkland Islands since 1833 was never a contentious issue. What was clearly controversial was Britain's claim that this 149-year period of continuous possession proved its right of sovereignty over the Falklands. This line of reasoning demonstrated a disregard for the rules that have to be met or satisfied before prescription can vest title.

The rules pertaining to acquisitive and extinctive prescription are slightly different. Acquisitive prescription, the mode advanced by Britain, does not support its claim to sovereignty because continuous possession fulfills only part of the requirements. Granted that the British occupation had been "long and continuous," it nevertheless failed to satisfy the critically important criterion of being peaceful; hence title cannot flow from acquisitive prescription. While British possession had been effective in the sense of being continuous, open, and notorious, at the same time the Argentines had protested continuously against that possession. In short, British possession had not been peaceful, and this aspect of the law must be fulfilled before title can flow from acquisitive prescription.

When the modern Argentine Republic was established in 1853, protests against British occupation of the Falklands continued, although they were not made with any degree of regularity. Following an Argentine note of protest on 31 July 1849, the issue was not raised again until 1888. Since 1946, however, "Argentina has not missed any opportunity of protesting against the British presence on the Islands."[78] An important observation is in order here. For a policy of nonrecognition, as demonstrated through protests, to be efficacious under international law, it must have a certain degree of intensity and periodicity. The Swedish jurist Ove Bring, in applying these criteria to the Falklands situation, concluded: "All in all, the Argentine protests have been made with such regularity and been of such intensity that there is no contesting that they are of legal relevance in the Falklands crisis."[79] Under these circumstances, it is very clear that

Britain's claim was not supported by acquisitive prescription. The picture changes, however, when we apply the rules pertaining to extinctive prescription. This mode involves possession, although originally wrongful, of such long term that it precludes the deposed state from asserting its claim. The quintessential aspect of this mode has to do with changing circumstances in world politics.

Diplomatic pressures were the only means available to Argentina up to 1920. The government in Buenos Aires could have resorted to military means, as it did in 1982, but open and unprovoked aggression would have been and still is contrary to international law and highly disruptive of world order. Nevertheless, Argentina protested, and for a time these protests were effective in blocking Britain's claim to sovereignty by extinctive prescription, had not changing political circumstances intervened. The establishment of the World Courts, initially as the Permanent Court of International Justice and later as the International Court of Justice (ICJ), changed the situation so that diplomatic protests were no longer sufficient to keep alive Argentina's claim to sovereignty. In order to avoid extinguishing its claim, Argentina should have resorted to the ICJ rather than continuing to protest. The fact of the matter was that Argentina never submitted its claim to the Court for judgment. Its failure to do so, to take advantage of the requirements prescribed by international law, has quietly ceded sovereignty to Britain by extinctive prescription. Thus by 1982, Argentina's claim was extinguished. The British jurist Rosalyn Higgins arrived at a similar conclusion when she pointed out: "No tribunal could tell her [Argentina] that she has to accept British title because she has acquiesced to it. But what the protests do not do is to defeat the British title, which was built up in other ways through Argentina's acquiescence."[80] There was therefore little doubt that Britain acquired title to the Falklands by extinctive prescription. In other words, it was in this mode that the strength of the British claims resided.

# General Assessment of the Disputants' Claims

Argentina has some good grounds on which to base its claim to sovereignty over the Malvinas. Foremost among them are occupation and British abandonment. Discovery and succession to Spanish rights are highly questionable. The contiguity argument has not assumed the status of a principle in positive international law, where its application could have a precedent effect. However, in spite of the weaknesses of the latter arguments, these weaknesses do not of themselves dilute the efficacy of Argentina's overall claims, especially when they are viewed against British arguments.

With very few exceptions, British academics, jurists, and politicians went to great lengths, particularly in the aftermath of the April 1982 invasion, to bolster their claims and diminish those of Argentina. In her 3 April 1982 speech to Parliament, Prime Minister Margaret Thatcher laid down the basic line: "We have no doubt about our sovereignty." Both Francis Pym, who became the foreign secretary, and Cecil Parkinson, the Conservative party chairman, trumpeted the "rock-solid" nature of the British claim. And a government publication of April 1982, *The Falkland Islands: The Facts*, presented the Tory line: "British sovereignty over the Falkland Islands rests on a secure historical and legal foundation."[81] A *Daily Telegraph* editorial during the latter part of April typified the situation in characteristic Tory fashion: "The British case is already clear. Britain is acting to uphold and make effective again her sovereignty over the Falkland Islands, a sovereignty which satisfies every known test of international law."[82] Along similar nationalistic lines, Sir Miles Clifford, a former governor of the Falkland Islands, expressed his views on the sovereignty issue thus: "Those who have occasion to conduct research into the history of this little colony can only confirm that our [British] claim to sovereignty is irrefutable."[83] Professor James Fawcett, an eminent British jurist, succinctly stated that "the territorial title to the Islands—the land and territorial sea and airspace—must be accorded to the United Kingdom."[84]

The above expressed views were a clear example of biased judgment and hasty conclusions. Their impact became all the more devastating as multitudes in Britain were galvanized into a state of euphoria. The aim undoubtedly was to reduce the Argentine claims to nil and, at the same time, to present the British case as being both justifiable and legitimate. Many were led to believe that Argentina had no claims after all. This was clearly not the case because Argentina did have some solid grounds on which to base its claims.

In June 1982, a study by the Geneva-based International Commission of Jurists forcefully pointed out after a thorough research into the dispute that the "Argentine claim is not as empty of merit as the British statements imply."[85] What was spectacularly revealing was a statement made by Peter Beck, a leading British historian on the Falklands dispute, regarding official British views: "In private, even British governments have oft-expressed doubts regarding the strength of the British case."[86] And a draft report of the House of Commons Foreign Affairs Committee conceded that "the historical evidence is finely balanced."[87] The inevitable conclusion therefore was that Argentina did have a basis for claiming sovereignty over the Malvinas Islands. When its claims were examined against those of the other disputant, however, it appeared that the weight had shifted in Britain's favor.

The modes of occupation and discovery did not give rise to a definitive title for Britain. As James Gravelle has stated, "Only by extinctive prescription can Great Britain claim definitive title to the Falkland Islands."[88] Even if we assumed that Argentina acquired definite title to the Islands by effective occupation or acquisitive prescription before 1833, Britain's claim to sovereignty since the 1920s was much stronger. This conclusion did not mean that the International Court of Justice or an arbitrator would rule in Britain's favor. If this were the case, then it would have been reasonable to assume that Britain would have willingly sought judgment from such quarters. The sovereignty issue remained complex and historically nebulous. Moreover, since the war of 1982, the issue has obviously become even more intractable and the attitudes of both disputants have hardened. Beck's insightful statement captures the essence of the problem: "Although both disputants have adopted a rather simple black and white view of the claims issue, most objective and informed studies of the legal and historical aspects of sovereignty tend to interpret the question in a somewhat grey and uncertain manner."[89]

Overall, the British case remains much stronger than Argentina's. In the end, however, what really counted was not the paper strengths of the respective claims, but the question of will and power. In 1833 and again in 1982, Britain had both the will and power to control the Falklands.

# Britain's Relationship to the Falklands Prior to 2 April 1982

During the decade or so prior to the Falklands War of 1982, there were a number of clear signs which strongly indicated that successive British governments were losing interest in the southwest Atlantic region as a whole and consequently in the future of the British possessions located in the Falkland Islands, the Falkland Island Dependencies of South Georgia and South Sandwich Islands, and the British Antarctic Territory.[90] That diminution of Britain's interest stemmed from the low priority Downing Street accorded the region and was brought about in part by the heightened emphasis decision makers placed on Continental issues. Britain's energies during this period were concentrated on Europe and NATO. One historian commented rather sadly that "there was no policy for the Falklands."[91]

In the analysis that follows, an attempt will be made to trace and highlight the important landmark events that underlined the Anglo-Argentine, and by extension, the Falklands' relationship. This approach will underscore some relevant aspects of Britain's posturing and pronouncements which gave rise to certain signals that boosted Argentina's confidence and helped lead to its invasion of 2 April 1982.

Among the many contributing factors, the following appear to have been very compelling, and to a great degree, these factors tell the story of Britain's relationship to the Falklands prior to the outbreak of hostilities in April 1982.

First, the British government's policy towards the Falklands demonstrated its lack of commitment to the region in material resources. Government officials and ministers were cognizant of the decapitalization of the Falklands' economy, which not only led to a drain of capital from the area, but also created a climate of political and economic uncertainty that discouraged further private investments. The flight of capital to the United Kingdom base was the catalyst that brought about the depressed condition of the Falklands' economy. Official U.K. policy did not attempt to stem the flow, and governmental aid to the area did not amount to much. The following table gives a breakdown of the disbursements for a five-year period. Note the years of relative overall decline:

### British Aid to the Falklands, 1976 to 1980
*(In Thousands of Pounds)*

|  | 1976 | 1977 | 1978 | 1979 | 1980 |
| --- | --- | --- | --- | --- | --- |
| Technical Cooperation | 261 | 357 | 355 | 473 | 427 |
| Financial Aid | 1,233 | 758 | 1,765 | 442 | 587 |
| TOTAL | 1,494 | 1,115 | 2,120 | 915 | 1,014 |

### Students and Trainees Financed Under the Aid Program, 1980

| Students | Trainees | Total |
| --- | --- | --- |
| 5 | 11 | 16 |

*Source: Overseas Development Administration, British Aid Statistics, 1976–1980.*

Britain's lack of commitment to the region also manifested itself in other areas, most notably that of the government's determined effort to promote a negotiated settlement with Argentina in the period after 1976. The British government's initiative of November 1980 "represented a significant transformation in the dispute, since the government indicated publicly its willingness to consider a solution involving Argentina's acquisition of sovereignty over the islands."[92]

This shift in official posturing reflected a softening of Britain's hitherto "uncompromising attitude." But more significantly, it indicated the government's desire to settle the dispute with Argentina so that trade relations could grow between the two countries. When the Tory government came to office in May 1979, it reasserted with a vengeance Labour's "commercial non-policy" with Argentina. One observer noted that "ministers, including Mr. Peter Walker and Mr. Cecil Parkinson, rushed to Buenos Aires to reassert Britain's reliability as a trading partner—especially as a supplier of arms."[93] Huge arms purchases were made by Argentina in the 1979–82 period, during which time the total Argentine external debt rose from about $8 billion in 1978 to about $37 billion in 1982. A great deal of these purchases were made in Britain. Little wonder that one London daily screamed, "how the islanders were almost sold up the River Plate."[94]

Criticisms of the Conservative government's policy surfaced in both Parliament and the media. An example of such concern was expressed by the tabling of an Early Day Motion in the House of Commons on 15 December 1981 that stated:

> This House declares its determination that the Falkland Islands and Dependencies shall remain under British rule in accordance with the wishes of the Islanders and that the British interests in the British Antarctic Territories shall be protected and advanced; draws attention to the importance of preserving the international cooperation enshrined in the Antarctic Treaty ... and calls upon Her Majesty's Government to demonstrate its commitment to maintaining a tangible presence in the area.[95]

The motion, which was endorsed by over 170 members of Parliament from all political parties by the end of January, was totally ignored by the government. Support for parliamentary criticisms was reinforced by articles and letters appearing in the press. These called on the government to step up its commitment to the region as a whole.[96]

Another factor leading to the Argentine invasion was the failure of successive Labour and Conservative governments to implement some of the major recommendations contained in the Shackleton Report of 1976. The report highlighted among other things the necessity for cultivating closer cooperation with Argentina, the reinvestment of profits by absentee-owned companies operating in the Falklands, the extension of the runway at Stanley, and a diversification of development strategy to help the local economy to extricate itself from its monocultural mold.[97]

The British government was becoming more aware of the important role Argentina would play in the long-term development of the Falkland Islands. Given their proximity to the mainland and the benefits to be derived from closer ties with Buenos Aires, such as low fuel costs, London was very willing to work towards a settlement with Argentina. Embarking on such a strategy meant that Britain's exports to Argentina would rise dramatically. This strategy must also be seen in the context of the British domestic economy. Reductions in overseas aid from 1977 onwards stemmed from a weakened domestic economy, and with the 1979 oil price increases, the situation was exacerbated to the point where the government pleaded poverty. The government's policy of little or no aid to the Falklands arose from the weak British economy. Moreover, the strategic environment as it related to the South Atlantic region in particular was perceived by the government as benign.

Critics saw this as an excuse the government used to avoid diverting resources towards costly infrastructures in the Falklands. In a House of Commons debate in February 1977, Anthony Crossland pointed out: "We cannot at this time accept more costly recommendations.... There are more urgent claims from much poorer communities."[98] Thus the recommendation to extend the runway at Stanley to accommodate intercontinental jets was shelved. Although cost was a consideration, it was definitely not the main reason. Crossland hinted at part of the explanation when he said, "There are more urgent claims." This stance by the government indicated that the southwest Atlantic was of low political and strategic priority to Britain during this period. A more fundamental reason, however, was the desire expressed by both Labour and Conservative governments to seek a rapprochement with Argentina.

In essence, the economic development of the Falkland Islands was seen to be inextricably tied to the mainland. Hence the display of interest towards a political solution and that, by implication, involved the sovereignty issue. Nicholas Ridley, minister of state at the Foreign and Commonwealth Office, claimed in December 1980 that the future of the Falkland Islands was blighted by the sovereignty dispute. Thus the Islands suffered from a process of economic and demographic decline in spite of references to their offshore resource potential.[99] The government, he claimed, was therefore willing "to work with countries of the region," especially Argentina, in order to promote the economic development of the Islands.

Another element of the Falklands situation was Britain's eagerness to cooperate with Argentina and not provoke its antagonism. According to

Beck, "Since 1976 successive British ministers have gone on record to argue for positive advantages of settling the sovereignty dispute as well as using the latter as a bridge for Anglo-Argentine harmony."[100] David Owen echoed the sentiments of the Labour government in April 1977 when he asserted that "the establishment of a framework for Anglo-Argentine economic co-operation will contribute substantially to the development of the islands and the region as a whole."[101] Crossland also advocated this strategy in his February 1977 statement when he said, "It is cooperation not confrontation which we seek to achieve."[102]

In spite of parliamentary criticisms of government policy towards the Falklands and strong opposition from the Islanders themselves, both the Labour Opposition and the Conservative government continued to adopt and advocate a policy aimed at rapprochement with Argentina. Implementation of this policy was met, however, with stiff resistance. Support for the Kelpers to remain British transcended political party boundaries in Britain. Any government would find it extremely difficult to muster a majority in Parliament for policies that were clearly perceived to be inimical to the expressed wishes of the Islanders. Further, the Falklands lobby in London became a powerful force in Parliament and in the press. Members of the lobby group—the Falkland Islands Committee—included not only politicians but also retired senior officers of the armed forces and influential business tycoons. Though totally unofficial, the Committee was nevertheless able to put together an extraordinary political and business coalition to keep the Falkland Islands British. One writer summed up the Committee's influence in these pointed words: "Government ministers saw the names of the Committee on the Committee's letterhead and fled."[103] The cross-party support for the Kelpers was impressive, and the Committee's role in rallying support for the Falklands assumed a greater degree of importance during this period.

During the early part of the Tory administration, the rapprochement line was vigorously pursued. In a speech in Parliament in December 1980, Nicholas Ridley stressed: "It has not proven possible ... to exploit these resources, either of fish or oil, because of the dead hand of the dispute with Argentina. We are seeking to find a solution in order to make that possible."[104] While that solution encouraged closer ties with Buenos Aires, it also involved ways of arriving at a political settlement of the sovereignty issue. Beck alerts us to another factor that seems to have influenced such a policy: "The Falkland Islands dispute is viewed increasingly in London from a regional as opposed to an imperial perspective: the resulting tendency to treat the dispute in a Latin American context has been reinforced by organizational factors within the Foreign and Commonwealth Office."[105] The reluctance, therefore, on the part of the British government to pump economic development aid into the region was quite evident, given the official line it was prosecuting prior to April 1982.

The situation in the Falklands was further influenced by the British government's policy to withdraw the ice-patrol ship HMS *Endurance* and the implications arising from the passage of the Nationality Act in 1981. In its analysis of British government policies which cast some doubt on the strength of British commitment to the Falkland Islands and their defense, *The Franks Report* (1983) identified the significance of two disparate events. The first was the passage of the Nationality Act, which included provisions that deprived most of the Islanders of full British citizenship. The second and "probably the most influential signal received in Buenos Aires"[106] was the decision to withdraw HMS *Endurance* in 1982. This decision was confirmed in Parliament in June 1981.[107]

The government's decision to withdraw HMS *Endurance* arose as a consequence of the 1981 Defense Review. Preoccupied with cost-effectiveness and "getting value for money," John Nott, the defense secretary, sought ways and means to trim off the fat from the defense budget. His decision to scrap the patrolling activities of HMS *Endurance* was met with stiff opposition from the foreign secretary, Lord Carrington, and also from the Islanders themselves. Carrington wrote to Nott on at least three separate occasions—5 June 1981, 22 January 1982, and 17 February 1982—expressing his concern at the decision and pointing out the symbolic role of HMS *Endurance*. When informed of the defense secretary's decision, the Falkland Islands Council held a joint meeting on 26 June 1981 and thereafter dispatched a message to Lord Carrington stating the following:

> The people of the Falklands deplore in the strongest terms the decision to withdraw HMS *Endurance* from service. They express extreme concern that Britain appears to be abandoning its defence of British interests in the South Atlantic and Antarctic at a time when other powers are strengthening their position in these areas. They feel such a withdrawal will further weaken British sovereignty in this area in the eyes not only of the Islanders but of the world. They urge that all possible endeavours be made to secure a reversal of the decision.[108]

The decision appeared irreversible. Nott's letter of 3 February 1982 to Lord Carrington confirmed the government's decision to withdraw HMS *Endurance*. Further, during Question Time in the House of Commons on 9 February 1982, the prime minister said that the decision to withdraw

HMS *Endurance* had been very difficult and that, in view of the competing claims on the defense budget and the defense capability of the ship, the secretary of state for defense had decided that other claims on the budget should have greater priority.[109]

HMS *Endurance*, an ice-patrol ship, served a useful purpose in the South Atlantic. It carried out rescue operations and provided logistics support to the British Antarctic Survey team. Lord Carrington pointed out that the hydrographic survey tasks undertaken by HMS *Endurance*, and the operation of its Wasp helicopters over a wide area of the British Antarctic Territory were an important aspect of the British claim to sovereignty.[110] One historian noted that "the ship's major contribution derived from its symbolic role in terms of providing a regular British physical presence in the Falklands and Antarctic region."[111] According to Lord Shackleton, it was clear that "flying the flag was the most vital and obvious symbol at stake."[112] The withdrawal of HMS *Endurance* was bound, he feared, to be interpreted as a relaxation of Britain's Falklands and Antarctic vigil. "It is not without significance that I have been approached by friends on the Argentine side, who have asked whether that means that the British were thinking of changing their posture generally," he stated.[113] And Lord Morris, in his contribution to the House of Lords debate on 16 December 1981, remarked that the decision had been "greeted with unalloyed joy in the Argentine press," a point also verified by the *Daily Telegraph* and by the official *Franks Report*.[114]

The ineluctable conclusion, therefore, of any survey of British policy towards the Falklands prior to 2 April 1982 must be that the official decisions taken and pronouncements made by both Labour and Conservative governments since the late 1970s indicated a diminution of interest and a dilution of commitment towards the southwest Atlantic region. One reputable historian explained the rationale in these words:

> During this period, domestic problems and international concerns nearer home relegated the problems of the south-west Atlantic to an increasingly marginal role in the political as well as in the geographical sense. The refusal to extend the runway at Stanley in order to allow access to inter-continental jets served to confirm Britain's isolation from its possessions in that part of the world, while by 1981 the preservation of *Endurance* was apparently not deemed worth £3 million, which was reputed to be its yearly cost.[115]

And Lawrence Freedman of Kings College fame argued that the British government was willing to offer neither compromise to Argentina, nor a credible long-term commitment to the Falkland Islands. "There was," he said, "a lack of political will in London either to solve the dispute once and for all in some deal with Buenos Aires, or else to accept full responsibility for the long-term security and prosperity of the Islands."[116]

It was therefore clear that pre–April 1982 trends in British policy encouraged Argentina to believe that its invasion would prove successful. It must also be noted that the Argentine invasion pointed significantly to internal factors. Insofar as the external factors were concerned, however, these arose mainly from the military junta's perceptions of Britain's relationship towards the Falklands and the southwest Atlantic region generally.

## Conclusion

Negotiations over the Falklands dispute have reached a stalemate because of the issue of sovereignty, and efforts to unravel the mystery surrounding this phenomenon and reach a compromise have so far proved unsuccessful. My attempt to explore the setting as it related to geography and history has not yielded any unusual results with regards to the sovereignty question. Moreover, from an international law perspective, there seems to be no clear-cut example that approximates the Falklands dispute. It is clear that "sovereignty has been a greater curse and a source of more conceptual confusion than even Clausewitz's dubious doctrine."[117] My analysis reveals the inadequacy of historical data and legal applications in solving the sovereignty question which occupied center stage in the dispute.

Historical experiences, particularly those from which Argentina learned after its humiliating defeat in June 1982, have tended to harden positions on the issue. Forthright conclusions spelled out in black and white terms have also continued to surface over the years after the war. In November 1985, for example, the former governor of the Falklands, Sir Rex Hunt, had this to say on the sovereignty issue: "Having read all I can about the history of the Falkland Islands, I have absolutely no doubt that our claim to sovereignty is the *just* cause, and the Argentine claim is the unjust."[118] Governor Hunt's classification of the claims, forty-four months after the war, was a classic example of escalating rhetoric and analytical paralysis. My investigation has revealed otherwise—sovereignty remains a grey area and should be examined from that perspective.

EDINBURGH UNIVERSITY LIBRARY

WITHDRAWN

# Two

# The Falklands War and
# the Use of Military Force

The Falklands campaign, which began with a successful invasion of the Falkland Islands by Argentine elite forces of naval commandos, the *Buzo Táctico*, on the morning of 2 April 1982 and ended with their surrender to British forces on 14 June, exactly ten and a half weeks later, was an unexpected war for both Argentina and Britain. In strategic terms, the conflict was a classic example of a limited war. One military historian described it as a "textbook example of a limited war—limited in time, in location, in objectives and in means."[1] Some journalists went so far in their description as to refer to it as "a freak of history."[2] But whatever nomenclature one utilized in one's description of that war and whatever lessons were ferreted out after the fighting was over, the following assertion was unambiguously clear: both belligerent states did not plan to go to war in 1982 over a piece of "disputed" real estate.

Although the territorial dispute over the Falkland Islands had been a long-standing issue between the two countries, neither side was prepared for the heavy fighting which subsequently followed and resulted in the loss of more than one thousand Argentine and British lives. But when "faced with this unanticipated conflict, Argentina and Britain were compelled to use the forces they had available to gain control over the islands. The conflict is thus a textbook example of how the doctrine and deployment of military forces are often adjusted in a crisis to fit the changing patterns of international relations."[3] Moreover, while neither Argentina nor Britain anticipated war, both found themselves locked into an escalating conflict from which neither one was able to extricate itself.

The question, therefore, of why Argentina and Britain had to resort to the use of military force has to be answered. Answers to this central

53

question will be explored at length in this and the following chapter. But before embarking on that exercise, I wish to offer a short conceptual overview of the terms *war* and *force*. An explication of these essentially contested concepts will provide clearer insights into the phenomena of interstate conflicts. The intention, however, is not to present an exhaustive study on conceptual clarification, but merely to tease out a few strands of meaning to which these two terms give rise.

War is a phenomenon that is as old as organized society itself. Man's capacity to hurt and maim, to inflict pain, and to deliver the means of destruction to far-off places has obviously risen to unprecedented levels, particularly in our technology-driven age. Thomas Schelling describes the effects of war in terms of "pain and shock, loss and grief, privation and horror … always in some degree, sometimes in terrible degree, among the results of warfare."[4] Others see it as "probably the most destructive and depraved state of affairs that can or does exist on earth. It is organized and systematic killing accompanied by rapine, robbery and other forms of social degradation."[5] The dictionary defines war as the state or fact of exerting violence or force against a state or politically organized body; especially a contest by force between two or more nations or states. And Quincy Wright, in his monumental *Study of War*, described war as "a conflict among political groups, especially sovereign states, carried on by armed forces of considerable magnitude for a considerable period of time."[6] He viewed it as "the consequence of a situation in which legal sanctions are unable to maintain an accepted system of law."[7]

There is no universally accepted definition of war. That much is widely recognized. Attempts have been made, however, to synthesize the different strands of meaning with a view to arriving at some meaningful consensus. Two views, mainly of a politicolegal orientation, have emanated from that exercise. One holds that war is a continuation of politics by other means; the other, that war is a breakdown of order.

The first view has been credited to Carl von Clausewitz,[8] whose ubiquitous assertion that war ought to be a continuation of political intercourse with an admixture of other means, has rightly become the most famous of all strategic aphorisms.[9] Clausewitz's major postulations on war have persisted in the writings and views of many military theorists and practitioners. Mao Tse-tung, who borrowed the Clausewitzian dictum, once affirmed: "War is politics and war itself is a political action…. Politics is war without bloodshed while war is politics with bloodshed."[10]

While Mao's view equated the legitimacy of a government's political actions with the legitimacy of war, a view which would justify the use of force for practically any purpose, the view expressed by Clausewitz remains conceptually valid and operationally relevant. War has been and still is basically a political activity. It is fought for politicostrategic objectives, and it results from policies pursued by states "in the belief that the use of armed forces will serve their interests."[11] Moreover, this perspective on war is consistent with the arms control approach, which believes that wars begin in the minds of men and that peace and stability are related functionally to both intentions and military capabilities. If nations wish to go to war, they will find the means to do so. The objective, therefore, becomes one of controlling those factors which prompt states to go to war.

The second view of war is a legal one. When looked at from this perspective, war is seen as a breakdown of legal sanctions and the bargaining process. It is "a test of strength by the last resort of acts which aim at extermination, destruction, or unconditional surrender."[12] The fact that legalists have ventilated their respective viewpoints of war for centuries has in no way obfuscated the essence of their basic arguments. According to the legal perspective, war is essentially the consequence of a situation where sanctions are incapable of maintaining order and the status quo. Hence it is this breakdown of the legal framework which is seen as a precondition for the phenomenon commonly referred to as war.

Apart from these two major perspectives, there are other views of war that warrant mentioning. The deterministic view holds that war, like any other event, can be explained by natural laws. The voluntaristic view, on the other hand, holds that war is entered into by an act of free will and that its consequences change the course of history. While there are merits in both postulations, the latter has gained considerable currency over the years among legal scholars and jurists.[13] The initiation of a war, therefore, seems to be an act of choice exercised by at least one of the belligerent parties. Other views relating to the causes of war are manifold. Some scholars argue that the underlying causes of war can be traced to the structure of power and alliance relationships in the international system.[14] Others trace the roots of war to political, economic, social, and psychological factors internal to the state. And Marxists argue that wars are caused by the capitalist system, which constantly strives to expand markets and investment opportunities in order to accumulate wealth and benefit the owners of the means of production at the expense of the masses. War has also been traced to attempts by political leaders to solve their internal sociopolitical and economic problems through the adoption of hostile foreign policy ventures, on the assumption that external conflict will promote internal harmony and consolidate political leadership.[15]

Unlike war, a phenomenon that is not a permanent state of affairs in international life, force remains a ubiquitous instrument of international politics. According to Fred Northedge, "force has played and continues to play a dominant role in international relations."[16] Its use for self-defense by a state is sanctioned by the United Nations Charter. The legitimate use of force, therefore, is not inconsistent with the norms of international law. But what exactly is force? Are the expressions "force of events" and "force of circumstances" consistent with our basic understanding of the term from an international relations or more pointedly from a military/strategic perspective? It is clear that this metaphorical usage of the concept is not what is contemplated in the politicostrategic framework.

The concepts *force* and *power*, often used interchangeably, are not synonymous terms. Force is distinguishable from power. While power is seen as "the capability of a person or group to make his or its will felt in the decision-making process of another person or group," force refers essentially to "physical restraint or [a] set of restraints."[17] Moreover, power is relational and acts at the level of the mind. The ability to exercise power stems from a perception of capabilities, whether military, economic, or diplomatic. In this sense power is seen as being synonymous with force. But the synonymity is related to the threat, rather than to the use, of force.

Force is also distinguishable from violence, although both employ physical means to achieve certain ends. Whereas the term *violence* is normally applied to the use of physical force by nongovernmental agencies, generally for private rather than public ends, the term *force* refers to actions having a higher degree of legitimacy than those involving *violence* and refers to "an action sanctioned by a certain community allegedly in the public interest and for the public good."[18] The use of military force by states for the attainment of politicostrategic objectives is, of course, not a new phenomenon. According to one study, "the weight of evidence is consistent with the hypothesis that discrete uses of the armed forces are an effective way of achieving near-term foreign policy objectives."[19] And this was precisely what Britain and Argentina did in 1982. Both countries used military force in order to achieve certain objectives. In Argentina's case, military force was the chosen instrument used for regaining "lost" territory. For Britain, it was more a case of defending its national honor and maintaining international prestige. The clash of arms not only led to what has been described as a "short and sharp" war, but to the creation of certain perceptions among statesmen about the strategic role military forces play in international relations.

Military force was used in the Falklands War as a deliberate and controlled instrument. It was also used judiciously. The Argentine invasion was more like a surgical operation—swift and fairly clean. The British military response, on the other hand, was no different, except in scale. This chapter examines the use of force by both belligerents. Britain's case will be explored at greater length in the following chapter, and the present chapter will focus mainly on Argentine motivations. It will be shown that Argentina's use of force was prompted by a number of factors, of which domestic economic and political issues and the possibility of wider strategic gains were crucial in the calculus of the junta's decision making. Britain, on the other hand, embarked on a three-pronged strategy of which the military instrument was the most credible and, being fully aware of the costs involved in launching Operation Corporate, did not hesitate to use force for perceived politicostrategic gains. Both cases underscored the gravity of domestic economic constraints, and both demonstrated that a course of action which defied economic rationality could be undertaken when perceived higher interests are at stake.

## The Road to Conflict: The Junta's Decision to Invade the Falklands

When the ruling Argentine military junta finally decided to invade the Falkland/Malvinas Islands on the morning of 2 April 1982, little did these officers know that their action would set in motion a train of compelling events that ultimately would lead to their own demise. The decision to use military force to "repossess" lost territory not only plunged Argentina into a nasty little war with Britain, but it also spelled disaster for the ruling junta. At the end of the seventy-four-day war, Argentina was defeated and the members of the military junta were totally disgraced. Following their humiliation by the British, a crisis of epic proportions occurred within the armed forces, which experienced pressure from the established political parties for a return to constitutional government.

The question of why the military junta decided to execute its invasion plans when it did in early April 1982 is a crucial and important one. But before considering this question, we must look into the recent socioeconomic and political history of Argentina in order to get a better understanding of the factors that shaped the junta's decision. It is necessary to go beyond the plethora of one-line explanations for such a complex issue. One such explanation contended that "the Argentine government was trying to divert attention from the country's monetary inflation."[20] Such a representative view, while being both simplistic and erroneous, has been widely circulated. It is, therefore, the aim of this section to present a balanced and comprehensive understanding of the forces that helped to shape the junta's decision to use force on 2 April 1982. The first step on that road that led to conflict was taken almost fifteen years ago, and it is appropriate at this time to reexamine the broader and deeper aspects of those forces that shaped the junta's decision.

Explanation in the social sciences does not come to us in a neat package of readily available immutable laws, but must be ferreted out from a consistent pattern of behavior and its linkages. Further, the task requires an exploration of the manner in which some ideas have become facts. Ideas come from thinkers and are put into practice either directly where thinking men assume power or indirectly where the powerful interpret the world and act in it according to the lessons they have learned. It is therefore this flowing stream of ideas which shape the explanations of international relations as offered by the scholar and guide the decision makers who conduct the policies. The recent politicoeconomic history of Argentina prior to 1982 splendidly underscores the power and fascination of ideas.

Preoccupied with the forceful idea of the "Argentine Question" and the relentless pursuit for answers, successive rulers of Argentina, both military and civilian, have embarked upon courses of action that have plunged the country further into disaster. Blessed with a temperate climate and endowed with vast natural resources, Argentina, the eighth largest country in the world, was before World War I economically closer to Canada and Australia than to any other Latin American country. A settler country of primarily European immigrants, it had a predominantly urban population and in 1913 boasted the highest literacy rate in all Latin America. By 1929, the year the Great Depression began in America, Argentina had also won the reputation of being a model democracy in the Western Hemisphere. Indeed, it was the envy of its neighbors until an unparalleled tidal wave of violence washed over it. As formulated by Raul Alfonsín before he became president in 1983, the question is why Argentina, a rich and democratic nation in the 1920s, reverted to a process that moved it toward underdevelopment, authoritarianism, and violence.

## Background to Military Rule

By the end of 1975, the civilian government of Isabel Perón was facing its worst crisis since the general elections of March 1973. Apart from internal disorders within the Peronist movement, there were also serious domestic economic problems confronting the government. The impact of the new economic austerity plan introduced in June 1975 was keenly felt among the working class. That plan involved, among other things, a new devaluation of the peso, increases in the prices of public goods and services—in some cases more than 100 percent—and a severe limitation on wage increases to under 40 percent, while inflation rose 102 percent from June to August alone.[21]

In a concerted effort to get the government to roll back prices, the working class took strike action. No sooner was the new economic plan unveiled than the country was plunged into a massive wave of strikes. Industrial action by the working class exacerbated the already fragile state of the economy in both macro and sectoral terms. According to one report, "the industrial sector was in deep depression, unemployment had shot up from 2.3 percent to 6 percent in Greater Buenos Aires, and to 7.5 percent in Cordoba and other centers of the badly hit car industry."[22] Moreover, the crippling inflation rate, which was now at an alarmingly high level, further decimated the standard of living of most Argentineans, particularly the urban poor and the working class. Real wages fell 26 percent between December 1975 and March 1976, an average of 8.6 percent per month.

Working-class mobilization against the government's monetary and fiscal policies was intensified and reached new heights in early 1976. Workers' demands and aggressively militant agitation became a matter of serious concern for the country's armed forces and the military economic elites. When in early March 1976 the new economics minister launched yet another austerity program that was more in line with International Monetary Fund (IMF) prescriptions, a fresh and spontaneous outbreak of civil disorder followed. The impact of widespread working class strike and militant actions severely jolted the entire country. Argentina's internal situation in March 1976 was chaotic and very frightening. It appeared that the government of Isabel Perón was unable to deal with the myriad of social and economic problems that confronted the country.

As the crisis deepened, it became clear to many that a military coup was imminent. Indeed, rumors of a coup began to circulate around the capital city weeks before the military seized power. Amidst the confusion and near collapse of the government, on 24 March 1976 the military overthrew the civilian government of Isabel Perón. The new leader, General Jorge Videla, justified the March coup as an end not only of a government, but also of a historic cycle—the cycle associated with Peronist and post–Peronist interference in and mismanagement of the economy.[23] This event marked the sixth occasion on which the military had seized power in Argentina. They had done so in 1930, 1943, 1955, 1962, and 1966. And on all those occasions things had not turned out well for the military.[24] This coup would turn out to be no different.

## Military Rule: The Domestic Context 1976–82

The excesses of Peronism had been such that when the junta seized power in a bloodless coup in March 1976, its action was greeted with a nearly universal sense of relief.[25] Support for the coup came mainly from the industrialists, large landowners, and financiers, who had refused to accept the reformist project attempted by Perón and were instrumental in shaping the junta's Malvinas policy. The extent of support seems, however, to have transcended this group of economic elites. According to one observer, "the coup was also welcomed by a sector of the middle class, alienated by the chaos and disorders of the previous years and who now saw a possibility of a restoration of law and order."[26]

Headed by General Jorge Videla, the new military government quickly set about the task of transforming Argentina's political system. In particular, it aimed at weakening decisively the power of the working class and its Peronist leadership. Through the execution of a carefully crafted policy, the new military leaders hoped to create the political conditions necessary for the restructuring of the economy. Juan Corradi, a noted Argentine sociologist, captured the junta's strategy in these succinct words: "Their objective was not merely to terminate the disorder of the Peronist years, but to reorganize the very basis of Argentine society."[27] He went on to list the elements that constituted the reorganization: abolishing terrorism, revitalizing the economy, and transcending the social stalemate. The junta's efforts to reorganize Argentine society were, however, a monumental failure. They plunged the country into a deeper state of social and economic chaos and repression that was unprecedented in the recent history of Argentina.

The military set about their tasks with considerable energy and launched what the new president referred to as "the third world war" against Communist subversion. This brand of unconventional warfare was not concentrated essentially against the guerrilla movement or "terrorists," as they were called in an attempt to justify their elimination and make their extirpation more readily acceptable to international opinion, but was directed to all and sundry. To be sure, that classification of "terrorists" included, according to the president's suggestion, anyone "who spreads ideas that are contrary to Western and Christian civilization."[28] The ax of repression soon fell upon a wide cross-section of people and included trade unionists, students, publishers, medical doctors, journalists, teachers, and political activists of all persuasions. Corradi's apposite remark correctly summed up the situation: "The military rulers have reduced the complex mores of Argentina to a simple dichotomy: friend or foe."[29]

While the military was actively engaged in prosecuting a war against "subversion," the newly appointed economics minister, José Martínez de Hog, an old Etonian and Harvard graduate, was attempting to restructure the economy. An export-led strategy became the main feature of his restructuring exercise. Exports were to provide the dynamism necessary to stimulate economic growth and expansion. Along with the export drive, the role of foreign investments was also seen as a crucial variable in the equation for economic recovery and sustained growth. Thus this two-pronged strategy of export promotion and foreign investments was given high priority in the government's newly devised economic plan. In its efforts to attract foreign investments, the government adopted certain legislative measures which, in the words of the new economics minister, "will give guarantees to the foreign investor which are unique in the world."[30]

Despite the attractive incentives built into the government's protective measures, the anticipated foreign capital did not come pouring into Argentina. Whatever amount came in, the greater share of it was not channeled into productive enterprises but was deposited instead into local banks in order to take advantage of the high interest rates offered. The attraction to foreign investors that such a short-term scheme provided was quite obvious. In an economic climate characterized by a combination of relaxed foreign exchange regulations and high interest rates on bank deposits, the inducement to owners of foreign capital to speculate on gilt-edged, short-term investments was very high. Ironically, this much publicized economic strategy became an index of failure. More than 40 percent of all foreign investment to Argentina during the period 1977–81 came from the United States. Britain's share was a mere 0.8 percent. As revealed in the following table, the foreign investment by country was highly skewed:

### Foreign Investment in Argentina by Country of Origin: 1977–1981

| United States of America | 43.5% | Italy | 14.3% |
|---|---|---|---|
| | | France | 9.6% |

| | | | |
|---|---|---|---|
| Netherlands | 9.2% | Canada | 1.3% |
| West Germany | 6.4% | Japan | 1.2% |
| Switzerland | 4.4% | Sweden | 1.2% |
| Brazil | 1.4% | Britain | 0.8% |

*Source: Argentina, Ministry of Economy, Weekly Economic Bulletin, 9 November 1981.*

In spite of the implementation of these measures, the economy failed to respond to the minister's formula. High interest rates and the dismantling of trade barriers were having a devastating impact on local industries. Many went bankrupt. By 1979 the country's external trade balance began to deteriorate, and in less than one year, it was in deficit by $2.4 billion. To compound the economic woes, Martinez de Hog made it a policy to increase the level of foreign borrowing. This line of action, he argued, was necessary to restore international confidence in the country's future.[31] It was this very policy of excessive foreign borrowing which by 1982 had soared to a record high of $40 billion that compounded the country's economic crisis.

Economic hardships, perceived to have been brought about by de Hog's tight monetary and fiscal policies, were unpalatable to the masses. In spite of the political repression which the military government was pursuing with a vengeance, the labor movement was becoming bolder and more militant in its demands for reforms and changes in government policies. Organized strikes were the order of the day, and their sectoral spread became quite noticeable: rail, oil, and banks in 1977, the motor industry and medical workers in 1978. In April 1979, there was a general strike in which 30 percent of the country's labor force participated. Military crackdowns and political repression were particularly severe during these periods of labor unrest.

The junta's strategy to abolish terrorism, an unconventional form of warfare carried out in large measure by dissidents, eventually led to state terror with the country's military forces in the vanguard. Suspected "guerrillas" were being systematically annihilated in a most brutal and bloody campaign that claimed the lives of thousands of innocent victims. It was the era of the generals' dirty war in Argentina, an era that witnessed the silent disappearance of thousands of Argentineans from all walks of life and from all ideological and political persuasions. Amidst this state of repression, mayhem, and disappearance, a deafening silence reigned, except on one occasion. In the winter of 1978, Argentineans were allowed to pour into the streets again to celebrate the World Cup Championship which the Argentine national soccer team had won. One analyst noted how skillfully the junta used this event to create a state of euphoria in the country. "The event," according to Juan Corradi, "was studiously exploited by the regime to make citizens forget their ordeals. Soccer came to mean fellowship on the cheap."[32]

At the end of the first five years of military rule, General Videla completed his term of office and transferred power to another general, Roberto Viola. The transition went smoothly and impressed many interested observers. But by 1981, the country had paid a very high price for military rule. Terrorism was almost abolished, but terror became part of the art of governing and fear was ubiquitous in the land. The economy which the junta had vowed to restructure and revitalize went bankrupt in spite of the implementation of free market policies. Social and political upheavals were at an all-time high. A country of 28 million people, rich in natural resources, self-sufficient in oil, and boasting the highest standard of living in all Latin America, was brought to the brink of total disaster by five years of military excesses. Argentina had changed, and the changes were distinct and very noticeable.

When General Viola took over the presidency in March 1981, Argentina was in the midst of its worst financial crisis since 1976. The country's foreign debt, which had stood at $19 billion at the beginning of 1980, rocketed to $30 billion by the end of that same year. Despite a resurgence in external financial flows (investment capital from foreign sources) and a concurrent rise in the volume of exports, the economy was still experiencing the devastation brought about by triple-digit inflation and high interest rates. "It [had] reached the point," noted one commentator, "where Argentines habitually invested half of their monthly salary, as soon as they received it, for a two-week period: incredibly it was a hedge against inflation."[33]

Sustained economic growth turned out to be an illusive dream. During Viola's short term in office, there was a further devaluation of the peso. This move, instead of making Argentina's exports more competitive on the international market, had quite the opposite effect. By mid–1981, all economic indicators were pointing to a deepening of the recession. According to one report, the country in June of that year "was shaken by its third serious financial crisis in three months, involving a major panic on the foreign exchange markets. Foreign reserves fell by U.S.$308 million in one day."[34] As the economic crisis deepened, cracks and divisions within the junta's support structure became evident. They also systematically eviscerated the system of law and accountability. Although Viola and his loyal group of supporters were attempting to seek some sort of accommodation with union and party political leaders, the hard-liners led by Generals Nicolaides and

Galtieri were completely opposed to any move that would lead to their relinquishing power. A return to civilian rule was, according to them, unthinkable. In fact, General Galtieri was openly opposed to Viola's "liberalization" program, and he found much support for his views, particularly among the cavalry officers. That support came at a propitious time, coinciding with the end-of-year promotions. At this time many senior officers loyal to Viola were asked to resign. In December 1981, after some painful negotiations in which the frictions among the military hierarchy became quite transparent, Viola was removed from office and Galtieri appointed his successor. General Galtieri's appointment signaled a triumph for the hard-liners or right extremists, who were in no hurry to steer the country towards a democratic path.

The internal coup which brought General Galtieri to power reflected the depth of the country's political crisis. During the repression or "dirty war" of 1976–1979, in which the guerrilla movement was vigorously attacked, there was a feeling and a show of unity among all branches of the armed forces. But these heinous activities could not have been sustained indefinitely because of the growing fear of failure among the military hierarchy. And with Galtieri's ascension to the presidency, the issue of finding a more permanent political formula for the country's future was intensified. Galtieri's survival rested on how skillfully he could play his cards on both the economic and political fronts. Bold and major initiatives in these areas were long overdue, and the new president was well aware of this.

Galtieri introduced a program of economic austerity aimed at cutting inflation and boosting exports and foreign investments. On the political front, he allowed some measure of liberalization and "also announced plans to bring in a statute which would outline the permitted limits for political party activity."[35] These new measures, while augmenting the president's populist appeal, also underscored his political ambition. Galtieri's charismatic appeal received a further shot in the arm when he publicly declared his personal assets and promised to return his presidential salary to the Treasury. Showmanship aside, Galtieri understood more about the psychology of mass appeal than his two predecessors. While he became a popular leader among his fellow countrymen, his support was not restricted to the domestic environment. It was in the arena of foreign policy that he began to play his hand much more assiduously. And it is to an examination of this policy which we now turn, but in the wider context of the junta's rule.

64

## Military Rule: Foreign Policy Issues

Throughout 1981 it was becoming increasingly evident that Argentina was going to take a hard line on a number of foreign policy issues. As commander of the army and a leading figure in the military junta, General Galtieri himself had played an important role in shaping Argentina's position towards a number of these issues. We shall examine three of them.

First, the Beagle Channel dispute with neighboring Chile was a significant issue. This long-standing dispute centered on the three small islands of Picton, Nueva, and Lennox, which are clustered at the eastern entrance of the Beagle Channel. In the Boundary Treaty of 1881 between Argentina and Chile, no specific mention was made of these islands.[36] Hence both countries have consistently cited different interpretations of the treaty to support their respective claims.

Argentina's case for wanting to exercise full control over the three islands stemmed from two considerations. The first was that Chile's possession of these three islands would give her the leverage for expansion into the South Atlantic and Antarctica. Commander Marshall Hall believes that such an "expansion would strengthen Chile's communication with the Antarctic Peninsula, as well as its stature as an Antarctic nation."[37] The second consideration involved a number of important military implications for Argentina. Argentina's second largest naval base is located at Ushuaia, some fifty miles to the west of Picton Island. Apart from being a large and important home base for the country's navy, Ushuaia is also the staging and support center for Argentina's Antarctic stations. Were Chile to be granted sovereignty over these three disputed islands, not only would the territorial sea baseline be shifted, but, by implication, this would also mean that Argentine ships coming to and from Ushuaia would have to transit Chilean-controlled waters.

Argentina's fears were well grounded. When the five-member international court to which both disputants agreed, which was appointed by the British Crown in 1971, awarded the islands of Picton, Nueva, and Lennox to Chile in 1977, Argentina declared the ruling null and void. In that ruling, the five-man arbitration committee accepted the arguments put forward by Chile. This acceptance of Chile's Pacific Ocean thesis meant that the disputed islands are located on the Pacific side of the boundary separating the two oceans and should therefore belong to Chile. Argentina's refusal to accept the committee's verdict and its subsequent military maneuvers and inflamed political statements nearly brought the two countries to the brink of war in 1978. The Argentinean armada deployed to Tierra del

Fuego in November was able to dominate the scene. This demonstration of strength or "gunboat diplomacy" forced the Chileans to back down from pressing their claims, and to agree to resubmit the case for arbitration to the Vatican. The junta's military move did pay off, and according to one observer, "the Argentine military thus benefited from its show of bellicosity."[38]

The junta's initiative vis-à-vis Chile with respect to the three islands in the Beagle Channel was aimed at forestalling a final settlement of the dispute. One analyst made the point that "the net result for Argentina [was] that it bought time."[39] By getting Chile to repudiate the arbitration committee's ruling, the junta not only scored a temporary foreign policy victory, but was also able to turn its attention to a more formidable and long-standing issue—the sovereignty of Islas Malvinas. If this contentious issue with Britain could be resolved in Argentina's favor, it would definitely bolster its diplomatic position and put it in a stronger bargaining position against Chile over the Beagle Channel dispute.

The second major foreign policy issue which centered on the ownership of the Falkland Islands was a long, drawn-out, highly contentious one. During the six years of military rule from 1976 to 1982, negotiations with Britain, while being characterized with some amount of intensity at times, were also gradually perceived by the junta as being futile. Richard Lebow points out that "the Argentine leaders had lost faith in negotiations with Britain and had concluded that they would never achieve sovereignty over the Falklands by diplomacy."[40]

Argentina, since 1834, had consistently protested against British occupation of the Falklands but did not actively pursue its sovereignty claim until the 1960s.[41] It was during the latter half of the 1970s that Argentina stepped up the intensity of its claim by embarking on a vigorous diplomatic campaign. That campaign coincided with, and was buttressed by, the doctrine of an expansive territorial sea that Argentine leaders found to be very supportive of their arguments. Indeed, one analyst noted that "from the 1970s on, speeches given by government officials on the annual 10 June Malvinas Day have emphasized territorial integrity or geopolitical mutilation. A typical speech in 1978 said, 'the distance across this sea separates us, but at the same time unites us with the [Malvinas].'"[42] Argentina's version of maritime law was not about freedom of the seas and the strength of historical precedents. It was a version which indicated a radical departure from the dominant views espoused by European states. Maritime law, and indeed the concept of an "Argentine Sea," was about the natural right that accrued to a coastal state to exercise jurisdiction over its patrimonial sea.

On the diplomatic front, a renewed assertiveness underscored Argentina's posture regarding negotiations with Britain. There was also a gradual escalation of military activities in and around the Falkland waters during this period. In November 1976, for example, Argentina established a military presence at Southern Thule on the South Sandwich Islands. In addition to all these considerations, signals emanating from London also helped to reinforce the junta's belief that the British government did not have a firm Falklands policy. Members of the junta believed that if they followed a course of action whereby they would commit themselves incrementally to the use of force, it was conceivable that they might just be able to get away with it. Lebow advances the point that "their strategy was to commit themselves step by step to military action in the expectation that this would succeed in eliciting some kind of British concession on sovereignty before they were compelled to act."[43]

By the time General Galtieri came to power in December 1981, the Falklands/Malvinas question was already a high priority issue on the junta's foreign policy agenda. The junta leaders' successful efforts in isolating the Beagle Channel dispute gave them more leverage to deal with Britain on the contentious issue of sovereignty over the Malvinas. The pursuit of a vigorous Falklands policy was therefore more than just another foreign policy issue. The military rulers saw it as having both a unifying and legitimizing effect.

The third major foreign policy issue related to the growing friendship between the junta and the U.S. administration. Ronald Reagan's successful election to the White House in November 1980 marked a new phase in the relationship between the United States and Latin America. During the early months of Reagan's presidency, Carter's human rights policy was dropped, and the new administration in Washington began to make strong overtures towards the anti–Communist, right-wing dictatorships in Latin America. In the context of U.S. involvement in El Salvador—in a fight perceived to be against international Communism, Argentine support and commitment were regarded in Washington to be vital. It soon became apparent that this rapprochement between Washington and Buenos Aires would bring mutual benefits to both administrations. The junta members, in particular, were most eager to embrace American overtures, as this would seem to end their isolation. Washington, on the other hand, was keen to secure the participation of a Latin American state in its Central American imbroglio. According to one observer, "the Junta's involvement would contribute, from the diplomatic point of view, to inter–American solidarity and, from the political and military point of view, Argentine troops and counter-insurgency specialists could be deployed more freely with none of the inhibitions on direct US involvement imposed by U.S. public opinion."[44]

This warming of U.S.-Argentine relations culminated in a series of activities undertaken by both governments in 1981. First, there were a number of high-level diplomatic exchanges between the two countries. Reagan's personal emissary, the multilingual Ambassador Vernon Walters, paid visits to Buenos Aires in February and September. Visits were also made by the U.S. Army commander in chief and by the U.S. ambassador to the United Nations, Jeanne Kirkpatrick, in April and August respectively. From the Argentine side, visits were made to Washington by General Viola in March and by General Galtieri in August and November. During his second visit to Washington, one commentator remarked, "Galtieri further cemented the relationship with the U.S. Defense Secretary Casper Weinberger described him as a 'magnificent person' and National Security Adviser Richard Allen called him 'an impressive general.'"[45] Second, in 1981 Argentina sent an estimated 200 military personnel to El Salvador, Guatemala, and Honduras under the guise that they were "advisers."[46] In return, the U.S. restored its military aid program to Argentina with the proviso that the junta should take steps to return the country to more democratic forms of government.

It was this change of U.S. policy, characterized by mutual short-term benefits and exchanges, that helped to strengthen the junta's Malvinas policy. Taken together, these three foreign policy issues formed the interlocking grid of the junta's larger policy objective. That objective centered on the ownership of large chunks of Antarctica. The realization of that larger objective hinged heavily, however, on the immediate possession of the Falkland/Malvinas Islands. By placing the Falklands and South Georgia in their South Atlantic setting, Argentina sought not only to emphasize a geopolitical context, but also to increase the size of its patrimonial sea and therefore its ultimate control over large areas of fisheries and seabed mineral resources. Moreover, in a strategic sense, control over the Falklands would give Argentina wider diplomatic and military options and boost its claim to jurisdiction over the continental shelf.

## The Invasion of 2 April 1982

The invasion of the Falklands by Argentine troops cannot be traced to a single factor. While it was true that the event was undertaken just when it seemed that the time was set for the junta's departure and it might have been intended to forestall an imminent nationwide strike, it cannot be ascertained with any degree of certainty that these precipitating factors constituted the explanation for the junta's use of military force on 2 April 1982. In fact, the presence of these conditions only helped to hasten the occurrence of that event. The reasons for the junta's decision to invade the Falklands were more fundamental and deep-seated.

Nef and Hallman advance three reasons for the invasion. They suggest that "the war was the result of the simultaneous convergence of three inter-related trends—systemic, national and psychological."[47] At the systemic level, the argument revolved around the "increasingly fluid and unstable nature of the international environment."[48] This proposition is nothing new. It is a given condition of the international system quite often referred to as political anarchy. Anarchy in this context is not synonymous with chaos, confusion, and total disaster, but refers essentially to the absence of an overarching political controller or world authority endowed with supranational powers to use force and to impose universal law and order. According to Barry Buzan, this "global anarchy is fundamentally different from anarchy in a group of individuals whose relations are totally without government."[49] International relations have always been and will continue to be carried out within an environment characterized by instability, tension, and anarchy. The fact that states have in the past and will in the future continue to prosecute their own national interest not only underscores the salience of political realism, but also highlights the potential for conflict in an anarchical system. Conflict avoidance or conflict resolution is not the ultimate goal that states strive towards in their interactions with each other. It is how they are able to manage and minimize the potentials for conflicts in their relations that is important. To be sure, conflicts are endemic at all levels of society. Given their ineluctability and pervasiveness, the best strategy devised so far in dealing with them involves skillful management.

The systemic argument raised by Nef and Hallman appears to be a weak one because the political structure of the international system is fundamentally anarchic. To apply this structurally universal precondition as a cause of conflict is stating the obvious. However, their second reason, that involving domestic or national problems, seems to be much more valid. Discussions above did focus on the domestic upheavals that resulted from the junta's economic and repressive political policies. Apart from the organized pressure brought about by the militant trade unions and other interest groups that deplored the junta's human rights record, there was also the more immediate and pressing problem posed by a weak and faltering economy. With triple-digit inflation and a steadily rising unemployment figure, the government's management of the economy was at best disastrous. The temptation therefore for the military rulers to act out of domestic considerations not only appeared enticing, but also had a definite payoff function.

The invasion executed in the early morning hours of 2 April 1982 was not merely a diversionary tactic. From the domestic perspective, it was undertaken with the purpose of buying time. This was the payoff function in that the junta turned a rapidly deteriorating and somewhat uncontrollable domestic situation to its advantage. One analyst noted very succinctly, "The regime's adventurism appears as a risky, but calculated, gamble not only to increase its prestige, but to ensure its very survival."[50] That the junta was seeking a way out of the domestic quagmire into which it had plunged the country was clearly a possibility. The invasion created, as no other act would, an immediate sense of national unity and solidarity. It completely transformed the junta's image among the rank and file in Argentina. As was noted in the *Guardian*, "If there is something that troubles a military regime more than the state of the economy, it is its image."[51]

The Malvinas issue produced consensus, unity, and purpose among all Argentineans. It was perhaps the single most potent force that could bring about cohesion and at the same time galvanize support for the junta. On this issue there was and still is but one view in all Argentina—*Malvinas son Argentina*. The junta members were keenly aware of the strength and depth of national feelings on the Malvinas question. Moreover, they believed that their planned adventure would strike the responsive cords of patriotism and loyalty among the masses. The move was also "generally regarded as a political strategy to ensure their continued rule."[52] And the *Economist* concurred that "the invasion was launched just as the popularity of Argentina's military rulers had tumbled to its lowest point since the coup of 1976."[53] There was no denying the impact of domestic political and economic factors on the junta's decision. But while these factors are compelling to a certain degree, they do not in fact constitute the totality of the explanation. The evidence would seem to indicate that it was the convergence and combination of several factors that led the junta to make the critical decision.

The convergence of domestic economic problems with the perceived pay-off benefits for the junta was bolstered by a third consideration—to bring an end to the years of frustration experienced in negotiations with Britain. In short, mounting domestic problems coincided with feelings of despair brought about by the rising frustrations over the negotiation process.

One analyst shared the view that "the Argentine Junta, dissatisfied with the progress of the negotiations [sought] to resolve the question of sovereignty once and for all by force."[54] And Robert Scheina, an American specialist in Latin American affairs, believes that the "war was caused by an unanticipated series of events heaped upon years of frustrations."[55] In addition to these factors, there was also a strategically compelling reason for the junta to invade. It involved the British government's handling of the South Atlantic issue. British policy towards the Falklands prior to 2 April 1982 clearly indicated a diminution of interest and a dilution of commitment towards the region as a whole. Lawrence Freedman argued that the British government was willing to offer neither compromise to Argentina, nor a credible long-term commitment to the Falkland Islands. "There was a lack of political will in London either to solve the dispute once and for all in some deal with Buenos Aires, or else to accept full responsibility for the long-term security and prosperity of the islands."[56] These manifest pre–April 1982 indications in British policy performed a significant role in encouraging the leaders of the Argentine junta to believe that the invasion would prove successful.[57]

In addition to the above considerations, there were also the critically important strategic issues of capability and military readiness. By the time General Galtieri came to power in December 1981, Argentina, with the aid of the United States and all major European suppliers, including Britain, had already developed an impressive capability in conventional weapons. The rapid growth and numerical strength of the Argentine armed forces make them the second largest in Latin America after the forces of neighboring Brazil. It was reported that as much as 35 percent of national spending was directed to military purposes and that the domestic arms industry, which was controlled by the military elites, employed about 41,000 people. Argentina's impressive military capabilities, built up during the 1976–1981 period, gave the junta leaders the confidence to launch the invasion.[58] When they did so in April 1982, the country's military might was at an all-time high.

The navy, which spearheaded the invasion, had a manpower complement of 36,000, slightly more than half the size of the British Royal Navy, and an impressive assortment of ships and aircraft inventory. The latter included "30 carrier-based Skyhawk and Super Etendard fighter-bombers."[59] The 20,000-man air force deployed four dozen Mirage fighters, about 70 Skyhawk fighter–ground attack aircraft, 11 Canberra bombers, about 30 Paris light strike aircraft, and about 60 assorted aircraft between seven air brigades.[60] Argentina's 130,000-man army was a formidable force.

It was organized into four army corps, which consisted of two armored, one mechanized, two motorized, one airborne, three mountain, and one jungle infantry brigades. This preponderance of military capability not only gave the junta leaders the leverage to project power, but also strengthened their confidence that they possessed the correlation of forces to capture and occupy the Falkland Islands and at the same time serve as a strong deterrent to the British.

Perhaps a final factor, albeit a precipitating one, involved the South Georgia incident. One analyst argues that the South Georgia episode, which involved the operation of a scrap metal dealer, a Señor Davidoff, was the trigger for the crisis.[61] And the Hoffmanns expressed the view that "the South Georgia confrontation [led] to war."[62] For a certainty Davidoff's commercial activities on South Georgia around the latter half of March 1982 were not planned by the junta. Davidoff's interest in dismantling the old whaling station at Leith lay in the profitability of the venture. His contract with the owners of the whaling station, Christian Salvesen Limited of Edinburgh, for an estimated 30,000 tons of scrap metal stood to net him a handsome profit in excess of $10 million.[63]

The fact that Davidoff chartered the *Bahía Buen Suceso* from the Argentine navy did not necessarily mean that a sinister motive or plot was behind his operation. The navy was responsible for supervising any Argentinean voyage of this kind in the Antarctic area. It appears, however, that Davidoff's commercial venture was seized upon by the navy, thereby giving the junta the opportunity to force the British government into making a firm announcement on the sovereignty issue of the Falkland Islands. Martin Middlebrook, a British military historian, contends that the link-up of the scrap merchant and a naval vessel allowed Admiral Anaya to control events throughout the crisis. He notes that "Galtieri and Anaya agreed that their plans to occupy the Falklands should be brought forward and that, using the pretext of the South Georgia crisis, they should occupy both the Falklands and South Georgia as soon as possible."[64]

Although the junta's decision to invade was taken incrementally, it nonetheless fitted into a larger strategy of a course that sought to escalate tensions with Britain. The manipulation of the South Georgia incident was one such tactic in that strategy. As a precipitating factor, this incident, skillfully manipulated by the junta, not only raised the stakes in the South Atlantic, but also set in motion a compelling train of events which forced the junta to execute its invasion plans without delay. Taken together, this convergence of the major fundamental factors with the critical precipitating ones, created the strike-out conditions which led the junta to take the final step in the decision-making process to invade the Falklands. Yet the employment of the direct use of force need not have taken place when it did in April 1982 but for the overwhelming presence of these precipitating factors. The reasons why Argentina used force to grab territory and the subsequent response by the British will go down in history as a classic case of mutual miscalculation. The Falklands invasion was a navy operation, planned and urged upon the other junta leaders by that service. And though a secret adventure, employing initially only naval forces, it nevertheless exposed the importance of Argentina's wider domestic and regional interests.

# British Military Response: The Task Force

## Introduction and Preparation of the Task Force

When the Argentine military forces invaded the Falkland Islands on 2 April 1982, an action which at that time was perceived to be a fait accompli, it triggered a set of events that were fraught with uncertainties. No one was sure what the outcome of that act of aggression would turn out to be. Neither could it have been ascertained then that Britain and Argentina would actually exchange blows in a war that would turn the South Atlantic region into a battleground. Of more lasting effect, though, were the political repercussions which followed in the wake of this act and their devastating impacts on the military junta.

What began as a routine exercise by the Argentine navy on Wednesday, 31 March 1982, and culminated in the seizure of British territory two days later was viewed by Downing Street as an act of unprovoked aggression. This British response caught the junta leaders unawares. They were not prepared for it and were clearly unable to deal with that response. One American observer noted that the "Argentine seizure of the Islands had pulled many of the levers of the subconscious British tribal memory."[65] Although hastily contrived, the British response was swift and decisive. As a matter of fact, Britain was not caught completely off-guard by the junta's decision, but was somewhat surprised by the timing of the invasion by the Argentine navy. Through its network of military intelligence gathering activities, Downing Street was aware of developments taking place in the South Atlantic. "The British Government," according to military historian Middlebrook, "had been alerted on Saturday, 27 March, to the probability of an Argentine invasion. News had reached London of the extraordinary

73

activity at Argentinian ports, of movements of troops by air inside Argentina, and of detachments of ships towards South Georgia from the supposed naval manoeuvres off Uruguay."[66]

The British response was twofold and included some preliminary military moves. Planning for a Falklands naval force started as early as the last half of March, when as a counter to a reported Argentine naval presence in Falkland waters, a task group of some three destroyers/frigates was first alerted to sail to the South Atlantic. One report confirmed that "preparations had started for the deployment to the South Atlantic of a limited number of Royal Navy surface units."[67] The second aspect of this twofold response was a diplomatic offensive that was quickly put into place. It included, among other things, a request for direct U.S. mediation and an immediate meeting of the United Nations Security Council to discuss the Falklands crisis. These initiatives, far from being alarmist and reactionary, were predicated on the belief that an armed Argentine attack on the Falklands was imminent. That perception was confirmed when Operation Rosario was successfully completed at 1100 hours on 2 April 1982.

Politically, the British government wasted no time in extracting the domestic support it badly needed for its proposed course of action. When Parliament was convened on Saturday, the day after the invasion, that act not only underscored the gravity of the situation the government faced, but was also meant to send an unequivocal and firm message to the population at large that the government was committed to restoring national honor and pride. In her historic opening speech, Prime Minister Margaret Thatcher declared in no uncertain terms that "aggression must not be allowed to succeed." Her adroit use of words and emotional appeal went a far way in creating the perception that British subjects had been made the unwilling victims of a fascist military takeover. It was politically prudent for Thatcher to seize the high ground and turn this embarrassing incident into a popular cause. And this she did with audacious ingenuity.

Amidst the calls for resignations which punctuated the debate in Parliament, a plan of action was unveiled. The prime minister announced measures that sought to impose immediate financial sanctions against Argentina and the preparation and departure of a large naval task force by Monday morning.[68] The Ministry of Defence hurriedly assembled a task force to carry out Operation Corporate, the name given to "the complete operation to move a Task Force to the area of the Falkland Islands, covering naval, ground and air battles around the Falklands and including the subsequent return to the U.K."[69] The decision to mount Operation Corporate was not taken when Parliament was convened that historic Saturday morning. The decision to do so had been taken one day before the Falkland Islands were invaded. Middlebrook confirmed that "Mrs. Thatcher accepted Sir Henry Leach's advice and the following day [1 April] the firm decision was taken to make the necessary preparations for the dispatch of a force to regain the Falklands."[70] Thus Downing Street's apparent assessment of the situation on the eve of the invasion turned out to be very accurate.

A "War Cabinet" was assembled to coordinate the activities of the various governmental departments such as treasury (which instituted financial sanctions), trade (which placed a total ban on Argentine imports), and defense. Members of the cabinet were Mrs. Thatcher; Mr. Whitelaw, home secretary; Francis Pym, foreign secretary; John Nott, defense secretary; Mr. Parkinson, paymaster general; Sir Robert Armstrong, cabinet secretary; Sir Anthony Acland, permanent secretary, foreign office; Sir Frank Cooper, permanent secretary, defense; Admiral of the Fleet Sir Terence Lewin, Chief of the defense staff; and Sir Michael Palliser, who had retired from the foreign office only a few days before, but who returned to serve as a special adviser.

Throughout the weekend following the invasion, men and war materiel poured into ships, some of which were either requisitioned or chartered. In a closely coordinated and massive logistics effort, the Task Force was made ready for dispatch in a very short space of time. Reminiscing on those hectic days, former defense secretary John Nott made the point that the entire exercise "was the result of close cooperation between the services, the Merchant Navy, the Royal Dockyards and commercial ports, the stores and transport organisations of the Ministry of Defence, and industry."[71] This remarkable achievement displayed the high level of planning and logistics capabilities found in Britain. It also underscored the country's ability and readiness to respond to crises once the decision to do so was made.

On 5 April, three days after the Argentine invasion, HMS *Hermes*, the flagship, and HMS *Invincible*, their decks lined with Sea Harriers and Sea King helicopters, weighed anchor and headed down the Solent on the morning tide. Their sailing, carried out in a blaze of glory and publicity, was part of a campaign designed to impress the Argentine junta leaders. It was a momentous day in British history, undoubtedly the most important for the Royal Navy since the fleet sailed for Suez in 1956. The two carriers were joined by other Royal Navy vessels, and, altogether, the naval force appeared to be a formidable one. By the day's end, there were two aircraft carriers, seven destroyers, five frigates, and four tankers or supply ships steaming towards the South Atlantic. This contingent which formed the original Falklands naval Task Force that set sail directly from the U.K. was later joined by a number of warships that were taking part in NATO's spring training naval exercises near Gibraltar.

The dispatch of such a formidable force was a clear indication that the government had the will to act decisively in a time of national crisis. It also indicated the unanimity of domestic political support for such a course of action. Moreover, it reinforced the importance of politicostrategic imperatives and their priority in the decision-making process. Massive increases in public expenditures entailed in this operation that ran counter to supply-side economics, part of the government's monetary and fiscal policy, were allowed. The Task Force's dispatch was unequivocally a decision for war. Its composition represented a credible and "potent instrument of war."[72] And Freedman rationalized that "from the start the task force had to look capable in principle of retaking the islands."[73] But once the fleet was dispatched, it generated both a psychopolitical and military momentum that made the possibility of war a real outcome.

## The British Three-pronged Strategy

Britain's naval effort was part of a larger continuing politicomilitary strategy, the object of which was to get Argentina to withdraw its occupation forces from British territory. As such, Britain's strategy rested on three planks: diplomacy, economic sanctions, and military force.

The diplomatic offensive began with a sustained campaign of public education about the history of the Islands and the British arguments for sovereignty. In this exercise, Britain portrayed itself as the victim of Argentine aggression. The real diplomatic pressure on Argentina began, however, in the Security Council at the United Nations, where Resolution 502 was passed:

> Deeply disturbed at reports of an invasion on 2 April by armed forces of Argentina, Determining that there exists a breach of the peace in the Falkland Islands (Islas Malvinas), [the United Nations]
> 1. Demands an immediate cessation of hostilities;
> 2. Demands an immediate withdrawal of all Argentine forces from the Falkland Islands (Islas Malvinas);
> 3. Calls on the Governments of Argentina and the United Kingdom to seek a diplomatic solution to their differences and to respect fully the purposes and principles of the Charter of the United Nations.

The near unanimous (10 for, 1 against, and 4 abstentions), passage of this resolution was an important diplomatic victory for Britain. Had

Argentina complied and peacefully withdrawn its forces, however, Britain would have had no option but to negotiate the sovereignty issue. The outcome could have been very different for Argentina had it in good faith complied with the provisions set out in Resolution 502.

The passage of this resolution also had a powerful effect on world opinion. The Argentine invasion was seen as an act of aggression that should be condemned. Moreover, the resolution, which was more in Britain's immediate favor, gave Britain the option to invoke Article 51 of the U.N. Charter. Britain could now claim the right of self-defense. This diplomatic victory provided the legitimacy for the Task Force. One military strategist made the valid point that Resolution 502 provided "much more than a valuable diplomatic advantage ... it served to integrate the military and diplomatic aspects of the British position" and "it helped to legitimize a resort to force if mediation failed."[74]

While diplomatic moves continued to gather momentum and also involved the United States (through Secretary of State Haig's shuttle diplomacy), both Argentina and Britain prepared for war. In Argentina's case, troops and reinforcements continued to pour in at Stanley, turning the Islands into an armed camp. Britain, on the other hand, continued to requisition more merchant ships and to prepare more vessels for the Task Force.[75]

On the day of the invasion, Britain froze all Argentine assets in the United Kingdom, stopped imports from Argentina, and banned the export of military hardware and supplies to that country. The call for economic sanctions against Argentina was made to the EEC, and in a surprise move characterized by speed and unanimity, the EEC's Council of Foreign Ministers granted Britain's request. The EEC members not only prohibited exports to Argentina, but on 16 April they also followed Britain in banning all imports from Argentina and fully supported Resolution 502. The imposition of economic sanctions was "intended to give a firm political signal of the EEC's displeasure over the Falklands crisis to Buenos Aires, rather than give Argentina the impression that the Community wishes to start a trade war."[76] This line of argument was underscored by the fact that the "sanctions" time frame was limited to only one month. Further, the exercise was designed to keep up the pressure on Argentina's crisis-ridden economy and to underline the country's diplomatic isolation.[77]

Prior to April 1982, trade between Argentina and the EEC was highly skewed in the latter's favor. Both West Germany and Italy had sizable investment portfolios in Argentina. They were also major suppliers of arms and military equipment to the regime in Buenos Aires. Britain, though a smaller trading partner with Argentina in aggregate monetary terms, enjoyed a favorable balance in percentage terms. The following statistics gave a fairly clear picture of Argentina-EEC trade for the year 1980.

### EEC-*Argentina Trade, 1980*
#### *(In Millions of U.S. Dollars)*

| | Exports to Argentina | |
| --- | --- | --- |
| EEC *Total* | 3,088 | |
| West Germany | 1,253 | (40.6%) |
| Italy | 635 | (20.6%) |
| France | 432 | (14.0%) |
| United Kingdom | 402 | (13.0%) |
| Netherlands | 183 | (5.9%) |
| Belgium/Luxemburg | 125 | (4.05%) |
| Denmark | 40 | (1.3%) |
| Ireland | 11 | (0.36%) |
| Greece | 1 | (0.03%) |

| | Imports from Argentina | |
| --- | --- | --- |
| EEC *Total* | 2,552 | |
| West Germany | 709 | (27.8%) |
| Italy | 498 | (19.6%) |
| Netherlands | 433 | (17.0%) |
| France | 296 | (11.6%) |
| United Kingdom | 266 | (10.4%) |
| Belgium/Luxemburg | 155 | (6.1%) |
| Denmark | 138 | (5.4%) |
| Greece | 52 | (2.0%) |
| Ireland | 5 | (0.2%) |

*Source:* OECD *Figures (1980)*

Apart from the military sales aspect, which had some impact on Argentina's ability to prosecute a sustained air war, the imposition of a short-lived strategy of economic sanctions on Argentina proved to be somewhat ineffective. Conventional wisdom holds that economic sanctions are not effective instruments in international relations. Both the Rhodesian and South African cases support this view. The important point, however, was that Britain never expected much to happen from the application of this instrument. Freedman argued that "there was little confidence in economic sanctions as a means of solving the dispute."[78] Neither was this instrument relied upon as a means of getting Argentina to comply with U.N. Security Council Resolution 502. The wider implications of economic sanctions involved crucial issues of support and solidarity for Britain and its graduated response to the use of military force.

The use of the military instrument was the ultimate weapon in Britain's armory of options. From the early days of the conflict, Prime Minister Margaret Thatcher knew that only through the use of force could British rule over the Falklands be restored. She had an uncanny ability to understand the dilemma facing the junta leaders—if they backed down, they would have to resign. The assembly and dispatch of a credible military force from the start was meant to support both diplomatic and economic measures. Through these measures Britain sought to avoid giving the impression that it was bent on using force from the very inception. Moreover, because of the three-pronged strategy, not only did international opinion become increasingly more favorable to Britain, but the retaliatory use of force was gradually seen to be very necessary. "It was," according to one strategist, "an instinctive reaction, driven by immediate political need rather than by forethought."[79]

From a military perspective, the dispatch of the task force was part of an attempt to make a belated reply to Argentina's military threats. Its credibility stemmed from the dynamics of composition and capability and was seen as a buttress to diplomacy. Politically, it provided the government with the necessary leverage to deal with domestic criticisms. In addition, the War Cabinet was determined to give the impression that Britain's military actions would be in accordance with international law. Hence the plethora of public statements detailing various aspects of operational plans. The use of military force definitely was to be seen as an incremental process. In fact the War Cabinet deliberately encouraged the idea that the exercise of military force would not be a haphazard undertaking but would follow a closely controlled process of escalation.

Apart from satisfying domestic and international opinions with regard to the proposed use of force, these public statements also encouraged the belief that the Task Force commanders were under political control. In other words, the instrument of force as exemplified by the Task Force would have an overriding strategic objective and thus would not be used indiscriminately. This theoretical rationale or ideal was difficult to operationalize, however, and, according to one analyst, the strategic reality was "quite unrelated to the logistical and operational dynamics which governed the use of the Task Force."[80] In short, the mobilization and dispatch of the Task Force created its own momentum which generated a compelling category of needs from which the logic of conflict was derived.

Finally, the dispatch of the Task Force chimed with a deteriorating domestic economic situation. British defense policy was under severe economic and budgetary pressures. The option to do nothing, though attractive under the circumstances, was no option at all given the importance of Britain's perceived politicostrategic interests. In the prosecution of those interests, Britain also was seen as demonstrating Western resolve by not allowing aggression to go unpunished.

## Logistics Support and Ascension Island

The speedy assembly and dispatch of the Task Force to the South Atlantic, a distance stretching over 7,500 miles, created a logistic tail that was fraught with problems. These problems, although not insurmountable, were nonetheless immense and included the maintenance of a long supply line stretching back to the U.K. In addition to the deployment of over fifty naval vessels, the Task Force was also supported by 54 ships chartered or requisitioned from 33 companies. Nineteen of these STUFT (an acronym meaning ships taken up from trade) vessels had helicopter pads fitted on their decks in a matter of days, and nearly all were converted for replenishment at sea.[81] The crucial role played by these ships constituted part of the formula for success. One report noted that these ships "carried more than 100,000 tons of freight, 9,000 personnel, and 95 assorted aircraft. From Devonport and Portsmouth alone, the Royal Navy shipped more than 30,000 tons of provisions, ammunition and other stores. The complete task force was stored for war in three days, with more than 80% subsequent availability of all major store items."[82]

From the inception of the British campaign to retake the Falkland Islands, it was recognized that success would depend in large measure on the quality and efficiency of the logistic support. The art and science of "getting the right men and materiel, in the right quantities, to the right place, at the right time" requires detailed planning and organization.[83] Accordingly, a logistics support "cell" was established at Northwood, a Royal Navy facility outside of London, and overall command for this ad hoc tri-service organization fell to a force logistics coordinator. The principal task of this unit was to oversee replenishment planning and logistic requirements for the Task Force. The establishment of this unit and the centrality of its operations not only helped to reduce confusion and bureaucratic inertia, but also guaranteed a very high level of efficiency. One analyst advanced the point that "having such a logistic 'czar' ensured optimum and economical use of sometimes scarce resources and the priority for the supply of the most urgent stores."[84]

Military considerations were paramount, but the truly massive logistics effort also had a distinctly political undertone. It eloquently underscored the British government's resolve to retake the Falklands. This fact was amply demonstrated by the scale and efficacy of the exercise. Captain David Kenney, a U.S. Naval Reserve officer, argues that "the visibility of Britain's massive logistical effort showed better than anything else its resolution to retake the Falklands."[85] It is conceivable that the synergistic effects brought about by the Task Force's credibility and the enormous logistics undertaking created a momentum that made the use of force ineluctable. Politically, it was the potency created by this synergy which the Thatcher government used as one of its tactics to attempt to persuade the Argentine junta to comply with U.N. Resolution 502. The junta officers, on the other hand, were politically unsophisticated in their reading of this and other signals. Their failure to do so did not stem from an inadequacy of proper information. It was a simple matter of blind stupidity on their part. They deliberately tuned out any information that did not dovetail with their grandiose plans—a classic case of defensive avoidance.

At the time of the Argentine invasion, Britain had no plans for a logistics support operation in the South Atlantic. The nonexistence of contingency and logistics plans was not a reflection of sloppy military management, but more a case of defense policy orientation where NATO served as the focal point. Britain's military effort was concentrated in Europe, and defense of the Western Front constituted its priority in military planning and force deployment. However, given its lack of a plan for defending the Falklands, the speed and efficiency with which logistics activities were undertaken clearly demonstrated the breadth and depth of Britain's military planning and resource capabilities. The British effort was a success story. The entire "operation benefited from the very experienced logistics organization which exists in the U.K."[86] Experience in logistics planning and implementation for long-range military exercise was gained particularly in 1970. In that year, 20,000 men were moved by air and sea to Malaysia to participate in jungle training exercises. That experience paid off handsomely when military and civilian planners devised and implemented plans to move an enormous volume of supplies across the country to the docks in time for the ships to set sail on 5 April 1982. By contrast, Argentina's capability to resupply its own occupying forces on the Islands with food, ammunition, and other war materiel proved critically inferior to the need.

The long logistics tail created by the dispatch of the naval Task Force heightened the importance of Ascension Island, which was seen as a midway point between Britain and the Falkland Islands. The importance of this little island to the British campaign cannot be overstated. One analyst noted that "it was crucial."[87] And another advanced the view that "it proved invaluable to the campaign."[88]

Seven miles at its widest point, Ascension Island is a 34-square-mile outcrop of volcanic rock located 4,225 miles by sea from Britain and 3,750 from the Falklands. The island had no native population nor any previous British military presence. Although a British territory, the island was leased to the United States, with the principal users of its 3,000-meter-long "Wideawake" airfield being NASA, USAF, and Pan American.[89] The number of flights in and out of Ascension did not exceed 250 in any one year, and these were handled by two aircraft controllers. At the height of the Falklands War, Wideawake was undoubtedly one of the busiest airstrips in the world, accounting for some 800 air movements in a typical day. All told, some 2,500 fixed wing and 10,600 helicopter flights were mounted from this "unusually quiet" airfield.

Ascension also served as a rendezvous area for the Task Force. It was here that the major redeployment and regrouping of men and ships took place. Moreover, "the island was also needed for the massive re-stow of stores and equipment that took place because of the hurried departure and the newly accepted logistic support plan."[90] And to facilitate the large number of aircraft using the Wideawake airfield, "the Royal Engineers laid a temporary pipeline running 3½ miles which, together with a pumping station and a 180,000 gallon bulk fuel installation, was completed in eight days. At peak periods, it delivered 300,000 gallons of aviation fuel a day in support of RAF operations."[91]

The importance of Ascension Island to the entire campaign lay primarily in the logistical role it played. As a midway point, it mitigated the logistical support problems arising from the 8,000-mile distance separating the Falklands from the United Kingdom. It is reasonable to conclude that its strategic location and the vital logistics support it provided made Ascension Island an integral part of the success equation of the British campaign. A high technology environment, as was the Falklands War, demanded great logistical depth. This fact was never lost on British military planners.

The mounting of the Task Force was a classic demonstration of the inherent flexibility of the amphibious option from both a political and military point of view. The British government was able to demonstrate its firm resolve not only to the junta, but also to its own allies in NATO and to the rest of the world by assembling and dispatching a militarily strong and capable force in a matter of days. And "the speed with which this was achieved remains one of the most striking facets of the entire operation."[92] Admiral John Woodward, the Task Force's commander, reminisced: "The speed at which the Task Force was assembled remains one of my lasting memories."[93]

A price, however, had to be paid in terms of the considerable restowing and cross-decking of men and materiel that took place later on this little island. It was clearly not planned that way, but, the delay in reaching the trouble spot gave diplomacy a chance. Ascension Island proved its worth in facilitating and sustaining Britain's logistics effort. Its availability as an anchorage for re-organization and as an airhead for supply was critical to victory in the South Atlantic operation.

# Legal Dimensions of the Use of Force in the Falklands War

The Falklands War provided a useful case study of the role legal principles play in the conduct of global politics. It gave an insight into the state and workings of the international system. Moreover, it also illustrated the dangers that arise when principles of law are neglected or applied selectively. One of these important principles involves the legality of the use of force. And it is this aspect or dimension of the use of force that I shall examine briefly in this section.

The use of force is a fact in international life. And the use of this instrument by society and states is not a new phenomenon but a long-established practice dating back to antiquity. The concern expressed by states about the use of force, however, particularly since the carnage experienced in World Wars I and II, reflects a preoccupation with the strategic role that legal principles ought to play in the use of this instrument. One of the chief aims of the United Nations Charter was to establish viable legal principles to guide international relations.

The principles which moved so many nations to express their concerns during the Falklands crisis were both clear and basic to the system established by the U.N. Charter.[94] Article 2 (3) obliges members to "settle their international dispute by peaceful means," while Article 2 (4) prohibits "the threat or use of force" against a state. This article, which lays down the basic rules, was vigorously upheld by the Security Council when Resolution 502 was passed. Apart from the prohibition it places on states regarding the use of force, Article 2 (4) also would seem to enjoin states to "vote for the rules" when they are clearly violated. In other words, when one state uses force against another in a clear-cut situation like Argentina's invasion of the Falklands, there is a strong tendency for other states to lean on the violator, as did so many against Argentina.

The legal principles emanating from Article 2 (3) and (4) also involve other important nuances. They have the capability to rally support for the injured party, with such support cutting across self-interest and alliance politics. For the aggressor this can be devastating. "Argentina's diplomatic isolation sapped its will to fight, as well as its ability to secure weapons, replacement parts, and credits."[95] In addition to serving as a focal rallying point, legal principles also have a strategic capability of deterrence. The regular implementation of principles over a long period of time tends to make certain conduct unthinkable. The deterrent capacity of legal principles is, however, not a sure thing in interstate relations. States continue to violate principles of international law and behavior with impunity. And when a government sees others successfully ignoring legal principles, it will not give those principles much deterrent weight when calculating the risks involved in the prosecution of its own self-interest. This was precisely what Argentina did. After Goa, West Irian, East Timor, the Western Sahara, and Afghanistan, the Argentina junta leaders believed that their invasion of the Falklands would cause but a mere ripple and would soon be forgotten. But they were wrong. The British military reaction, which was short, sharp, and costly, can be justified on the basis of its reinforcement of legal principles which are so crucial to peace and stability.

## Argentine and British Use of Force

The relevant norms of international law as clearly delineated in the U.N. Charter (1945), the Rio Treaty of 1947, and the Organization of American States Charter (1948), made Argentina's forceful seizure of the Falklands on 2 April 1982 illegal.[96] This understanding and perception was not shared in Buenos Aires, however, as Argentina continued to justify its use of force. In doing so, it relied on three general arguments.

First, Argentina asserted that continued British occupation of the Falkland Islands represented an act of aggression against Argentina and its territorial integrity. Apart from being a silly argument, this line of reasoning also lacked legal substance. Argentina's security and hence sovereignty were clearly not under any threat from Britain's occupation of the Islands. Argentina's feeling of being threatened could be justified only if the

Malvinas were indeed its rightful territory. Historically and legally, they were not. Moreover, the 150-year historical record of British occupation of the Islands was completely absent of any overtures or incidents on Britain's part that could be interpreted as being threatening to Argentina's security.

Second, Argentina had reiterated the point that it had searched for and exhausted peaceful methods of settlement as recommended by Article 33 of the U.N. Charter. These efforts were undertaken prior to its use of force. While this claim may appear to be a valid one, there are a few problems associated with it. To begin with, the U.N. Charter does not say that a party to a dispute can use force after it has made a good faith effort to settle a dispute by peaceful methods. The obligation to refrain from the use of force remains absolute, even if the parties concerned have sought and exhausted all forms of peaceful settlement. Further, Argentina did not submit her case to the International Court of Justice (ICJ) for a ruling. This procedure is enjoined on all member states of the U.N. Interestingly, it was Britain that offered to submit its dispute with Argentina over the Falkland Island Dependencies of South Georgia and South Sandwich Islands to the ICJ in 1947. Argentina, on the other hand, never even intimated, let alone submitted, its dispute to the U.N. Security Council for an opinion. This was a necessary step that Argentina was obligated to follow, having reached an impasse in the sovereignty negotiations with Britain. Article 37 of the U.N. Charter is very clear on this matter, stating: "Should the parties to a dispute of the nature referred to in Article 33 fail to settle it by means indicated in that Article, they shall refer it to the Security Council."

The third major plank on which Argentina justified its case for the use of force stemmed from the reservations it claimed were made with regards to the Malvinas when it signed the U.N. Charter. According to one legal researcher, however, "no such reservations were ever made."[97] Apart from that fact which the relevant documents do substantiate, had any reservations been made by Argentina when it signed the U.N. Charter, these reservations would have been rejected by the other signatories. But more importantly, reservations are not legally valid, particularly in the face of rejection, whether total or partial. Alberto Coll set the record straight when he said: "It appears that [what] the Argentine government loosely calls its reservations to the Charter concerning the Malvinas were no more than unilateral statements, made at the time of Argentina's signing of the Charter and addressed primarily to domestic public opinion which have no legal effects on Argentina's obligations under the Charter."[98]

In sum, the major obstacle to all of Argentina's justifications was definitely the strict prohibition of the use of force spelled out in the U.N.

Charter. The use of the instrument of force as a means of effecting change in international relations is not sanctioned by the Charter. Argentina's justifications were legally invalid and politically dangerous. If other states had followed Argentina's example, a new wave of political turmoil and security instability would have been unleashed upon the international system, given the plethora of active disputes about islands and other territories in the world.

What of Britain's use of force? The case here is quite clear. Britain's military response to Argentina's seizure of its territory was justifiable under international law. This justification stemmed from Article 51 of the U.N. Charter, which states:

> Nothing in the present Charter shall impair the inherent right of individual or collective self-defence if an armed attack occurs against a Member of the United Nations, until the Security Council has taken measures necessary to maintain international peace and security.

In the Falklands War, Article 51 could be construed to mean that Britain had the right of "individual self-defence." One legal writer made the point that "the United Kingdom was fully entitled under Article 51 of the United Nations Charter to resort to such measures [force] as were considered necessary by way of self-defence in response to an armed attack, in whatever part of its territory that attack occurred."[99] Coll advanced a similar view when he said that Britain's "use of force was legal, resting on the right to self-defence which, as Article 51 indicates, antedates the Charter, rests on juridical foundations independent of the Charter, and is sanctioned by the Charter."[100]

An important caveat, however, is relevant. The right to self-defense does not confer upon states the right to an unlimited use of force. Their use of this instrument must be linked to, and guided by, principles of proportionate means, as James Fawcett, an eminent British jurist, has explained: "Measures and actions taken in self-defence must be confined to the reversal of the armed attack and its effects, and must in the scale of, for example, weapons used, targets attacked, and effect on civilians, be proportionate to the achievement of that aim."[101]

The British use of force, as triggered by the self-defense provisions contained in Article 51 of the U.N. Charter, required a level of violence that this obligation would permit an offended state to use in its response to aggression. Had Britain, for instance, bombed the Argentine mainland, such an act would not only have been unjustifiable under the circumstances, but would have been disproportionate to the objectives Britain was seeking.

In other words, the extent of one's defensive measures must be proportional to the degree of aggression one has suffered. A close examination of the facts reveals that the British use of force was generally proportional to the degree of aggression initially carried out by Argentina. This proportionality factor was particularly accented in Britain's conduct of its military operations, with the exception of the *Belgrano* incident. In spite of this incident, however, the overall conduct of the British military campaign strongly suggested that the objective was attained by a proportional use of force. Britain accepted the norm that any disproportionate use of force beyond the requirements of self-defense could embitter future relations with Argentina.

Finally, Britain's strategy in restoring the status quo ante, particularly in the context of Argentina's refusal to comply with U.N. Security Council Resolution 502, necessitated the use of force. Professor Rosalyn Higgins, an eminent British legal scholar, has expressed the view that Britain had to resort to the use of force as the only means of restoring its own right, and at the same time, acting as the enforcement authority for the Security Council's call for withdrawal.[102]

## Conclusion

The war in the South Atlantic in early 1982 represented the dramatic and tragic culmination of a long-running international dispute. Although the battle for the Falklands was decisive in purely military terms, the larger question of a peaceful settlement still appears to be an elusive one. The use of force by both Argentina and Britain not only underscored the anarchical structure of the international political system, but also raised serious concerns for the long-term development of the Islands and of Antarctica. Sooner or later, Britain will have to enter into some form of meaningful dialogue with Argentina, given the depth of feelings Argentineans have towards the issue of the sovereignty of the Falklands. Argentina, on the other hand, still faces the formidable task of re-structuring its domestic ideology towards the Malvinas. Fifteen years after the war, the feelings on both sides still run deep. While the probability of some meaningful and beneficial accommodation on the future of the Islands taking place between the two sides appears rather small, one should not rule out the possibility of some form of radical change taking place at some point in the future.

Apart from the above considerations, it is worth highlighting the more salient and immediate issue of the use of force in the Falklands War of 1982.

For Argentina, the context that provided the strike-out conditions for the junta to use force straddled the boundaries of both the domestic and international environments. When the military leaders decided to embark upon the Malvinas landing, the internal situation in Argentina was fraught with political uncertainties and characterized by a multitude of economic and social woes. One Argentine analyst summarized the domestic situation well when he said that there was "an uncontrollable worsening of the economic crisis; contradictions in the armed forces and disintegration of the bourgeois front; isolation of the military, monopolist, and financial pinnacle from the rest of the society; and great advances in the mass movement and the struggle for democracy."[103] The dynamics of the entire internal political situation were such that a social explosion appeared imminent. One commentator noted that the new president's position "was at once imperiled by a financial crisis that soon exploded into a thunderous economic collapse."[104]

The external environment, particularly that aspect dealing with the junta's counter-revolutionary alliance with the United States and Argentina's interventions in Bolivia and Central America, contributed to its regional great power ambitions. Indeed, the military leaders were driven not only by a sudden patriotic impulse to seize the Malvinas, but also by the need to strengthen their national and international position. Moreover, the Malvinas issue appeared promising to the junta and thus gained increasing primacy.

For Britain, the situation and issues at stake were quite different. The use of military force, though legal, proportionate, and highly reactive, was part of a larger strategy that included diplomatic pressures and economic sanctions. In the end, it was the use of military force that secured Britain's objective, but at a tremendous cost. It is therefore a valid conclusion that economic considerations were pushed aside for higher politicostrategic objectives. When the decision was taken to recapture the Islands, Task Force commanders were not only prepared militarily, but they also had the full confidence and support of Downing Street.

The use of force in the Falklands War also illustrates the critical problem of mutual misperception that have so often arisen in international relations. One British analyst made the sobering point that "international crises often arise not from deliberate provocation or frontal challenge to a state's interest, but from miscalculation and misperception."[105] Such was the case in the Falklands War.

# Three

# British Motivations to Recapture the Falkland Islands

Conflict is an integral part of the anatomy of international politics. It stems in part from both the anarchical structure of the international system and from the prosecution of individual state interests. For analytical purposes, it can be examined at three different levels. At the individual level, "conflict between demands and activities within the group is a necessary characteristic of group life connected with the existence of politics."[1] At the systemic or international level, conflict is endemic and a necessary aspect of international life. It is not an alien phenomenon in either the practice or the study of international relations. What is noticeably conspicuous, however, is our inability to resolve or manage conflicts successfully, despite the accumulated knowledge and wisdom of *Homo sapiens*. Our failure to do so stems in part from the complexities of international life and our still partial understanding of human nature and behavioral dynamics.

Predicting state behavior is not an exact science, especially in conflict situations. The assumption of rational behavior on the part of a country, however desirable this idea may appear, is not a given state of affairs. The proposition that states do and will continue to prosecute issues that are perceived to be in their national interest holds true. But how that prosecution will take place is fairly unpredictable. Moreover, in a conflict situation, a state's behavior is not only difficult to predict with exactness, but it is equally difficult to arrive at the reasons which impelled its action. An example of the latter proposition was the numerous and sometimes absurd pronouncements made by the Soviets about the real motivations behind Britain's decision to recapture the Falklands. Some observers stressed nostalgia and a desire to defend British prestige, as well as Britain's desire to demonstrate resolve to defend its possessions against anticolonial movements.[2] Others disagreed and stressed British investments in the Falklands, as well as the natural resources, especially oil, allegedly available in the region surrounding the Islands.[3] Another popular view drew attention to the vast quantities of raw materials which are believed to be present in the surrounding waters. Possession of these strategically positioned islands would make possible the control of the sea lanes in the entire South Atlantic.[4]

The Americans also saw British motivations differently. For Alexander Haig, the U.S. secretary of state at the time and a key actor in the diplomatic negotiations following the Argentine invasion, the issues were Western resolve, combined with pride and patriotism.[5] However, for some members of the National Security Council and some of the president's aides, "the dispute in the Falklands had to do with oil and could be resolved by reaching an agreement to split up the drilling rights."[6]

It is clear from the above brief discussion, that ferreting out precise reasons for a state's behavior is not based on simple calculations of rationality. It is a complex exercise which requires close attention to both the psychology and rationality of decision making, as well as a suspension of judgment regarding definitive explications. The most that the analyst can hope for are plausible explanations. Notwithstanding this caveat, however, analysts, in their relentless search for the truth, are driven to explore and analyze a wide range of issues and their relationships. Monocausal explanations are difficult to sustain in the social sciences. The dynamics of state behavior within the international system would seem to suggest the interplay of two or more explanatory variables in any one situation.

The British decision to recapture what they perceived to be lost territory after the Argentine invasion of the Falkland Islands was a superb example of how not to rely on monocausal explanations. It was a response that ought to be seen within a larger framework that encompassed the worlds of both domestic and international politics. Within the parameters of that larger picture, one is able to work out and explain the modalities of British motivations. For it is clear that "the causes and character of the Falklands conflict are [still] widely misunderstood."[7]

This chapter examines some of the pertinent issues or motivations that lay behind the British decision to recapture the Falkland Islands. It should be pointed out at the outset that it was this decision which led to the seventy-four day war in the South Atlantic. Our focus is not on the decision-making process per se, but on the considerations that impacted on the decision. In other words, what were some of the issues and motivations that helped to shape and prompt the decision to retake the islands?

Several hypotheses will be examined. It will be shown that no one hypothesis is sufficiently adequate to explain British motivations. The explanatory power of one or two would appear, however, to be more convincing than the rest. Nevertheless, it is only through an examination of several of the arguments that a clearer picture surfaces. We begin by looking at the conflict from the classic North-South dimension and end by an examination of some compelling issues relating to democratic principles and strategic interests.

## A North-South Conflict?

The idea of a North-South classification of the conflict began to circulate even before the war ended on 14 June 1982. Foremost among the proponents of this view was Johan Galtung. Having examined and dismissed several hypotheses about the conflict, ranging from the internal projections of both governments, democracy versus dictatorship, to an East-West confrontation, Galtung settled finally for a North-South dimension to explain the nature of the Falklands War:

> The conflict is a North-South conflict of a new type, and the first of its kind. The classical North-South conflicts have centered around civil and political rights in the struggle against colonialism, and around economic, social and cultural rights in the struggle against neocolonialism. This conflict is about territory as such because of historical and geographical rights. But more importantly, it is a country in the South against a country in the North. And that serves to align the forces.[8]

Galtung's classification was taken up and expanded by Anthony Barnett, who devoted an entire chapter of his book *Iron Britannia* to "a war in the Third World."[9] He too saw "the war over the Falklands [as] a North-South clash, [and] not a South-South one,"[10] and also investigated political causes of the war.

The textbook North-South classification has its roots in the structuralist framework of international relations. Unlike realism and pluralism, structuralism is not a product of academic international relations. It does, however, draw upon a rich heritage of classical theory. This includes the early Christian and humanist concerns with justice and the fate of the individual, the Kantian philosophy of morality, the dialectics of Hegel, and above all, the historical materialism of Marx and Lenin.[11] Moreover, this

91

framework's importance to social scientists in all countries and in all fields stems from the insights it provides to basic Marxist thought. According to Michael Banks of the London School of Economics, it is "The bridge between economics and politics, the latent solidarity of groups whose objectives are linked by common circumstance and the progressive unfolding of historical changes in response to technological development and its expression in laws, ideologies and governmental institutions."[12] Structuralism also incorporates imperialism and variants of dependencia. It is within these two latter subsets that the Falklands War can be examined.

Such an examination, however, will not be capable of generating any fruitful or worthwhile insights into British motivations. The Falklands War had nothing to do with nostalgic imperialist ambitions or with a desire on the part of the North to teach the South a lesson. It pointed to other considerations. The anticolonial rumblings emanating from Buenos Aires were not efficacious insofar as juxtaposing the two sides. As noted in the *Times of India*, "There can no longer be any doubt that General Galtieri hoped to get away with the occupation of the Falklands by stirring up anti-colonial sentiment in the Third World and thus blocking any favorable action by the United Nations. But as it happened, things took a different course. Most non-aligned countries did not look at the issue as Buenos Aires would have expected them to."[13]

The geographical argument as it relates to the alignment of forces would seem to exemplify from the outset a North-South arrangement. But such an alignment was short-lived and came about as a consequence of the conflict and not because of any intrinsic desire or motivations of Downing Street. The British response, while prompting an initial North-South line-up, clearly was not motivated by such considerations. It would appear that the North-South alignment stemmed more from political ideology and diplomatic posturing than from law and international morality.

Another dimension of a North-South alignment manifested itself in the economic sphere. The discernible trade sanctions imposed by the North (EEC and USA), on Argentina would seem to suggest such an alignment, although it is worth noting that Australia and New Zealand also imposed sanctions. The EEC trade embargo on Argentina could have had a staggering effect, particularly if it had been extended in time. Argentina's annual exports to the EEC were valued at $2.3 billion, a large percentage of its total export sales. Without these revenues, it would have been difficult for Argentina, which had reserves of about $5 billion, to pay the nearly $10 billion in annual interest and other charges on its foreign debt.[14] Notwithstanding this consideration, the point needs to be made that although both

Britain and Argentina are modern industrial states, the former is a member of an integrated economic community and a military pact. Support for Britain from most countries within the industrial bloc, which are incidentally located in the North, stemmed from several considerations. Apart from a demonstration of alliance or EEC solidarity, there was the general perception of a "grave wrong" being done to Britain. Argentina's forceful seizure of the Falkland Islands was seen as being both unlawful and an act of unprovoked aggression. Britain, at the same time, was adjudged the aggrieved party. It was portrayed as a victim of Argentina's military aggression carried out by a fascist dictatorship that had an appalling record of human rights abuses. Thus it would appear that the short-lived economic support which produced an apparent North-South line-up was not prompted by a conspiracy involving the North ganging up against the South. This support flowed from considerations of law, morality, and economics.

What of the South's support for Argentina? Did the Latin American and other "South" countries see the conflict from such a perspective? To begin with, Argentina did not consider itself as a developing Third World country. It was not a member of the non-aligned movement, and more importantly, its record of voting at the U.N. General Assembly strongly indicated a "Northern" proclivity. Argentina's leaders and diplomats portrayed their country as a "developed" and "modern" state with an almost 100 percent European or white population. Mention is hardly ever made of the thousands of indigenous Indians who live on the fringes of society or of the tens of thousands who were systematically slaughtered by the European colonists and their descendants. By 1982, Argentina's cup of human rights abuses was overflowing and most Third World states had already distanced themselves from the country. Moreover, Third World solidarity did not swing towards Argentina during the Falklands War, particularly because of its close relations with South Africa. Argentina, a rich white nation, had shown no inhibitions about "cuddling" up to the apartheid regime in South Africa. The day it invaded the Falklands, its rugby team was playing the Springboks on their home ground.

From an international law perspective, Britain's reaction was described as legitimate self-defense. This perception knocked away the foundation of the Argentinean claim that the Inter-American Security Pact of 1947 (also commonly referred to as the Rio Pact) was applicable. The Rio Pact, the formulation of which was influenced by the onset of the Cold War and, to a certain extent, by the Monroe Doctrine, lays down the norm that the American states can decide on concerted defense measures in the event of external aggression against any one of them. The question, however, of that norm in the Rio Pact never came to a climax in the Falklands War. And that was partly because the Latin American countries were not particularly willing to consider military action in the cause of continental solidarity and partly because several states in the region found it extremely difficult to brand the British operation as aggression.[15]

Mexico, a regional power with considerable influence, remained neutral. Venezuela and Guatemala, on the other hand, were vigorous supporters of Argentina's military use of force to repossess its "lost" territory. Despite these overtures, neither was willing to make a tangible commitment in terms of troop deployment and other materiel support to Argentina. Venezuela's support was a somewhat peculiar affair. A country noted for being very critical of military governments in the Southern Cone, Venezuela became one of Argentina's staunchest supporters. That support, however, was not for the junta but the returning of a favor. When Venezuela was attacked by European powers in 1910 and blockaded because of its external debt problems, Argentina came to the rescue with the Drago Doctrine, which made standard the practice of not allowing countries in debt to be invaded by their creditors. Venezuela remembered, and 72 years later rallied in support of Argentina.

The Commonwealth Caribbean, including Guyana and Belize, who have ongoing territorial disputes with Venezuela and Guatemala respectively, strongly supported Britain. Chile, a neighboring state to Argentina that has a long-standing territorial dispute with it over the Beagle Channels, criticized Argentina's use of force as a means of settling international disputes.[16] Moreover, Britain's early diplomatic success with the passage of Security Council Resolution 502 had the effect of splitting the Latin American votes in other forums. Support for Argentina in the OAS was at best minuscule. This was of some significance, particularly in the light of the strong tendency demonstrated by Latin American states to hang together in the face of external interference in the hemisphere.

Support for Argentina from the South was low and mixed. Most countries, especially those in the region like Chile, Guyana, and Belize who have territorial disputes with militarily stronger and more powerful neighbors, disapproved of Argentina's use of military force. From the larger international perspective, disapproval of the junta's human rights record had been widespread. Many fledgling Third World democracies, jealous of their image, did not want to be seen supporting Argentina against Britain. One Chilean academic told this writer that Chile had grasped at the opportunity to support Britain if only to be seen in a different light.[17]

What then of the North-South hypothesis? It is clearly one that means different things to different people. In a more fundamental sense, the North-South scenario falls short as an explication for British behavior. The clash of arms between Britain and Argentine forces can be labeled as neither a colonial war nor a war of national liberation. It did not involve an indigenous population waging a war for greater autonomy. The clash of arms was over a piece of disputed real estate occupied by British subjects which had been seized by force. The clash, while prompting a temporary North-South alignment of support in geographical terms, was nonetheless an encounter between two modern industrial states. The fact that one was located in the North and the other in the South was more a question of geography than one of politics and ideology.

As an explanatory variable impacting on British motivations to recapture the Falklands, the North-South hypothesis is clearly inadequate. The arguments subsumed under this variable are clearly not sufficient or forceful enough. British motivations had very little to do with North-South arguments. On a peripheral note and one that merits some interest for the North, however, there is the view expressed by the Sunday Times: "NATO never wavered publicly in its backing for the British military campaign. There was another, more cynical, reason for this enthusiasm: The South Atlantic was to prove the best testing ground ever devised for the ships, planes and missiles on which NATO forces rely."[18]

The Falklands War has also invoked some amount of cynicism among Third World leaders. It was seen by some of these leaders as significant for the unity it created among many Western democracies in terms of economic sanctions imposed on Argentina. Moreover, that level of unity was perceived from the perspective of a North-South scenario. Such a perception was not unfounded, particularly in the light of an earlier experience. When the Soviet Union invaded Afghanistan in December 1979, the countries of Western Europe, while condemning Soviet behavior, did not impose economic sanctions on her. The editorial of one issue of the *International Defence Review* puts it this way: "Third World representatives [have] pointed out [that] the Falklands crisis has proved a far greater unity between industrialised western nations over imposing economic sanctions against a developing country than they were able to muster against the USSR when it invaded Afghanistan."[19] The two cases are clearly distinguishable. While the perception of a North-South alignment remains firmly entrenched among some Third World countries, it is hardly conceivable that such a perception played a role in British motivations.

# Economic, Geopolitical, and
# Strategic Importance of the Falklands

Britain's continued desire to occupy the Falkland Islands prior to the outbreak of hostilities in April 1982 cannot be explained simply by reference to their economic value. Indeed, the presence of half a million sheep together with a population of 1,800 humans would hardly provide a strong incentive for war based on the economic attractiveness of the Islands. Before dismissing these arguments outright, however, it would be worthwhile to examine in some detail a scenario based on the potential economic importance of the Falklands and the surrounding waters.

## Economic Factors

In his 1982 report, Lord Shackleton pointed out quite emphatically that "the Falkland Islands do have a resource development potential."[20] Part of that potential was realized in 1986 when revenues received through the granting of fishing licenses exceeded all expectations.[21] There are a number of reasons why the Islands and surrounding waters are potentially economically important. These range from hydrocarbon deposits to fisheries and seabed minerals. Let us examine these in more detail.

During the decade when oil was king, 1974–84, rumors were rife about the hydrocarbon potentials of several geographical areas, one of which was Antarctica. Motivated by the lure of big profits, many oil companies prosecuted their surveys and drilling operations with enthusiasm. The Malvinas basin was the scene of many such surveys. "The whole basin has been seismically surveyed, including an extensive survey by BP in 1979, and drilling has taken place in the Argentine sector."[22]

Three international oil companies, BP, Shell, and Esso, undertook drilling operations through various contractual arrangements with YPF, the Argentine state oil company. Their findings revealed some seven hydrocarbon sites, of which about four have been tentatively identified in the Malvinas region. One of these, called the Magellan Field, stretches over the mainland of Argentina to Tierra del Fuego and the surrounding channels and islands. Exploitation of this field could prove relatively easy because the area covers dry land and relatively shallow waters. Some parts of this field cannot be drilled, however, given the state of the territorial dispute between Argentina and Chile. With the Argentine/British dispute remaining unsettled, oil companies are scared away by what they perceive to be a politically unstable situation.

The second field, called Malvinas North, is located to the north and slightly west of the Falkland Islands. It lies mostly in quite deep and rough waters. Drilling operations carried out by Esso "revealed two finds, both uncommercial."[23] This does not mean, however, that the Malvinas North field is a potentially dry one. Given the high cost of drilling in deep waters and the price of crude today, such an exercise could be very uneconomical. One cannot, however, rule out the possibility of any future exploitation, particularly if crude oil prices should cross the $40 per barrel mark.

The third field, Malvinas South, lies to the southeast of the Islands, partly in the rough sea over the continental shelf and partly in the shallow waters of the Burwood Bank.

The existence of oil in the Falklands area has been the subject of a long debate. It seems clear that the region is potentially rich in hydrocarbon deposits formed in sedimentary basins around the surrounding waters of the Islands.[24] Exploitation of these potential resources could prove to be quite costly, however, especially in the Malvinas fields, where part of the oil lies in very deep and rough waters.

As for minerals and fisheries, the Law of the Sea idea of a 200-mile Exclusive Economic Zone (EEZ) has fueled speculation about the potential deposits of vast amounts of minerals in and around Antarctica. One optimistic writer noted that "the Antarctic is exceedingly rich in fish resources, minerals and oil."[25] In the wake of the 1974 oil crisis, statistical estimates of Antarctica's petroleum and gas potential triggered an awareness of the continent's marine and mineral resource potential. This potential is relevant to the view advanced by Russett that, as the international scramble for access to increasingly scarce resources heightens, marginal areas like Antarctica will begin to attract attention from governments and entrepreneurs.[26]

The example of the North Sea clearly demonstrates the feasibility of harnessing offshore resources in difficult conditions. The problems envisioned in an Antarctic operation for mineral and oil exploitation would be more formidable, however. Moreover, another problem makes it hard to achieve an accurate assessment of the situation. According to Beck, "the general lack of knowledge about Antarctica renders it difficult to evaluate its material possibilities, and at present, its resource value tends to be more potential than real."[27] But what of the Falklands area and its surrounding waters? According to the Law of the Sea doctrine, the Islands can lay claim to vast areas of marine resources.

There is a vast marine potential in these offshore waters (that part of the Patagonian Shelf adjacent to the Falklands) and in the Southern Ocean (the area south of the Antarctic Convergence). The 1982 Shackleton Report noted that "the potential yield of the fin fish and squid resources for the entire Patagonian Shelf is estimated at about 4–5 million tons a year."[28] As for the Southern Ocean, the potential yield is even more impressive. This area is known to have the largest resources of krill in the world, with a sustainable yield estimated at from 50 to 150 million tons per year.[29] It is also believed that the biological wealth of the Falklands oceanographic region accounts for as much as 10 percent of the international shellfish market. A leading fisheries expert at the FAO, John Gullard, has said that "the Falklands area is one of the world's most productive fisheries."[30] It is interesting to note in passing that at the time of Argentina's invasion in 1982, both Russian and Polish fishing trawlers were using facilities at Port Stanley.

Other potentially exploitable resources include tourism, wool and skin processing, and kelp. The latter commodity, found in large quantities around the coasts of the Falkland Islands, is suitable for the extraction of alginic acids, which are used in a wide range of industrial and pharmaceutical applications. For Britain, however, these resources in the South Atlantic represented only a long-term, potential economic interest. Against this background, we now return to the economic scene in early 1982. How was the Islands' economic situation generally regarded in Britain? An answer to these questions can be gleaned from three points.

First, up to March 1982, the Falklands' economy showed little signs of coming out of its downward spiral. Two major reasons accounted for this situation. They were a fall in the export price of wool and the steady flow of funds out of the Islands. While the impact of the latter was cushioned slightly by aid flows after 1976, there is no denying the overall effect these outflows had on the economy. In short, private sector investment suffered greatly.

Second, depopulation of the Islands had occurred, and morale was low among the poorer inhabitants. The population situation was aggravated further by the acute shortage of young women.

Third, there had been hardly any change in the structure of the economy since 1976. The 41 large sheep farms were still in the hands of absentee landlords. Moreover, the economy remained monocultural, depending primarily on the export of wool. Economic diversification, much talked about, had not yet taken place. In early 1982, the state of the Falklands' economy looked very dismal. When this reality was placed alongside the reluctance of both Labour and Conservative governments to implement the major recommendations of the 1976 Shackleton Report, the future prospects of the Islands looked even bleaker. The 1982 report made the sobering point that "the internal economy of the Falklands is in grave danger of collapsing in the next five years or so without continued support and/or development."[31]

Not much had changed since 1976 when the Shackleton team visited the Islands. The main theme of the 1976 Shackleton Report was dependency: the dependency on the Falkland Islands Company (FIC) for trade and the personal and psychological dependency of the people who lived there, many virtually enserfed to the company. The FIC exerted a virtual monopoly over land ownership, shipping, food supplies, and banking. Economically, the colony was a territory totally dependent on imports (which the FIC controlled) for most of its consumption and capital goods.

Official British interest in the economic development of the Falkland Islands was overshadowed by a larger geopolitical concern. For both Argentina and Britain, "it was not the economic attractiveness of the Islands that provided a compelling impulse for the parties to resort to force."[32] It can be argued that it was the economic implications arising out of the Argentinean claim that mattered for British decisionmakers. The Argentinean claim to sovereignty over the Falklands carried with it a "claim to jurisdiction over the continental shelf."[33] The implications from such a claim were very far-reaching. They would deter any oil company from embarking on any substantial investment in offshore mineral exploitation without firm undertakings acceptable to the Argentine government. Argentina's claim to parts of Antarctica would also be bolstered as a result of it having sovereignty over the Falklands, and, the loss of the Falklands would make the British Antarctic Territory (BAT) less secure for Britain.

Thus, while no obvious economic attractiveness of the Islands impacted directly on British motivations to recapture them, it was the wider economic implications that would seem to have had some effect. The extent of that effect, however, is a moot question. We now turn to the geopolitical and strategic considerations.

## Geopolitical and Strategic Arguments

The strategic importance of the Falkland Islands and their surrounding waters was never a contentious point. That importance was recognized over a hundred years ago when the Falkland waters became a focal ocean turning-point in world trade. Many analysts, especially after the 1982 conflict, have alluded to the strategic importance of these islands. David Brown referred to them as "a convenient station near Cape Horn."[34] Captain Joaquin Stella of the Argentine navy not only underlined the area's strategic importance "as an alternative to the Panama Canal,"[35] but also indicated other nodal points of significance. These included "fisheries; natural resources; maintenance of the sea lines of communication; bases, and support positions; and access to Antarctica."[36] Beck saw the Islands' strategic importance, especially for the United States and NATO, "on account of their location near the sea lanes around South America, their potential as an unsinkable aircraft carrier; the possibility of the closure of the Panama Canal, and the emerging Soviet interest in the wider South Atlantic region."[37]

For the Argentine military leaders, the Falkland Islands' strategic importance was seen in a wider geopolitical context. Geopolitics "offers the reality of a geographic basis to political action, ... it helps to bring abstract strategic concepts down out of the clouds."[38] It can also be viewed as the common meeting ground of military geography, strategy, and diplomacy. The Falklands were seen as "the key to the defence of the South Atlantic," particularly in the context of a military alliance involving the United States, South Africa, Argentina, Brazil, Uruguay, and Chile.[39]

The geopolitical significance of the South Atlantic was underscored by the idea that there should be a South Atlantic Treaty Organization (SATO). Supporters of this idea argued that SATO would be vital for Western shipping lanes because those ocean-going freighters that are too large for the Panama Canal must go around Cape Horn. Moreover, such a security mechanism would provide an access route to Antarctica and a source of economic wealth, particularly oil and seabed minerals. Also, it was suggested that "the danger to this area was the Soviet threat to shipping, or the 'encirclement' of the Atlantic basin by left-wing governments (Cuba to the north, Angola to the east)."[40]

The SATO failed to come to fruition because of a lack of political commitment of the actors involved and because of the varying ideological orientations and interests of the parties. Moreover, the intellectual premise for SATO was based on a faulty assumption of a Soviet threat to the South Atlantic. The threat was grossly exaggerated and could not have been sustained for any lengthy period. Perhaps the greatest problem facing the formation of SATO was Brazil's reluctance to be associated with South Africa in a close military pact. Brazil believed that bigger export markets could be won by cultivating closer relations with black African countries. Brazilian-Nigerian bilateral trade was a case in point.

Argentina's leading role in SATO negotiations was not without purpose. The aim was to get Britain out of the South Atlantic. By involving the United States in a South Atlantic pact and by stressing the necessity of the Falkland Islands for a military base, the Argentines were making a strong case for British withdrawal from the region. They believed that the Islands were a key factor in the security of the South Atlantic and that by regaining them, they would perform a great service for the "Western Christian" and anti–Communist world. In short, the Argentines wanted Britain out and were confident of getting U.S. support.

Another area of geopolitical interest was the nexus between the Panama Canal and the southwest Atlantic. In the event of the canal being closed, the latter area would be utilized for ocean transit. Menaul made the point that "the Falklands, together with South Georgia and Ascension in the South Atlantic, form an essential link with Diego Garcia in the Indian Ocean (through Simonstown in South Africa) in a chain of defences protecting the vital sealines of communication around not only the Cape of Good Hope, but also Cape Horn in the event that the Panama Canal should be denied to the West."[41] Apart from the beneficial link which arose between the two transit points, the South Atlantic waterway was strategically important in its own right, and particularly in the context of a changing perspective on the Panama Canal. The latter, according to a recent report "is no longer crucial to U.S. strategic or economic interests."[42] Some analysts contended that the Canal was not a vital defense asset because of the U.S. Navy's focus on larger aircraft carrier battle groups and a "three-ocean" navy. Moreover, aircraft carriers and submarines do not transit the Canal, so its importance as a military shortcut has been diminished.[43]

What then of the Falkland Islands and their strategic importance to Britain? To begin with, their geographic propinquity to Antarctica serves to bolster British claims to parts of that vast continent. Moreover, they are seen as the gateway to Antarctica and as providing an essential base for Britain's Antarctic role. This idea of placing the Falklands in a wider regional context was alluded to in the 1982 Shackleton Report: "While naturally our major concern has been the Falkland Islands and their inhabitants, we have sought to draw attention to wider and longer-term issues in the South Atlantic and the Antarctic."[44] Second, the Islands are vital for the service facilities they offer to fishing vessels. Increasing exploitation of the fishery and other marine resources of the region accentuates the need for service facilities which Port Stanley provides. Third, in the period before the Falklands War, the British believed that in the event of any outbreak of hostilities of an East-West dimension, access to, and more crucially control of, the Falkland Islands would prove advantageous to the West. Given the Soviet Union's power projection capabilities before the Falklands War and its access to Angola, there was no denying the strategic importance of the Falkland Islands to the West. The Islands, apart from serving as a key refueling and resupply base, also could be used as a base and platform for launching air attacks. Fourth, the phenomenal growth of the USSR as a naval power during the 1970s, after its development of a major long-range nuclear submarine fleet, was seen to pose a global threat.

While no one disputes these considerations, the question remains: Were they important factors in British calculations to use force? Did the members of the War Cabinet take a systemic view of their impending military action or were they overtaken by the pressing needs of immediate developments? Straightforward answers are easy to come by, but their accuracy is another matter.

British foreign and defense policymaking is not completely devoid of systemic thinking. History demonstrates the long-term view and cost-benefit approach inherent in British policymaking. However, while such an approach was used in the past, can it be said with any degree of certainty that a thorough cost-benefit approach was used in order to arrive at a course of action which called for the recapturing of the Falkland Islands?

The British decision finally to use force is believed to have been taken incrementally. This was the view Parliament wanted disseminated. In such a context, time was on the decision-makers' side. They had sufficient time to undertake a cost-benefit analysis of the options and, in so doing, must have given consideration to several factors. Goldblat and Millan were quite explicit in their belief when they asserted that "the reasons for opening hostilities were geo-political."[45] If by the opening of hostilities they meant the Argentine invasion, then such a claim would not be unfounded. However, one could give too much weight to the contribution of the geopolitical/strategic factor in the British calculation, particularly in the context of the Islands' forceful seizure and the widespread public outrage in Britain which that act triggered. It was unambiguously clear that the Thatcher government was reacting to events that had taken place nearly 8,000 miles away. But distance and location were not the problems facing the government in the initial stages of the imbroglio. The importance of location, which is intrinsic to geopolitical/strategic analysis, was subsumed under the gravity of the situation. The government's problem centered around the need to assuage public feelings and cushion the blow to British pride. These considerations aside, it is plausible to conjecture that geopolitical/strategic factors did play a role, however minuscule, in the determination of the government's decision to recapture the Falkland Islands. Their repossession, however, has transformed the Islands and the South Atlantic into a strategically important area for Britain and the West.

The systemic variable, already referred to, appears to have formed a part of the decision-making matrix. According to Haig, "Margaret Thatcher never saw the problem as a narrow issue exclusively between Britain and Argentina. Almost messianically, she viewed it as a test of Western fiber and determination."[46] By placing the issue in a wider systemic framework, it is obvious that the prime minister's decision was guided by geopolitical/strategic considerations. The impact of these considerations on the overall decision to recapture the Islands can be measured, however, only in the light of other explanatory variables. The sections that follow consider these variables.

## Domestic Economic and National Honor Considerations

It is tempting to equate British motivations for recapturing the Falklands with the strong impulses unleashed by domestic political and economic forces prevailing in Argentina before April 1982. It is abundantly clear, as argued in the preceding chapter, that the deteriorating sociopolitical situation and the ruinous state of the Argentine economy did provide a motivation to the junta leaders for taking military action. The idea that external diversions could be turned to as a temporary and palliative tactic, particularly in the face of domestic upheavals, was not unfounded. But insofar as the British response was concerned, it would be extremely difficult to sustain the hypothesis that domestic economic considerations played a decisive role in shaping the government's decision to recapture the Falklands. Notwithstanding this, the fact remains that at the time of the South Atlantic crisis, the British economy was in a terrible state, with all the major indicators showing the extent of the problem. Was it the case though, that like Argentina, the British government was forced to take military action in order to divert attention from domestic economic and political concerns? While the situation facing Downing Street was not so grave as to force the government's resignation, the Falklands diversion was indeed welcomed from the standpoint of a UK-EEC showdown. The country's self-defined sovereignty was decisively violated when the EEC decided Britain's food prices against its wishes. It appears that the Falklands imbroglio saved Thatcher from a fight with the EEC, where all of the UK's economic weakness showed most damagingly. She could ill-afford to fight on two fronts at the same time. The larger question of domestic economic problems remained, however, and the arguments seemed compelling.

## Economic Considerations

When Margaret Thatcher arrived at 10 Downing Street in May 1979, unemployment was officially put at the 1.3 million mark and was falling. At the outbreak of the Falklands conflict nearly three years later, it had rocketed to 2.9 million and was rising. The squeeze on British industry was traumatic. Between 1979 and 1981, manufacturers' international competitiveness had deteriorated by 50 percent. In order to survive, some companies were forced to slash profits to the bone, while others borrowed heavily from their banks to stay afloat. The greatest ever one-year decline in British output occurred in 1980.[47] The steep rise in interest rates aggravated the economic situation and eroded the competitiveness of most manufacturing companies. The government's attempt to slow down the rate of inflation, a goal it managed to achieve in a modest way, was "combined with deteriorating unemployment and trade."[48]

In the face of this deteriorating economic condition and the stark reality of the international recession, the government pursued its supply-side economic policy with a vengeance in an attempt to get British industry to perform. Obsessed with the idea of "company-led growth," the government developed a strategy based on boosting company profits. It was believed that if companies could spend more on fixed investment and stock building, they would halt the economy's decline. This idea, while being theoretically sound, was difficult to implement in light of the adverse economic circumstances prevalent at the time. The overall climate, characterized by "deindustrialization, a massive increase in unemployment, a surge in the export of capital, the regressive reform of taxation and decrease in real wage incomes," was not conducive for the successful implementation of the government's strategy.[49] For years, British companies had been quietly hemorrhaging to death. According to the *Economist*, their pretax real rate of return on capital fell from 11.7% in 1964 to 5.4% in 1974; by 1981 their real return had fallen to 2.0%, well below returns in other industrial countries.[50]

This was the economic situation in which the government found itself in 1982. It was widely held that its economic policies, among other things, were directly responsible, but the government did not see it that way. The

chorus "if the policies ain't hurting, then they ain't working" became a familiar refrain of government ministers. The need for greater industrial
efficiency and output was seen as the way out of the economic quagmire.
Despite the debilitated state of the British economy at the outbreak of the
Falklands War, it cannot be compared with Argentina's. The Argentine
economy was on the brink of collapse when it invaded the Falklands. Added
to this reality was the grave and sordid state of political and social life in
the country. The very fabric of society was under siege. Such was not the
case in Britain. The British government, while faring disastrously in the
opinion polls, was not confronted by the type and scale of problems that
faced the junta. In short, the domestic political and economic situations in
the two countries were not the same. The policies of both governments
were different, as were the circumstances under which they operated. On
the other hand, the Falklands issue provided a point of convergence for both
governments. Both saw the strong element of political opportunity and
seized it. For Buenos Aires, the capture of Las Malvinas from British control meant a new lease on the junta's life and legitimacy. For London, the
recapture of lost British territory from a totalitarian dictatorship saved the
government from the political consequences of doing nothing. According
to Lord Carrington, "outrage would have directed itself against any government which took so supine an attitude."[51] Haig opined that "it was clear
that the survival of Mrs. Thatcher's government was at stake."[52] That survival was not predicated so much on getting the economy right, however,
as it was on the government's ability to act quickly, forcefully, and decisively. Downing Street's quick action in dispatching the Task Force not
only underlined the gravity of the situation but also demonstrated the government's decisiveness and willingness to stand up to aggression. While the
need to create such a perception was prompted by political expediency,
there is no denying the role played by the domestic economic situation.
Although economic considerations were not decisive, the political decision
to recapture the Falklands was taken against the background of an economy that was both debilitated and in a "doldrums" state. This is not the
same as saying that the depressed state of the economy was the origin of
the government's political decision. Because of the depressed state of the
economy, however, such a decision had a clear payoff function of diverting
the focus of attention away from the economic debate and towards the war
mobilization effort.

   What then of the domestic economic circumstances? Did they provide very strong motivations for the government's decision? The short
answer is no. Nonetheless, this is not to dismiss economic circumstances

outright because they played a minor role in shaping that decision. It was very clear that by the end of 1981, the Thatcher government was cornered, and it found accidental salvation in turning to the Falklands crisis. This much cannot be denied. Moreover, the government's decision to retake the Falkland Islands in the face of severe domestic economic pressures demonstrated the potency and continued relevance of wider politicostrategic developments. In short, the U.K. government pursued the war despite economic difficulties at home. Defense policy was clearly not constrained by domestic economic considerations. Further, the decisionmakers had no way of knowing at this initial stage how long the war effort would last and how much it would cost. (See Chapter Four for the costs of the war.) Despite these very real uncertainties, the government did not waver in its commitment to go ahead with its plans for the repossession of the Falkland Islands. We turn now to an examination of national honor considerations.

## National Honor Considerations

Wars are begun not on the basis of abstract principle but because of anger and errors of judgment rising out of the frailties of human nature. Anger and outrage are powerful emotions. In the Falklands situation, the tendency to be carried away by the emotions of the moment was not peculiar to Argentina alone. The British outrage and euphoria demonstrated the uncontrollable power of emotions. The Falklands War was a classic case of emotional outbursts. It underlined the enduring relevance of such concepts as pride, prestige, and national honor in the international relations of states. It showed also that when such ideas are taken to excess and become all consuming, the consequences can be disastrous.

Before examining these ideas within the context of the government's decision, we pause to consider a related concept—island people—which the prime minister skillfully weaved into the fabric of the national honor cloth.

In her speech marking the opening of the emergency debate in Parliament on that historic Saturday morning, Prime Minister Margaret Thatcher made the following remarks in her final appeal:

> The people of the Falklands, like the people of the United Kingdom, are an island race. Their way of life is British; their allegiance is to the Crown. They are few in number, but they have the right to live in peace, to choose their own way of life and to determine their own allegiance.... It is the wish of the British people and the duty of Her Majesty's Government to do everything we can to uphold that right. That will be our hope and our endeavour and, I believe, the resolve of every Member of the House.[53]

Thatcher's remarks were quite explicit. Many journalists trumpeted this idea of "island people," and some believed that it was one of the major factors that propelled Britain into war with Argentina. For instance, the *Nairobi Daily Nation* stated: "The war was fought because the Argentine rulers sought to subjugate the Falklanders, of British descent, by force of arms after they made it clear that they wanted to remain part of Britain."[54] Similar sentiments were expressed in an Italian daily: "The two thousand inhabitants of that territory [the Falkland Islands] are ethnically and linguistically English. They want to remain English and above all, do not wish to become Argentine."[55]

For the concept of "island people" to be credible as an explanatory variable, however, one has to examine it in its wider perspective. It must include such nuances as ancestry, wishes and rights, allegiance and language, and customs.

The ethnic makeup of the Falklanders has never been a contentious issue. They were and are almost wholly (over 95 percent) of British origin.[56] Their traditions and way of life are British, as are their educational system and constitution.

In December 1977 a motion adopted by the Falkland Islands Legislative Council explicitly stated the desired wishes of the Islanders: "This House wishes it to be conveyed to Her Majesty's Government that the people of the Falkland Islands have shown overwhelmingly that they wish to remain British."[57] Respect for such wishes was also expressed by U.N. General Assembly Resolution 1541: "The right to self-determination might be met by the people becoming an independent state, or being freely associated with another country, or being integrated with another country, provided that the choice was freely and publicly made by the people."[58] In a ministerial statement in 1980, the House of Commons reaffirmed its respect for the wishes of the Falklanders, noting: "Her Majesty's Government's policy with regard to independence for remaining territories for which it has responsibility is to respect the wishes of the local inhabitants as expressed through their elected leaders."[59]

The contentious issue underlining the debate on "wishes" was whether the Falklanders qualify as a *people*. The term *people* is a difficult concept to define, and no definition has been agreed upon in the UN. It was on this issue that the Argentineans took a firm and recalcitrant posture. They do not see the Kelpers as a people, endowed with the rights to express their wishes in determining their future. They see the territory as being more important than the people. Such a view had been expressed openly at the United Nations in 1965 when the Argentine delegate made it clear that

107

"there is not the least doubt that the territory of the Falkland Islands is much more important than the population."[60]

The British, on the other hand, have taken a more considered view of the issue, basing their judgment on historical facts. The overwhelming number of inhabitants of practically all South American states (exceptions being Guyana and Surinam) are descendants of European settlers. The indigenous Indian people have been, to a large extent, systematically eliminated. And as James Cable has noted, "particularly in Argentina, an indigenous people has always been an endangered species."[61] This was not the case in the Falklands, however, because there were no indigenous inhabitants of these islands. This made them unique insofar as the "people" issue was concerned. Thus the present inhabitants of the Falkland Islands, the Kelpers, have the same right to be accepted as a people as those who live in other South American countries.

This British posture, diametrically opposed to the dominant Argentinean view, was a strong catalyst for galvanizing support among Members of Parliament. It transcended party lines and gave a dogged tenacity to the government's negotiating stance. Moreover, the government's strong desire to respect the wishes of the Kelpers, thereby according them the status of a people, meant that open conflict with Argentina seemed inevitable. The Thatcher government was not prepared to negotiate away the wishes and rights of the Falklanders. Respect for their wishes to continue to be associated with Britain remained paramount. And it was this very issue of wishes which dogged negotiations throughout the conflict. Thus when Argentina invaded the Falklands on the morning of 2 April 1982, Britain could not have acquiesced in what it perceived to be the colonization of some of its people.

Linked to the idea of "wishes" are other nuances like "rights" and "small size" which were perceived to be very important. The journalist Christopher Dobson summarized it well when he said:

> Argentine troops had landed and seized British territory, island territory moreover, and the British themselves were more comparable to those of the British in 1939—a comparatively small island in a hostile world. If the idea were allowed to get around that islands might be seized, would not the British themselves be in danger? That was the reasoning behind the mood of somber understanding. That is why the Falklands crisis was so different from any other of the dangerous affairs which had confronted the nation in recent years.[62]

Apart from the above considerations, British motivations, it would seem, were influenced also by pride and prestige. Cable, while recognizing that "a nation's response to foreign coercion is inevitably influenced by its international standing,"[63] made the forceful point that had Britain "submitted to Argentine coercion, even on an issue which affected no vital British interest, she would have lost much of her credibility either as an ally or an enemy."[64]

National pride and international prestige are important independent variables in international relations. They matter a great deal more to medium powers than they do to either a superpower or a minor power. Superpowers do not have to aspire to greater influence and status within the international political system. They already have those qualities by virtue of the sheer statistics of their military and economic strength. The minor powers, if they can be called powers, are not too concerned about fighting to preserve their international standing. They know their place in the pecking order. It is the medium powers which are more awkwardly placed within the global system. How they are perceived by the other powers is extremely important to them. Their standing in the world matters greatly, and it depends as much on their reputation as it does on their measurable assets. They cannot afford humiliation, least of all at the hands of another power in that debatable middle ground between a superpower and a minor power.[65]

When Argentina, a middle power of a lower order than Britain, seized territory belonging to the latter, the blow to British pride and prestige was overwhelming. According to Lord Carrington, the foreign secretary at the time, "the invasion of the Falklands has been a humiliating affront to this country."[66] And in that historic Saturday (3 April 1982) debate in Parliament, George Foulkes echoed the sentiments of the House when he said "our country has been humiliated."[67]

The humiliation was felt in a very acute way. Britain was no ordinary medium power. It was once a great power which controlled a third of the world, and that was not too long ago. Nevertheless, the blow to British pride also had other implications. It awakened the warrior spirit of the British people, a people who had thought that this spirit had died with the end of empire. The British saw that they had to react to this invasion, which had the potential to undermine Britain's credibility as a medium power of the first order. Had Britain backed down from what was widely regarded as "naked aggression," the perceptions that most countries had of Britain would have changed significantly. The image of Britain as a no-nonsense, law-observing, pluralist democracy was important and had to be upheld. Maintaining that image was crucial for Britain's continuing pivotal role both within the NATO alliance and the EEC. David Watt argues that if

Britain had failed to act forcefully, its position within the NATO alliance and within the EEC would have received less consideration in the future and its claim to a permanent seat in the U.N. Security Council would have been weakened.[68]

The invasion of the Falklands by Argentina had the potential to produce British humiliation and British loss of pride and international prestige. A price had to be paid for the restoration of Britain's image and credibility. And that price involved going to war with Argentina, though the entire South Atlantic issue did not involve an obvious national interest. Carrington made it clear in his memoirs that "the Falklands represented no vital strategic or economic interest for Britain."[69] According to an American analyst, the issue was not one of national interest but of national pride: the British public was not prepared to tolerate the blow to national pride that the Argentine invasion represented.[70] And the government had to act in a way that sought not only to assuage domestic public outrage, but also to give a clear signal that it was in a bellicose mood. Whether the effort to create that perception smacked of political opportunism was another matter. The government's reaction did demonstrate, however, its firm resolve to deal with the crisis in a very decisive manner.

In sum, it appears that national honor considerations impacted very heavily on the government's decision to recapture the Islands. Of the many considerations examined so far, this one is indeed very compelling and offers a powerful and persuasive explanation of British motivations, although it should not be seen in complete isolation. The words of the prime minister given in a special interview to the *Daily Express* reveal the cogency of this variable: "It was understood right from the outset that the honour of our people and our country was at stake."[71] It is clear that the Thatcher government pictured itself in a political corner in which national honor considerations would not permit either appeasing dictators or meekly accepting invasion. National honor on several planes was involved: politicomilitary standing, bargaining reputation, and domestic and international image. Thatcher shared with Haig a concern for the credibility of a NATO country.

# Defense of Democratic Principles

At the height of the Falklands crisis, Thatcher, speaking on a BBC "Panorama" program on 26 April 1982, described the diplomatic impasse in these crisp words: "The sticking point for us is the right of self-determination." She then went on to explain what she meant by self-determination: "The Falklander's loyalty to Britain is fantastic. If they wish to stay British, we must stand by them. Democratic nations believe in the right of self-determination.... The people who live there are of British stock. They have been for generations, and their wishes are the most important thing of all. Democracy is about the wishes of the people."[72]

Following the early signs of a breakdown in diplomatic negotiations between Argentina and Britain, Thatcher, in reminding Parliament about the gravity of the situation that lay ahead, pinpointed some of the principles that Britain was defending:

> The principles that we are defending are fundamental to everything that this Parliament and this country stand for. They are the principles of democracy and the rule of law. Argentina invaded the Falkland Islands in violation of the rights of the peoples to determine by whom and in what way they are governed. Its aggression was committed against a people who are used to enjoying full human rights and freedom. It was executed by a Government with a notorious record in suspending and violating those same rights. Britain has a responsibility towards the islanders to restore their democratic way of life. She has a duty to the whole world to show that aggression will not succeed and to uphold the cause of freedom.[73]

From the above considerations, we can delineate at least three democratic principles which the Conservative government upheld and showed a determination to defend. These were "the right of self-determination," "the sanctity of the British way of life," and the imperative that "aggression should not pay."

These principles were reinforced again by the prime minister when she addressed Parliament on 20 May 1982. It was a crisis moment in the negotiation process. Argentina had rejected finally the latest British proposals. Those proposals, according to Mrs. Thatcher,

> preserve the fundamental principles which are the basis of the Government's position. Aggression must not be allowed to succeed. International law must be upheld. Sovereignty cannot be changed by invasion. The liberty of the Falkland Islanders must be restored. For years they have been free to express their own wishes about how they want to be governed. They have enjoyed self-determination. Why should they lose that freedom and exchange it for dictatorship?[74]

Thatcher was not the only one in the War Cabinet to uphold these democratic principles. Francis Pym, the newly appointed foreign secretary, remarked in Parliament that "the preservation of peace depended on the international community supporting the principle of self-determination and punishing those who violated it."[75] Pym also made it clear that Britain was prepared to use force in the exercise of its rights of self-defense. "Not to be prepared to do this," he told the House, "would be irresponsible since it was in the interest of the whole free world that the rule of law should be upheld and that aggression should not prevail."[76]

Support for Thatcher's "defense of democratic principles" posture came from several quarters. Hastings and Jenkins believed that "the Prime Minister was determined that the Falklands conflict should be seen as a noble and principled crusade."[77] And Laffin also felt very strongly about this matter of principle. For him, "Britain went to immense trouble and expense to fight a war in the South Atlantic purely because of its concern for the freedom of an independent people."[78] In editorials in several newspapers across the globe, this theme was well orchestrated. A few examples reveal the extent to which the "defense of principle" argument disseminated:

> Margaret Thatcher is fighting for a principle, not territory.[79]
> However few their numbers, Falklanders are also entitled to self-determination.[80]
> The British Government, with sacrifice of blood and treasure defended far more than land and liberty. They defended the principle of legitimacy.[81]
> Britain, by defending a principle without which international life would become impossible, has done the international community an exemplary favor.[82]
> An example to the world of identifying principles and being prepared to fight for them.[83]

Words like *principle, wishes,* and *freedom* were used extensively by the prime minister throughout the Falklands conflict. In parts of her speech quoted above (containing 260 words), these key concepts were used ten times. And of the five editorials quoted, four used the word *principle(s)*. The contextual use of these concepts would seem to strengthen the hypothesis that the defense of democratic principles did provide the overriding motivation for the British use of force. Indeed, one analyst appeared to be quite explicit in his assessment when he said: "Let there be no doubt about it. The war in the Falklands was fought, on the UK's part at least, for the sake of people—the Falklanders themselves, and their right of self-determination."[84]

But what of these principles which Mrs. Thatcher was promulgating and defending? Are they credible and did they matter? The principle of self-determination is fundamental to democracy, but it is not one which is absolutely supreme. A people has the democratic right to be the arbiter of its national identity. That wish of the population is very important, but it is not absolutely paramount. To the British government, self-determination was not a negotiable proposition, and self-determination as expressed by the Kelpers meant a reimposition of British rule. Herein lay a major stumbling block in the negotiation process. The government's unyielding stance on this issue of self-determination not only hardened its negotiation position but gave the general impression that the government was fully prepared to defend the principles it was advocating. But is it always so?

It is illuminating to reflect on the Diego Garcia episode. In 1966 an Anglo-American military agreement attempted to turn the island of Diego Garcia in the Indian Ocean into a U.S. military outpost. The island was inhabited by just under eighteen hundred settlers. Diego Garcia had been their home for decades. They were never consulted by the British government with regards to their wishes. After the agreement was signed, these Ilois people were forcibly deported to Mauritius over a thousand miles away and dumped into squalor and poverty. It is interesting to note that both Labour and Conservative governments had, in succession, approved the wholesale removal of these island people, quite against their wishes. They were not even compensated. They had to wait sixteen long years for the paltry sum of 4 million pounds, which was then divided up among the 1,200-plus remaining survivors.[85] Could it be any more obvious that the bipartisan attachment in the British government to the principle of self-determination for small island communities does not exist, or at the very least, is racially selective? For it is abundantly clear that the Ilois people of Diego Garcia are "black," whereas the Kelpers are "white." Obviously, attachment to a principle ought to cut across racial boundaries. The behavior of successive British governments towards the Diego Garcians strongly suggests that principles like self-determination, wishes, and freedom for island peoples have been used selectively. Margaret Thatcher, being a "conviction" politician, clearly found it politically expedient to prosecute the war with Argentina by portraying it as a defense of democratic principles. However, a caveat is in order here. The Falklands issue is clearly distinguishable from both the Diego Garcian and Hong Kong cases. It was and still is a domestic political issue. The Falklanders are British, and Argentina's invasion was construed as a barbaric and reprehensible act against a small number of defenseless British subjects. (See Chapter Five for more on this crucial issue.) While the inhabitants of Hong Kong were accorded the same status as that of the Kelpers by the passage of the Nationality Act in 1981, the fact remains that the overwhelming majority of these people are not of British stock. The Sino-British accord, reached in December

1984, would seem to suggest the selective application of such principles as wishes and self-determination.

That portrayal of the Falklands War as a war of principles mattered a great deal to Britain's international image. It mattered more to the prime minister. The British military response could not be allowed to be seen as a sabre-rattling exercise or as an opportunity for revenge. It was crucial to the government that its response should be seen as a fight for principles. No opportunity was lost in the British propaganda campaign during the war. The defense of democratic principles and the rights and wishes of small island communities were elevated and transformed into virtues for which it was worth dying. Peter Kellner referred to Thatcher's war of "bogus principles."[86] It was not the principles themselves, however, that were bogus or ridiculous. It is a good and noble thing to resist aggression and fight for freedom and to defend a democratic way of life. It is also a good thing to side with democracy against dictatorship. However, the Thatcher government's behavior in some respects would seem to suggest a concern for something else and a lack of consistency. Take for example the close ties Britain had and still has with dictatorships. Prior to the South Atlantic conflict, the Thatcher government was steadfast in its efforts to cultivate relations with the notorious military dictatorship in Argentina. Clearly, such relations were not actuated by a desire based on the pursuit of principle, but by the motivation for profit. The South African case was another example. It was a racist and diabolical minority dictatorship that the Thatcher government seemed to find appealing. Downing Street's close embrace of Pretoria was not based on genuine principles but on the economic benefits which that relation brought to Britain. It was concerns like these which cast deep suspicions on the government's escalating rhetoric in early 1982 and undoubtedly undermined the credibility of official statements. In his usual sharp style, Barnett advances the view that "the Falklands were a perfect stage for the exercise of principle because they were so utterly removed from the complications of substance."[87]

What of the principle "aggression should not pay?" It was a statement that carried the most conviction both domestically and internationally, and from the legal standpoint, it gave legitimacy to the British use of force. The outraged domestic audience and a not too gullible international community had to see the British will to use force not only as a test of Western political resolve, but as a sort of evangelical crusade against aggressors. The idea that aggression should not pay also involved the notion that aggression should not go unpunished. It was this latter notion, subsumed in the larger idea, that formed part of Thatcher's quiver of symbols. Indeed the symbolic interactionists' general assumption that "humans perceive and interact in reality through the use of various symbols" is relevant here.[88] Thatcher's skillful use of symbols, opportune in time and remarkable in clarity, transformed the crisis by inculcating notions of right and wrong.

That aggression should not pay was made to be seen as a simple black and white issue. The United States, like most other countries, bought the idea. Admiral Stansfield Turner made the point that the United States has generally accepted the British contention that it went to war in order to defend the principle that aggression does not pay.[89] And Haig conceded that "the British demonstrated that a free people have not only kept a sinewy grip on the values they seem to take for granted, but are willing to fight for them, and to fight supremely well against considerable odds.... Principle triumphed."[90]

In her aggressive use of symbols, Thatcher was aware of the critical time factor. At the outset, she did not command, even in her own cabinet or party, widespread support for her vision as embodied in her ideals. The opportunity to seek a negotiated settlement, or to appear to seek one, gave Thatcher the time she needed for both public and international opinion to rally around her ideas. Moreover, Thatcher was strengthened by media polls showing that a majority of Britons were in agreement with her hard line on the Falklands before her government had firmly adopted it. In the end the British military response and subsequent victory was hailed as a triumph for Western democracy and as a lesson to future would-be aggressors. The fight for symbols, if it can be called that, also boosted Britain's international standing. That idea was not lost on some members of Parliament. Alan Clark, one of the more hawkish of the "war party" on the Tory benches, told an interviewer that in his view the Falklands War "has enormously increased our world standing. You asked about world opinion—I mean, bugger world opinion—but our standing in the world has been totally altered by this. It has made every other member of NATO say 'My God, the British are tough.'"[91]

To what extent then were the British motivated by a desire to defend democratic principles? To deny the impact of these principles completely would be both politically naive and intellectually myopic. Those principles were elevated and transformed into symbols that aroused passions, inspired zeal, and commanded respect. They flowed from a leader who practiced "conviction" politics and who had a penchant for reducing complex issues to straightforward and simple equations with two known variables—right and wrong. Haig recognized the powerful attachment Thatcher displayed towards these principles. When he put forward to the British the U.S. plan for a multinational force on the Islands to provide interim administration, Thatcher declined it as politically unacceptable to Britain in that it did not address immediately the issue of "self-determination":

> I pressed on the question of an international force on the islands and setting up some sort of administration and providing for self-determination. The notion was too woolly, Mrs. Thatcher said. The House of Commons would never accept it because she was pledged to restoration of British administration, which meant the courts, public services, and all the normal apparatus of government. No vague international presence would substitute for this essential authority. She feared that we were talking about negotiations under conditions of duress, which would be a terrible insult to Britain. In any case, she felt that Argentina would never accept self-determination because all the islanders wanted to remain British. As for sovereignty: British sovereignty was a fact. It continued no matter what the Argentines had done or may do.[92]

To the British, and in particular to Thatcher, "self-determination was non-negotiable, and self-determination, as expressed by the Kelpers, meant re-imposition of British rule in the Falkland Islands."[93]

The defense of democratic principles was not the primary reason why the Thatcher government wanted to restore British sovereignty over the Falklands, but these principles gave legitimacy to the British diplomatic and military efforts. They subsumed the more efficacious national honor considerations and in doing so, played a vital strategic role. Edward Thompson, drawing upon the skills of a historian, saw the real motivations for the war: "The Falklands war is not about the islanders. It is about 'face.' It is about domestic politics. It is about what happens when you twist a lion's tail.... [It is] a moment of imperial atavism, drenched in the nostalgias of those now in their late middle-age."[94] And Admiral Turner drove home the point with precision and accuracy when he said: "The prime reason Britain responded so quickly and decisively was that Prime Minister Margaret Thatcher's political fate was on the line. Her government had failed to deter the Argentine invasion. She had a choice between explaining her error or retaking the islands by force. She chose the latter and then encouraged public feelings about fighting for principle."[95]

# Conclusion

The question of why Britain fought for distant and rather unimportant islands which it had failed to defend is still being asked today. The

Argentine junta's total failure to predict the British reaction not only plunged the two countries into a nasty little war but brought about the demise of the junta. The British, on the other hand, were able to regain their lost territory, and with this victory came a fresh resurgence of pride and a strengthening of the Conservative government. But the question of why Britain fought this war still remained. For many, including lords Pym and Carrington, the answer was fairly simple and straightforward. Pym described the conflict in these words: "British territory had been invaded and British citizens captured. Strenuous efforts were made to secure the withdrawal of hostile forces by peaceful means, but when Argentina refused to accept any reasonable arrangement there was no alternative but for our forces to recapture the islands."[96] For Carrington, the motivation to act flowed from "the effect on world opinion and British prestige if nothing was done."[97]

The U.S. secretary of state, Alexander Haig, who was tireless in his mediation efforts to find a peaceful solution, never wavered in his conviction that "the Argentines had been guilty of aggression and must not be allowed to get away with it or there would be dire consequences for the rest of the world."[98] And from the *Strategic Survey*, we read: "For all the flexibility which the British government had shown, the dispute was widely seen in Britain as one of principle."[99] It was a principle that related to acceptable international behavior—"Argentina should withdraw her forces from territory which she had seized illegally and in the middle of negotiations."[100]

Unlike the Soviet decision to emplace missiles in Cuba, which to this day remains a complex foreign policy issue, the British decision to recapture the Falkland Islands in 1982 is less fraught with ambiguities. While there appear to be several plausible explanations for British motivations, only two sets of considerations emerge as dominant. On the one hand, there is the "defense of democratic principles hypothesis" and, on the other, "national honor" considerations. These two hypotheses are not mutually exclusive. Indeed, the concept of national honor also involves the notion of political principle. It is a concept that is less concrete than national interest—political, economic, or military—but no less real or important. It is the assessment and implementation of collective values for international behavior. And this overarching interest in "political principle" is particularly important in territorial wars and politicomilitary disputes.

National honor, it should be recalled, is a political phenomenon and a very important factor in decision making. That importance is underscored by the fact that national honor tempers or contradicts concrete national interest in favor of standing in the international political system. And, according to Kinney, "it has both domestic and international sources and results—a 'toughness,' or the easy resort to force."[101] In short, territorial goals tend to involve more national honor considerations than concrete national interest. Moreover, national honor is more divisible and less subject to non-zero-sum solutions. And when it incorporates ideas relating to "political principle," the consequences can be explosive. In such a situation, the concept can contain the seeds of confrontation.

The defense of democratic principles was never the dominant or overarching motive that lay behind the British decision to recapture the Falkland Islands. Democratic principles were portrayed and paraded by the government as a symbol for which it was worth fighting. But behind that showcase lay the real motivations—national honor considerations of pride, prestige, and international image.

Like the Argentine junta, Margaret Thatcher also grabbed the opportunity to assuage her disgruntled domestic constituency and to bolster Britain's international image by her single-minded determination to retake the Falkland Islands. Her tactics involved, among other things, a strong crusade for the defense of democratic principles. This tactic of transforming the British response into an ideal gave Thatcher the leverage to prosecute her interests with great finesse. The real motivations behind that tactic were not, however, the concerns of a North-South conflict or the short-term economic and strategic importance of the Falkland Islands, but the compellence of national honor. As Douglas Kinney notes, "More than most territorial disputes, ... the Falklands has become a question of the National Honour of both Argentina and the United Kingdom."[102] The Falkland conflict, it would appear, involved the need to preserve both Thatcher's political fate and British honor and prestige. These elements were perceived at the time to command the high ground of interest for the political directorate. And in that context, they assumed a strategic significance for the government. It is clear that anxiety over the economic cost of the war exerted no discernible influence in British decision making. The reasons for embarking on the recovery of the Falklands stemmed from wider political considerations. These were pursued regardless of Britain's economic weakness and the likely costs envisioned. Lord Lewin, a member of the Falklands War Cabinet, confirms that at no time was economic cost ever a consideration.[103]

Moreover, the Falklands crisis created a unique opportunity for the Thatcher government. It gave the government the opportunity to extricate itself from the political consequences of the difficulties into which it had plunged the country and, at the same time, to face up to an aggressor under the cover of defending principles. Whatever the motivation, one fact remains unassailable: The Falklands War not only gave a strategic motivation to defense policy, but breathed new life into the idea that states will fight for what they perceive to be higher political gains. Thus the Argentine invasion of the Falklands not only raised the politicomilitary temperature in the South Atlantic waters, but also represented to the British government a grave external problem which required decisive action. And the government's response showed little regard for the economics of war. If anything, it showed the salience of external developments and, by implication, the role which ought to be played by defense policy.

# *Four*

# British Defense Policy
# After the Falklands War

Within a year of the Argentine surrender, the British government took a major decision to restructure the defense of the Falkland Islands. Prior to the seventy-four-day war, this effort had consisted of a handful of marines whose presence was intended to act as a trip-wire deterrent. The failure of this policy led to the general agreement that any future defensive capability had to be credible and substantive, not merely symbolic. The new arrangements which the government agreed to put in place "involved the construction of an airfield capable of taking long-haul aircraft so as to allow rapid reinforcement in time of need, an early-warning detection and interception capability, ground-to-air missile defences, and enough rapid-response capability to be able to contain minor landings."[1]

The implementation of this arrangement not only pointed to a fundamental change in policy direction but also involved a substantial commitment of monetary and material resources for the future defense of the Islands. British policy towards the Falklands was now based on one major objective, and that was "to ensure the future security and welfare of the Falkland Islanders."[2] And this preoccupation with the defense and security of the Falklands after their recapture underlined a wider strategic imperative in British defense policy.

In the aftermath of victory following the Argentine surrender, the British government undertook a number of specific tasks in a course of action which later attracted the name "Fortress Falklands." That action or policy, apart from demonstrating the paramount importance of strategic concerns, also revealed the faulty assumptions inherent in the economic debate about British defense policy. The enormous cost incurred as a direct result of this new policy was not predicated on economic considerations of

121

affordability or opportunity costs, but on the strategic imperatives of security and perceived national interests. In short, cost considerations were pushed aside for what the government perceived to be higher strategic gains.

British defense policy after the Falklands War clearly illustrates the strategic rationale for a state's behavior. For the past two decades, students of British defense policy have been bombarded with the economic and resource constraints arguments of the debate. As one analyst noted, "the history of British defence policy is an attempt to reconcile the mismatch between resources and commitments."[3] The economic arguments were indeed compelling, and no attempt would be made here to minimize their importance. However, a focus on those arguments subsumed under the economics rubric as being primary and overriding in the formulation of British defense policy has tended to obfuscate the larger picture. Defense policy also must be formulated and digested in a strategic context. For it is precisely that context which will determine to a large degree the broad spectrum of defense policymaking.

The strategy for American armed forces is determined by a perception of the nature of the international environment and the political commitment to America's role in that environment. That strategy must necessarily take account of the changing nature of the world as well.[4] This argument also holds true for British strategy. After World War II, the most basic structural feature of defense policymaking to which decision makers had to respond was the changing nature of the strategic environment.[5] The Falklands War pointed to a number of important forces that were shaping the nature and character of those changes. This chapter will attempt to highlight, among other things, some of those forces and to demonstrate one of the central arguments of this book—the salience of wider strategic concerns in the formulation of British defense policy. The relevance of those concerns was amply illustrated by British post–Falklands defense policy. But before embarking on that exercise, we pause to examine briefly the state of British defense policy just before the Falklands War in order to provide the reader with some amount of relevant background information. This will be followed by an analysis of costs associated with the "Fortress Falklands" policy, lessons of the war, and the effects which they had on British defense policy.

# British Defense Policy Before the Falklands War: The Way Forward, 1979–81

The electoral victory that brought the Conservative party to power in the spring of 1979 was accompanied by a tremendous wave of enthusiasm coming particularly from the defense establishment. During their last three years in Opposition, the Conservatives, under the leadership of Margaret Thatcher—a first for a woman in British political history—were vocally assertive in defense and security-related issues. Indeed, the 1979 party manifesto pledged to strengthen Britain's defenses and work with allies to protect mutual interests in an increasingly threatening world. The in-coming government not only advocated a robust defense posture but gave it considerable priority in their planning. This posture was consistent with the general perception that the Conservatives' defense ministers were expected by their party to strengthen the country's military capabilities. That exercise would necessarily call for an increase in resource allocation for defense, a strategy which members of the new government had already agreed upon even before they took office. As part of this program, the government was committed to the task of improving the situation relating to "pay comparability," military hardware, and the numerical strength of the armed forces. The contentious issue of restoring "servicemen's pay to full comparability with that of their civilian counterparts was fulfilled within days of the general election victory."[6]

Thatcher's ambitious plans and good intentions, to which she had a firm commitment, coincided with the twin-headed economic problems of inflation and slow growth. The second explosion in oil prices in the summer of 1979 not only triggered the world recession but had a devastating impact on the British economy. The collapse of several companies and the subsequent loss of jobs which followed in the wake of this situation were on a larger scale than some in the government had anticipated.[7] Less than six months after this shock, the Soviet Union invaded Afghanistan. The invasion, while having an immediate jolting effect on NATO leaders, also underscored the general perception of Soviet military aggression and the precarious nature of the international political system. It also reinforced the concept of a strong Western resolve predicated on nuclear deterrence.

The effects of the global recession, though not immediately felt in Britain, continued to stymie the economy in spite of the country's North Sea oil windfall, which helped to buffer the shocks temporarily. Against these economic and international political concerns, the government was still committed to implementing the main features of the defense program which it had inherited from the Labour party. Its first Defense White Paper, which bore the title "Defence in the 1980s," confirmed this.[8]

## Background to the 1981 Review

A year after Thatcher took office, things had begun to go awry—the recession was finally beginning to bite. In addition to some adverse external developments, Thatcher's rigorous pursuit of a monetarist economic strategy exacerbated the domestic situation. The idea behind this economic theory of "monetarism," as expounded by Milton Friedman, was a simple one. Inflation was caused by printing too much money, and by limiting the money supply, inflation would be controlled, productivity and competitiveness increased, economic growth restored, and unemployment gradually reduced. Thatcher was not only fascinated by the major assumptions contained in this theory, but went head over heels implementing them. Her mistake was the resolute application of monetarism in the face of a recession, and it proved to be quite costly.

The government's failure to manage the economy in terms of reducing the money supply and at the same time coming to grips with the recalcitrant problem of inflation led to budgetary revisions of public expenditures. Education and some social programs bore the brunt of the burden of this adjustment. Defense, the seemingly untouched area for the Conservatives, was not left unscathed. Projections were revised downwards. It appeared that the government was experiencing severe difficulties in managing the defense program. Michael C. Chichester and John W. Wilkinson offer three reasons which brought about the state of affairs which the government faced: First, the escalation in the costs of new weapons and equipment, well in excess of the general rate of inflation; second, the increase in fuel costs which took place almost without interruption throughout the first two years of the Thatcher Administration; and third, the substantial increases in forces' pay.[9]

To the above reasons, Greenwood added a fourth—many contractors' bills came in earlier than scheduled.[10] This meant that "money poured out faster than had been anticipated and some panic measures had to be taken to arrest the flow."[11]

These factors directly affected the government's continued ability to sustain the present levels of defense spending. As a result, it embarked on a quick-fix program that involved deep cuts in the procurement of ammunition, fuel, oil, and spare parts. Even day-to-day activities relating to training and deployments had to be drastically curtailed. Greenwood summarized the situation well when he said: "It was made obvious that even the levels of funding in the government's original budgetary projections for the early 1980's were inadequate to sustain a programme of the scope, or on the scale, of that to which it was committed."[12] As the unfolding picture became more and more transparent, it became increasingly clear that new measures had to be quickly taken.

A different approach, underscored by rationality and prudent financial management, was inevitable. Such a program would seek to bring about more balance and consistency in defense spending and force structures. In short, the time had come for the governmental powers to carry out a reshaping and restructuring of British defenses. Against this general background, characterized in the main by economic recession, inflation, and ambitious plans for great power status, entered John Nott, the new secretary of state for defense. When he took up the defense portfolio in January 1981, it became evident to him and many others that a thorough review of British defense policy was not only essential but imminent.

## The 1981 Defense Review

The conduct of a far-reaching review of the United Kingdom's defense program and budget in 1981 culminated in the publication of a white paper that bore the title *The United Kingdom Defence Programme: The Way Forward.*[13] The appearance of the new blueprint was followed by months of animated discussions and keen criticisms that stemmed from members of the wider defense community. Being accustomed to a sort of "cheese-paring" exercise that sought to make ends meet, the defense establishment was unprepared for the reshaping plans prescribed by the new defense secretary. Nott's prescriptions as presented in *The Way Forward* constituted a fresh and radically different approach to the defense dilemma facing the nation.

What Nott put under scrutiny were plans for the continuation of the existing force structure, force levels, and reequipment. These plans incorporated provisions for the four major and one minor roles that the government, like its predecessor, was determined to execute. Greenwood provides a neat summary of the essential features of these roles as follows:

(a) Retention of a strategic nuclear retaliatory capacity, provided now by a force of four nuclear-powered ballistic missile submarines (SSBNs), and to be provided in due course by four (or possibly five) new British-built SSBNs serving as platforms for American-made Trident (D-5) missiles.
(b) Continued provision of the forces for defence of the U.K. base. These include the coastal defence forces, the home defence contingents, and the air defence "mix."
(c) Maintenance and modernization of the major contribution to NATO's ready forces for maritime warfare in the Eastern Atlantic.
(d) Maintenance and modernization of the national contribution to NATO's ground and tactical air forces for operations in the area of Allied Command Europe. These forces include BAOR and Royal Air Force (Germany); and a minor role involving
(e) Modest provision for non–NATO commitments.[14]

The program to sustain the above roles ran into serious difficulty for reasons already mentioned. What Nott set about to do for the British defense effort in *The Way Forward* was simply to take the existing program apart, carefully examine the components, and then reassemble the parts in such a way that the new whole became more effective and dynamic. In short, Nott's exercise was no more than a bold and innovative attempt to reshape British defense policy: "to curtail the scope of the nation's defence dispositions so that the funds actually available should not be spread too thinly and to restore balance to the stock of capital equipment."[15]

Behind Nott's synthesizing exercise lay the crucial issue of "sustaining power" or "effective capability" for a medium power like the United Kingdom. In other words, Nott was able to ferret out some of the striking disproportionalities inherent in British defense plans, and having exposed these, he immediately set about restructuring the program. The exercise was indeed financially astute and strategically compelling. The rationale for it was summarized in two key paragraphs of the White Paper:

> First, even the increased resources we plan to allocate cannot adequately fund all the force structures and all the plans for their improvement we now have.... Our current force structure is however too large for us to meet this need within any resource allocation which our people can reasonably be asked to afford. The effects—at a time moreover when economic recession led to intensified activity in industry on defence work and so caused extra difficulties in managing the defence programme—were seen in 1980/81, when harsh measures to cut back activity and stop placing orders on industry still could not prevent a substantial overspend; and similar problems, which will call for urgent corrective action, are already emerging for 1981/82.
>
> The second reason for change, partly related to the first, concerns balance within the programme. Technological advance is sharply changing the

126

defence environment. The fast-growing power of modern weapons to find targets accurately and hit them hard at long ranges is increasing the vulnerability of major platforms such as aircraft and surface ships. To meet this, and indeed to exploit it, the balance of our investment between platforms and weapons needs to be altered as to maximize real combat capability. We need to set, for the long term, a new force structure which will reflect in up-to-date terms the most cost-effective ways of serving the key purposes of our defence effort. The best way of enhancing the deterrent effect of our armed forces, for example in raising the nuclear threshold, is to give more resources to their hitting power in combat. This means that the structure we set must be one which we can afford to sustain with modern weapons and equipment, and with proper war stocks. This is less glamorous than maximizing the number of large and costly platforms in our armoury, but it is far the better way of spending money for real security value. Moving in this direction will mean substantial and uncomfortable change in some fields. But the alternative, of keeping rigidly to past patterns, would be a recipe for overstretch, inadequacy and waste—it would leave us the certainty of attempting too much and achieving too little.[16]

Central to the Review was the need to contain the cost of the Trident nuclear missile program in the defense budget over the next 15 years. Billed at an estimated cost of £5–£6 billion, the Trident program did occupy center stage in the debate that followed the release of *The Way Forward*. Nott, along with the prime minister, was convinced about the rightness of the decision to buy Trident as the replacement for the aging *Polaris* fleet in the 1990s. The new Review incorporated the Trident system as its base but also pointed out the need for immediate cuts in spending.

Another conviction of the secretary for defense was the need to look forward over the next ten years in order to assess the future defense requirements as a basis for commitments to be put in place now. This "look-ahead" strategy was operationalized in a few main projects, including the Tornado multirole combat aircraft, the Nimrod early-warning aircraft, the Royal Navy's antisubmarine carriers, the Rapier air defense missile, and the final stage of the Chevaline development of the Polaris missile warheads.[17]

Apart from what came out of the reshaping exercise in terms of cuts and commitments, it appeared that the navy bore the brunt of Nott's knife. But a second look would reveal otherwise. The decision to reduce the nominal size of the fleet was not to be seen as an end in itself, but more so as a means to an end. Having fewer vessels afloat but keeping them in operational readiness was much better than having a plethora of stock just on an inventory listing. Greenwood made the sobering point that "with fewer hulls, more money could be devoted to those that remained: to give them up-to-date weapons systems, to buy fuel and stores to enable them to provide a presence-at-sea (rather than the presence-in-port which is all that many warships had provided through much of 1980–1981)."[18]

Insofar as the naval outfit was concerned, the Review sought to bring into effect a smaller and better equipped operational surface fleet. There were, however, other views on this issue. Wyllie saw the cuts in a wider strategic framework: "the naval cuts ... suggests that the Thatcher administration continues to attach the highest importance to deterrence on the Central Front at the cost of power-projection capabilities on the high seas."[19] The logic of Wyllie's argument was underscored by the white paper's renewed emphasis on Britain's NATO commitments.

We now turn to the cuts. They can be summarized in the following ten points:

> 1. Reduction in the Royal Navy's frigate and destroyer force from 59 to 50. With six frigates already laid up, and eight of the fifty to be withdrawn to standby, the effective reduction by 1984–85 will be more than 20 ships.
> 2. Chatham dockyard and base to be closed in 1984 and considerable curtailment of Portsmouth, although the naval base there will be maintained.
> 3. Only two of the new Invincible aircraft carriers to be retained, although *Ark Royal*, launched in August, to be completed and no decision taken on her future until 1984–85.
> 4. The aircraft carrier *Hermes* to be phased out. The two amphibious ships, *Fearless* and *Intrepid*, to be disposed of earlier than planned, but their 7,800 marines to be retained.
> 5. The Royal Navy to lose between 8,000 and 10,000 men by 1986. Naval shore establishments, fuel depots and stores to be reduced as well as some army and air force support areas.
> 6. The Gibraltar dockyard's future to be reviewed.
> 7. The strength of the Army to be cut by around 7,000 to 135,000 over the next five years.
> 8. Some 2,000 mainly administrative jobs to go as one divisional headquarters in Germany is brought back to the U.K.
> 9. BAOR, at present over-strength, to be kept at 55,000 as provided for under the Brussels Treaty. Eight brigades will be organized into three operational divisions, as they were before the 1974 defense review.
> 10. The RAF is expected to lose 2,500 men over the next five years and the Jaguar force based in Germany and the U.K. will not be replaced. Its role will be shared between the Tornado strike aircraft and the AV-8B American version of the Harrier which is to be ordered for the RAF. [20]

There were also a number of new and positive developments set out in the defense secretary's statement to the House when he unveiled the Review. These included an undertaking to increase defense spending by three percent in real terms over the next four years, a doubling of the air-to-air missile stocks, an order for AV-8B advanced Harriers, and new improvements to be carried out on Chieftain and Challenger tanks. The prescriptions outlined in Nott's reshaping exercise were not simply about applying extra funding to enhance the combat endurance and hitting power of frontline forces. They also highlighted the perennially perceived problem of resource constraints and the urgent necessity for structural adjustments to the entire defense program. For the navy, it spotlighted the questionable judgments and assumptions implicit in the naval plans and some of the striking disproportionalities embodied in them.

The new orientation in British defense policy was now being more technologically driven. And in that context, the outcome constituted a reshaping exercise that called for structural changes in both hard and software. Moreover, the exercise also underscored the Eurocentric orientation of the government's policy—a policy which both economic circumstances and perceived politicostrategic imperatives allowed. The Continental commitment was perceived as vital to Britain's security, and official statements regularly described the forward defense of the Federal Republic of Germany as the forward defense of Great Britain itself. A restructuring exercise need not, however, be driven only by reduced economic circumstances. The need to reshape and restructure must necessarily flow from strategy. This, it appeared, was what took place in 1981.

No sooner, however, had the exercises been completed and the raging debates subsided, than an Argentinean general, 8,000 miles away, landed troops on a piece of British real estate. This event took place at a time when the government had run more than half its course and was faring disastrously in the opinion polls. When General Galtieri invaded the Falkland Islands on 2 April 1982, however, the fortunes of the Thatcher government were completely transformed. The event not only placed Nott's blueprint under severe strain, but as the ensuing months were to reveal, it also tested the assumptions that underscored his strategy. With remarkable dispatch, an impressive Task Force was assembled and put to sea—en route to the trouble spot, 8,000 miles away.

## Cost of the War and "Fortress Falklands" Policy

The ten and a half weeks of Britain's most unexpected war in 1982 transformed the Falkland Islands from an unconsidered and somewhat neglected colony to a heavily defended fortress. Before the Argentine invasion in April 1982, the territory had an extremely low priority in British defense plans, and the reasons for this diminution of interest flowed more from strategic considerations than from economic hardships or budgetary constraints. Nott's defense review in 1981 not only continued to accord priority to NATO commitments, but also spelled out the provisions necessary to meet these commitments. These provisions called for, among other things, a restructuring of maritime assets. It was believed that for Britain to cope with the Soviet threat in the eastern Atlantic area, a restructuring of naval capabilities was necessary. Nott's restructuring called for fewer but more heavily armed naval platforms, and he stated, "It is no use building more ships if we cannot afford the latest weapons."[21] That exercise, to be sure, involved a huge outlay of funds. The rationale behind this appeared to be more strategic than economic in nature.

The priority given to British NATO commitments was buttressed by the benign environment of the South Atlantic; there was no compelling reason to beef up British defense capabilities in that part of the world. One must see the South Atlantic aspects of British defense policy against this background. At the time when the announcements were made about what can be interpreted as a diminution of defense capabilities in the South Atlantic, strategic imperatives nearer home were uppermost in the minds of Whitehall decision makers. Once Argentine troops landed on British territory, however, the South Atlantic was immediately transformed from a backwater area of low strategic importance to one of perceived great importance. This shift in British defense policy, as underscored by the decision to recapture and defend the Falkland Islands, pointed more towards the systematic changes that had taken place. The force and salience of those changes demonstrated the strategic imperatives that were inherent in the formulation of British defense policy.

## Cost of the War

When challenged in the House of Commons on Thursday, 8 April 1982, on the question of the costs of regaining the Falkland Islands, Thatcher emphatically replied: "I took a decision immediately and said that the future of freedom and the reputation of Britain was at stake. We cannot therefore look at it on the basis of precisely how much it will cost."[22]

The prime minister's clear pronouncement not only raised the stakes in the South Atlantic, but also had the effect of minimizing the consequences of cost. By aligning the principles of freedom and national pride to the larger issue of security, Thatcher was able to advance a plausible reason for the commitment of resources to the "liberation" exercise.

The cost of the war has been put at £800 million. This amount of money did not appear to be too high in comparative terms.[23] However, when it was viewed from the perspective of a failed deterrent policy and stiff domestic budgetary constraints, the cost was indeed very high. A credible defense capability on the spot would have been insignificant in terms of extra cost when compared with the actual cost of liberating the Falklands. Moreover, the economic arguments put forward to justify the cuts in defense resources vis-à-vis the South Atlantic were overturned completely by changing strategic circumstances. The Thatcher government was firmly committed to restoring the status quo ante regardless of the monetary cost. That commitment flowed from a strategic and political imperative and involved perceived core national interests.

Implicit in the £800 million figure were allocations for logistics, ammunition, fuel, medical supplies, communications and intelligence, rents, contingencies, and so forth. The Ministry of Defence has not provided a detailed breakdown of that bill. Conceivably, that would be an almost impossible exercise, and the reason is clear. In the heat of the crisis, with its rapidity of movements, no one was able to put an exact cost on everything pertaining to Operation Corporate. While this initial cost remained fairly significant, the price put on postliberation activities was indeed staggering. Those activities fall within three broad categories of expenditures— garrison costs, infrastructure and other capital costs, and equipment replacement costs.

The cost of deploying troops in the South Atlantic and of maintaining a fortified garrison on the Falklands had been put at £544.5 million for the period covering the fiscal years 1983–84 and 1985–86.[24] Over the same period, infrastructure and other capital costs would have amounted to £445.5 million or about 45 percent of the aggregate of these two categories. The remaining category, equipment replacement costs, has been put at £870 million for the same period. Overall, these costs amounted to £1.86 billion and were envisioned to be the additional defense costs arising from the Falklands War for the period including the fiscal years 1983–84 and 1985–86. The following table shows the breakdown.

### Types of Costs by Years
*(In Thousands of Pounds)*

|  | 1983–84 | 1984–85 | 1985–86 |
|---|---|---|---|
| 1. Garrison | 233.2 | 183.7 | 127.6 |

|  | *1983–84* | *1984–85* | *1985–86* |
|---|---|---|---|
| 2. Infrastructure & other capital costs | 190.8 | 150.3 | 104.4 |
| 3. Equipment Replacement | 200.0 | 350.0 | 320.0 |
| TOTALS | 624 | 684 | 552 |

*Source: House of Commons Third Report from the Defence Committee,
session 1982–83,* The Future Defence of the Falkland Islands, *HC 154, 1983.*

The equipment replacement category was by far the largest in the breakdown. Within that category, the biggest chunk went towards the cost of acquiring four Type 22 frigates. The official estimate, put earlier at £870 million, had been revised upwards and now stood at over one billion pounds. Bloom's article in the *Financial Times* of 15 December 1982 expressed it well: "New orders for defence equipment amounting to over £1 billion ... are being placed by the Government as a direct result of the Falklands conflict."[25]

Compiling information from several official sources, Dillon has been able to give a fairly accurate portrayal of the expenditures in this category.[26]

| *Replacement of Equipment* | *Cost* |
|---|---|
| 4 Type 22 Frigates | 705 |
| Equipping and fitting of 4 Type 22 Frigates | 132 |
| Replacement of logistic landing ships | 46 |
| Aircraft, including 12 Phantom F 4Js, Chinook helicopters, 6 Sea Kings ASW helicopters, and 7 Sea Harriers | 108 |
| Weapons and ammunition stores | 53 |
| Other items (spares, support, etc.) | 125 |
| TOTAL | £1,172 |

The category relating to infrastructure and other capital costs had as its centerpiece the new strategic airfield to be located at Mount Pleasant. The estimated cost of this item was initially put at £200 million, but had to be revised upwards. The current total estimated cost for the Mount Pleasant complex now stands at £395 million (September 1984 prices).[27] That princely sum should not be taken, however, as being final. According to a report issued by the National Audit Office in November 1984, "The final out turn on ... contracts cannot be predicted confidently even during construction.... The final cost of the airfield contract is therefore vulnerable to considerable risks."[28]

In addition to outlays for the Mount Pleasant complex, an appropriation of £5 million was earmarked for road construction and improvement works. A subset of the capital expenditure category was what could be termed "economic reconstruction" costs. These costs included immediate rehabilitation and compensation of civilian losses, and a six-year postwar development expenditure plan. Together they amounted to £46 million.

A comprehensive expenditure portfolio for the ten-year period 1982–93 at average 1983–84 prices was in excess of £4 billion. This level of expenditure was hardly envisioned when the decision to launch Operation Corporate was taken. The following table outlines the breakdown:

### Falklands War Expenditures, 1982–93
#### *(In Millions of Pounds)*

| Item | Cost |
|------|------|
| War Costs | 800 |
| Economic Reconstruction | 46 |
| Road Construction | 5 |
| Capital Costs | 2,005* |
| Garrison Running Costs | 1,594.5 |
| TOTAL | £4,450.5 |

*Included replacement of equipment and other capital works.*

By 1992, when the final expenditure bill was presented, the figure was well in excess of £5 billion. That sum included the total expenditure for launching the war, the cost of "Fortress Falklands," and the economic aid extended to the Islands since 1982. The government's commitment to outlays of this magnitude cannot be traced to economic arguments of affordability, but stemmed from a resolute political will which was reinforced by changing strategic imperatives. No one disputed the fact that the British economy was declining and thus could ill-afford such high levels of expenditure which clearly have an opportunity cost. The rationale for this policy pointed towards the direction of strategic realism. Menaul concedes that the defense of the Falklands was a new and relatively heavy burden to Great Britain at a time when its economy was stretched to the limit.[29] He then makes the important point that "nevertheless, that commitment must be met even at the possible cost of stinting other significant responsibilities."[30]

There is another dimension of cost which is not readily quantifiable. No price tag can be placed on the 255 British lives lost during the campaign. Nonetheless, it was a price that had to be paid to achieve the government's objective of restoring British sovereignty to lost territory. During

Question Time in the House of Commons on 15 June 1982, The prime minister was emphatic in her pronouncement when she said: "We went to recapture the islands to restore British sovereignty."[31] Moreover, that cost, apart from others, has hardened negotiating attitudes, particularly towards the contentious issue of sovereignty. The cost in terms of loss of life has attracted great psychological attention to the virtues of the defense of the national interest.

Material loss is another area that warrants some mention. The loss of naval and air assets has not been devastating for Britain.[32] The Argentine losses in both men and materials were significantly higher than those of its adversary. In several ways, the British forces experienced luck. More British naval platforms could have been sunk had more Argentine bombs exploded. Given the absence of aircraft early warning capability in the Task Force, the loss of six ships was minuscule compared with what could have happened.[33] As one observer has noted, however, "The heaviest costs of the war lie in the future."[34] Those costs arise from the government's decision to commit substantial resources for both the immediate and the future defense and security of Britain's interests in the South Atlantic area. Out of that commitment came the policy known as "Fortress Falklands."

## The "Fortress Falklands" Policy

The "fortress" idea was already emerging in the last days before the Argentine surrender on 14 June 1982.[35] Suggestions of a negotiated settlement, an act of magnanimity on the part of the victor for the vanquished, or an Argentine participation in the future development and running of the Falklands were all treated as "sell-outs" or as "betrayals of honour" in the context of a resounding military victory. The government's firm attitude had little to do with emotions of the moment. It pointed more towards an appreciation of the new developments that were unfolding. Thatcher had taken a big gamble with her decision to use military force for the recapture of the Falklands. Flushed with victory, she was neither magnanimous nor in a mood for negotiating. The future defense and security of the Falklands was a priority item on the government's agenda.

That commitment was reaffirmed on several occasions. For instance, on 24 October 1983, three weeks before an Argentine resolution calling for sovereignty negotiations was to be debated in the United Nations General Assembly, the British Ministry of Defence announced: "Until such time as Argentina renounces the use of force in pursuit of its claim to the Falkland Islands and is seen genuinely to have done so, it will be necessary to maintain an appropriate garrison to defend the islands against the military threat posed by Argentina."[36]

The implementation of this plan involved a massive outlay of resources and demonstrated the government's commitment to defending its perceived national interest. This dramatic turnaround of policy was hardly explicable in economic terms. Prior to the Argentine invasion, the cost accountant philosophy which lay behind the cuts was dominant in Whitehall. And while the plea of poverty argument did have some merit, the fact that the South Atlantic region as a whole was given low strategic priority in London would seem to explain the government's pre–Falkland War policy. Moreover, when the change of circumstances did take place after June 1982, financial costs were pushed aside. But while it was conceded that exact figures were not available at that time, there was no denying some awareness on the part of the government of the approximate level of expenditure entailed. Fortress Falklands policy involved a massive appropriation of human and material resources. The big question was why the government embarked upon such a course of action.

The British economy was still undergoing painful shocks brought about by high inflation and interest rates. Tight monetary and fiscal policies were still being pursued by the Exchequer, and the effects of these measures were keenly felt in Whitehall (Department of Defence). An economically debilitating environment would not readily allow for increases in public sector spending. In order to keep inflation down, the chancellor had to employ other instruments besides high interest rates, one of which was tight control of public sector spending. The domestic economic and political situation in Britain was not reversed when General Galtieri landed troops on the Falklands. And the British victory ten and a half weeks later also did not help to alter or improve the economic situation. The Falklands campaign was a very costly undertaking and, as one analyst put it, "no price was too high to achieve victory in the South Atlantic."[37] It is apparent that a policy of fiscal constraint more in keeping with a cost accountant philosophy was quickly pushed aside when the government embarked on its Fortress Falklands policy.

It is conventional wisdom in international relations that when external developments impinged on domestic politics, the former are given priority, particularly when those developments are perceived as threats to vital interests. Although Argentina's forceful seizure of the Falkland Islands did not pose a threat to the security or territorial integrity of the United Kingdom, it constituted a loss of British overseas territory and also a serious

135

blow to British pride and prestige in the international community. More-over, the invasion was seen as an act of unprovoked military aggression which should not be allowed to go unpunished. These concepts were ele-vated and transformed into lofty ideals by Downing Street. They took on a different meaning and were aligned to higher considerations of national interest. Whatever the government's motivations in seeking to recapture the Islands and, in turn, to commit itself to defending them in the future, one thing appears certain—domestic economic and budgetary constraints succumbed to higher considerations of national interest.

The economics behind the government's decision to provide for the future defense and security of the Falklands points to an appreciation of strategic changes in the external environment. The Fortress Falklands pol-icy, which involved retaining a considerable British armed presence on and around the Islands, carried a price tag in excess of £4 billion for the period 1982–92. Justifications for such levels of expenditure particularly when the economy faced several other demands, can be traced to higher foreign pol-icy considerations. Such considerations, which included an awareness of the changing nature of threat in the strategic environment, seem to have been dominant in the calculations of the government. This is not the same as saying that the perceived locus of threat suddenly shifted from the European to the South Atlantic front. While the two geographic areas were distin-guishable in a legion of respects, they both have a common denominator.

The threat to Western Europe and by implication to Britain, and the threat to the Falkland Islands—a British overseas territory—pointed to a perceived hostile environment. NATO's defense capabilities, predicated on the strategy of flexible response and forward defense, mirrored the com-mon perception of a formidable external threat. The perception of that environment in turn dictated a strategy with implications for defense resource allocations. During the height of the Cold War, high defense spending for military buildup and weapons acquisition was justified in NATO member countries on account of the perceived hostility of the external environment. In late 1989 that environment changed dramatically with the collapse of the Berlin Wall and Communism. And with the dawn of a new era came the concomitant need to restructure defense commitments.

Fortress Falklands policy was justified not only because of the per-ception of a hostile threat from Argentina, but also more generally because of the changing nature of external threats. In their defensive use of force which this policy underscored, the British have served the broader cause of international stability and peace by preventing gain from military aggression. The British sustained their credibility within NATO and maintained the image of a firm resolve. Moreover, the centrality of Britain's role within NATO gained further legitimacy. In short, the British were seen as still having the will to fight for what they perceived as vital strategic and political interests. The Fortress Falklands policy also underscored the importance of major powers having in readiness certain key capabilities to deal with Third World contingencies. The unexpectedness of that war points to that fact, and the pursuit of present policy demonstrates an awareness of, and readiness to deal with, changes taking place in the international environment.

The dilemma facing British defense policy was well documented. Menaul summarizes it well when he asserts: "Great Britain faces a dilemma in that rising costs, declining economy and persistent demands for reduced defense spending place chronic pressures on all British governments, of whatever political cast, to tailor defence priorities in accordance with the yardstick of economics rather than of strategic realism."[38] The Falklands War and the pursuit of the Fortress Falklands policy would definitely seem to have overturned that economic yardstick. It is clear that the South Atlantic commitment has imposed a burden on Britain's defense role within NATO, but as long as the political will to continue paying for the garrison there exists, then the garrison will continue. We now turn towards an examination of some of the major lessons of the war and their relevance for British defense policy.

## Politicostrategic Lessons

The Falklands War was the first large-scale naval encounter using modern weaponry since World War II. Air-to-surface antiship missiles, antiaircraft/antimissile missiles, homing torpedoes, and a wide assortment of other advanced weapon systems and devices were used in actual combat for the first time. Also, for the first time in many years, a large-scale amphibious assault was carried out under a very strong enemy air threat.[39] It was a strange little war, fought in one of the most remote corners of the globe. Nonetheless, the interest and excitement generated by this war were unequaled in modern times. Before the Argentine surrender on 14 June 1982, there was a rush to pinpoint the salient lessons—tactical, strategic, or technological. According to Anthony Cordesman, "the initial rush to produce 'lessons' from the fighting produced results about as reliable as if Robin Goodfellow had been reporting on the British and Don Quixote had been reporting on the Argentines."[40]

The field day enjoyed by the military pundits and strategic specialists was understandable. It was the first time in the jet age that a Western fleet had encountered massive air opposition. Moreover, the Falklands War had the unique distinction of being the first real naval war since 1945.[41] Apart from everything else, it was a war of military innovation, one that did not match the popular scenarios illustrated by the image of a world divided between East and West because it was between two Western countries. For the British, the Falklands War provided a veritable storehouse of lessons ranging from tactical and strategic to military and technological. In his delineation, Jeffrey Record groups the lessons into three broad categories— "manpower, operations, and hardware."[42] The lessons of the war have been sought by many observers and participants. The war itself has assumed an importance for analysts of foreign and defense policy far beyond that accorded to the many other incidents of open international violence and nascent conflicts. One of the primary analytical tasks has been "to sort out from the many general and predictable verities the critical variables unique to this particular conflict."[43] That task is made all the more easy by the benefit of well-informed hindsight.

For the United States, the Falklands War is rich in lessons, richer than most of the other recent conflicts. The U.S. forces are similar to those of the British, and the war provided a test of machines, concepts, and manpower which simulation or training exercises simply cannot provide. For the Argentines, hard lessons were learned about the significance of tactics, strategy, and professionalism in military manpower. For the British, this analytical exercise has led to lessons about military hardware, force structure, and the value of alliances. It has also led to a critical awareness of the broader politicomilitary lessons about the necessity of keeping the instruments of national power in rough parity with the political dictates of international commitment.[44]

Whatever lessons are learned, their utility can be meaningful only in a strategic context. Lessons relating to force structure, tactics, and military hardware must be digested in a strategic environment. It is no use building up forces and acquiring weapons with the latest technology if there is not a clear scheme for their employment. The concern of some military planners and politicians with short-term defense budgets has overshadowed the determination for a long-range strategy. The development of capabilities without politicomilitary guidance could have disastrous consequences. The role of strategy, therefore, is to transform the total capabilities of a state into instruments of policy. In its simplest form, it is strategy that must tell the military planners what it is they must create capabilities to do, and what they should plan to use those capabilities for once they are in hand.[45] Thus strategy is the vital link in the transformation of national policy into concrete objectives, and national decision makers responsible for formulating policy must not become prisoners of events. In the context of defense, this means that defense policy must be flexible enough to meet the unexpected. This is, undoubtedly, one of the major lessons to be learned from the Falklands War.

In this section, an attempt will be made to explore and analyze some of the politicostrategic and military implications of the war within the context of the central thesis of this book. It will be shown that it is dangerous when decision makers and planners focus only on one scenario, however demanding it might be. In short, defense policy must be given the flexibility to meet the unexpected, particularly in the context of a mercurial international environment.

## Deterrence and Defense

It is generally agreed by those who have evaluated the Falklands War that an Argentine invasion could have been deterred had a credible British defense capability been in place. While it may be plausible to argue the advisability of a larger than token military presence, given the delicate nature of negotiations between Argentina and Britain at the time and the low strategic priority Britain accorded the area, the fact remains that a country's interest must be adequately protected. That protection need not, however, approach the point of being overwhelming or too intimidating. Cable has made the point that what was needed years ago was not a garrison or a naval presence capable of defeating an all-out attack but sufficient forces in place to make serious fighting inevitable.[46] Such a course of action, Cable believes, would have convinced Argentina—and mere words unsupported by visible preparations never convince anybody—that the Falklands could only be seized at the cost of war.[47] What was needed on the part of the British was a demonstration of resolve and capability.

A visible and credible deterrent capability in situ not only made strategic sense, but would have been highly cost-effective. Jeffrey Record, a senior fellow at the Institute for Foreign Policy Analysis, supports this view when he says:

> The deterrent value of forces on the spot is undeniable, and in retrospect, it can be convincingly argued that the junta's refusal to believe that the British would fight for the Falklands was fatally encouraged by the absence

**139**

of all but a token British force presence on the islands or in the South Atlantic prior to the Argentine invasion. It is highly doubtful whether the junta would have taken on a properly garrisoned Falklands supported by visible robust British sea power in the area.... The deterrent value of on-station forces is surpassed only by their war-fighting value.[48]

The failure of Britain to implement a credible deterrence plan before the conflict[49] and the consequences of that failure have added a timely relevance to the notion that "it is almost always better to deter a war than to fight a war, even if the war ends in victory."[50] The emerging lesson, particularly for British policymakers, is that in today's world, perceptions of military strength and a willingness to use that strength for the defense of vital interests must be clearly communicated. International relations among states would be less traumatic and more free of unsavory tactics if communication could be made clearer and was stripped of its obfuscating jargon. The real world of international politics and diplomacy does not, however, operate by a simple network of rules and standard operating procedures. The international system is not only anarchical, but full of complexities. One very noticeable and distinguishable reality of that complex system is the unrelenting drive of states to defend their vital interests. There are no easy answers to the questions of what Britain should have done or could have done. It was reasonable to expect a clear indication of an unwavering military obligation. After all, it was British sovereign territory that was at stake. By implication that meant a defense capability for deterrent purposes. The provision of just a token presence without special intelligence efforts and plans for rapid reenforcement was an invitation for trouble. Even these measures might not have been credible to deter Argentina from launching its invasion, but it is clear that what was needed was a credible defense capability on-station that would constitute a deterrent.

What of the economic arguments? Was not the question of non-affordability one of the major reasons advanced by the government for not beefing up the defensive capability of the Falklands prior to the invasion? Should the British government dispatch adequate levels of forces to all its overseas territories to fend off would-be aggressors? Such decisions should be based more on the strategic environment than on the economics of cost and affordability. British leaders had clear evidence of Argentina's bellicose behavior prior to 2 April 1982. They chose, however, to ignore those warnings, and the consequences turned out to be very costly. If the strategic rationale for a deterrent posture appears compelling, economic considerations should play a subordinate role. The Falklands invasion showed how difficult and expensive it can be to recover from a misjudgment of the size of force needed in place as an adequate deterrent to local aggression.

## *Importance of Allies*

The South Atlantic war demonstrated that bilateral alliances are still extremely important. It showed that dependence upon individual allies for access to facilities along extended lines of communication is a problem that all countries face.[51] In times of war, a favorable solution to that problem by a state can result in victory or defeat. Moreover, the war demonstrated Britain's need for alliance support, particularly that of the United States. According to Zakheim, "Britain clearly required the goodwill of the United States—apart from any material support it might have received—if it was to prosecute its South Atlantic operations successfully."[52]

United States support for Britain had two distinct features. In the first place, there was early military support even before the fighting commenced. This form of assistance occurred especially in communications and intelligence. In addition, "there had, in fact been," according to a well-informed insider, "a massive de facto tilt toward Britain from the very first day in the Pentagon itself."[53] Lehman explained that the tilt was the inescapable result of the "special relationship ... and not the result of any bias or any specific political decision."[54]

The second feature of U.S. support was its political decision taken on 30 April 1982 to support Britain openly. That official posture opened the way for U.S. material support, which amounted to roughly $100 million in sales to Britain.[55] Part of that package included the versatile and lethal AIM-9L Sidewinder missiles. According to one report, the Sea Harriers, armed with their U.S.-made missiles, not only "formed an effective first line of defense against incoming Argentine aircraft ... but of the 27 kills in the air, 23 are known to have been achieved by AIM-9 Sidewinder missiles alone."[56]

Support from other NATO member countries, though minimal, was nonetheless a morale booster. France, in particular, provided valuable information to the Task Force on defense against the deadly Exocet missile. Senegal and Sierra Leone opened their airport facilities to the British for refueling, but the major alliance support came from the United States. It is a moot question now whether that support was a critical factor in Britain's success. One thing was clear, however—U.S. support for Britain's prosecution of the war was not only a psychological boost to the latter but "added further credibility to the British claim that aggression simply could not be tolerated as a means of solving long-standing diplomatic disputes."[57]

Britain takes its bilateral ties seriously. Moreover, the Falklands War demonstrated that alliance support can be meaningful politically as well as militarily. There is also a powerful strategic rationale for alliances, particularly in a bilateral framework.

## *Arms Sales: To Friend or Foe?*

When arms sales are undertaken, there is an implicit assumption on the part of the supplier that such sales will not result in the supplier having to defend itself against the system it has sold. The explicit assumption, on the other hand, embraces the notion of friendship. That is to say, an arms-supplying state should sell its arms only to "friendly" states, or at least to states that are not "unfriendly." These guiding principles do not, however, hold universal sway. The rationale and motivations for arms sales vary from supplier to supplier.

The South Atlantic conflict demonstrated in a most graphic way that there is no guarantee that the supplier nation will never face its own weapons or those of its allies in future combat.[58] This is one of many inescapable lessons, and one that is well worth remembering. It drives home the point that arms sales ought to be a vehicle for national security and should be guided by that policy.

There is also the foreign policy dimension to arms sales. In many instances, arms sales are used to gain leverage and influence. Both superpowers have sold arms for these reasons. The Soviets in particular have shown a greater willingness to sell arms for political reasons. Andrew Pierre makes the sobering point that it is probably no exaggeration to conclude that arms transfers have been the most important instrument available to the Soviet leadership in dealing with the Third World.[59] The political and ideological motivations do have a solid foreign policy basis, although the Soviets on occasion do sell arms because of the economic benefits attached to such sales.

In the age of perestroika, the economic motivation was primary for the Soviet Union. However, unlike the Soviet Union and even France, Britain's arms sales policy was more cautious and was not seen as an instrument of foreign policy. The economic benefits accruing to arm sales were regarded as the motivating factors. Pierre summarized it well when he said, "arms sales, in short, are seen less as an instrument of foreign policy than as a commercial benefit or economic need."[60]

The economic motivation of British arms sales assumes a unique potency, particularly in the context of a weak economy. Arms production and sales contribute not only to the creation of jobs and research and development expertise, but also to gross domestic product and to a favorable balance of payments. Thus the promotion of British arms is a serious business. Healey underscored that seriousness in Parliament when he said, "It is not only our right but our duty, to ensure that British defence industries have a market which enables them to survive and have a proper share of the international market."[61]

In the Falklands War, British forces were operating against some of the weapons systems (e.g., Blowpipe) produced by their own industries. Argentina's acquisition of sophisticated British and other West European (mainly West German and French) arms was facilitated in 1980, when the curtailment order was rescinded by Thatcher. After President Reagan urged Congress in 1981 to lift its ban on arms sales to Argentina, the latter stepped up its acquisition very dramatically. In a context characterized by a certain level of open-market operation and unrestrained policy, Britain pursued its arms sales to Argentina with a vengeance. The motivations were clearly economic and the consequences equally so.

There is no way of telling whether countries that are one's friends today will turn out to be friends tomorrow. In the deadly business of arms sales, this maxim ought to be taken more seriously. When the Shah of Iran was forced to abdicate the Peacock Throne, the loss of F-14 aircraft and other sophisticated weapon systems drove home the truth to many Americans that greater caution and selectivity should be applied when selling arms abroad. The Falklands War underscored this point. If anything, the war has shown the danger of indiscriminate arms sales because prior to the outbreak of hostilities, Britain was one of Argentina's best suppliers.

## Military and Technological Lessons

The Falklands War provided the opportunity for Britain to test many of its sophisticated weapons systems in a real combat environment. These ranged from the integrated communication command and control (C3) systems to the individual weapons. Cordesman asserts, "It was a test of technology that is likely to be far more complex by the next conflict, and which is likely to make three-dimensional chess look like Pacman by comparison."[62] Aspects of military strategy and doctrines were also tested. The net effect has been the production of a sizable body of information ranging from official reports to individual reflections on the military and technological lessons of the war. This book will examine briefly three of these lessons. Attention will be paid to the "intelligence and warning" lessons in the conclusion of this section. In that way, a fairly broad spectrum of lessons will be examined.

## Relevance of the Naval Surface Fleet

The Falklands War demonstrated that surface ships are necessary to project power at a great distance and that those same surface ships can be sunk by a determined enemy. The ships of the Royal Navy are designed not merely to float, but to carry out and accomplish missions which no other set of platforms can do. "The issue," according to one strategist, "is not whether the surface ship remains viable, but rather what sort of surface ship represents the best combination of survivability and mission effectiveness."[63] The central argument, therefore, would seem to revolve around the concept of large versus small carriers, or CTOL versus V/STOL.

That debate dating back to the 1960s is still evolving. In the United States, it has taken the dimension of large versus small CTOL carriers. With the retirement of American World War II carriers and with the cost of 90,000-ton nuclear-powered Nimitz-class carriers being $5 billion each, many argue that the navy should build small 40,000- to 60,000-ton CTOL carriers. Thus "small" now includes both V/STOL and smaller CTOL carriers, while "large" usually indicates the nuclear-powered ships capable of carrying high performance navy planes such as the F-14, A-6, and larger AEW (early airborne warning) and ASW (antisubmarine warfare) planes.[64] In the Falklands War, the debate between the V/STOL and CTOL (i.e., the older version of small versus large) is more applicable.

John Lehman, Jr., a former U.S. naval secretary, was one of the first advocates of the view that the Falklands War strengthened the argument for large surface ships (carriers). He contended that the battles showed that only large carriers can be viable in a future war because only these can support adequate airborne early warning and interceptor aircraft.[65] On the other hand, there were individuals like former senator Gary Hart and Admiral Elmo Zumwalt who advocated that the destruction of the *Sheffield* proved exactly the opposite point—big and highly expensive surface warships are also extremely vulnerable.[66]

The wisdom of Lehman's claim was borne out by both the Falklands War and World War II. In the latter war, the U.S. Navy did not lose any aircraft carrier weighing over 30,000 tons. In the Falklands War, the two V/STOL carriers HMS *Hermes* and *Invincible*, because of their small size and resulting limited capability, were not only unable to maintain air superiority, but also lacked sustained AEW capability. This problem was emphasized repeatedly in the government document *The Falklands Campaign: The Lessons*. Together these carriers had an air complement of twenty Harriers and forty helicopters of various types. That inventory of air assets on board the two V/STOL carriers proved wholly inadequate to establish control of the skies above the Falklands theater of operations. By contrast, the U.S. Navy CTOL carriers, with their E-2 Hawkeye AEW aircraft that have a 200-mile range with six hours on station, would be more than capable of providing and maintaining air superiority and early warning in such a situation.

The general lesson in this debate is that air superiority is an absolute necessity in a power projection capability mode. If the Royal Navy had lacked even the limited V/STOL carriers, it is doubtful whether the British would have been able to wrest the islands from Argentina.

"The absence of early warning," according to one analyst, "was manifest virtually every time a British surface ship was sunk."[67] However, these lessons were not viewed in the same way at the British Ministry of Defence (MOD). British spokespersons have argued that the Falklands War was a "unique event" that is irrelevant to their general requirements because Royal Naval and British defense policy reflect the realities in northwest Europe.[68] The European strategy involved a concentration on ASW capabilities, based on V/STOL carriers. The anti-air-warfare-carrier fleet was dismissed as expensive and unnecessary. The rationale was that these V/STOL carriers would not have to operate too far away from land-based air forces, which would quickly respond in the event of help being needed.

This assumption is operationally unsound. The experience of World War II suggests that a dependence on land-based aircraft is not a guarantee for a highly effective military operation. Moreover, their use, when available, was not entirely successful in this case. As for the West European scenario, one analyst suggests that "it [is not] impossible to imagine that the most important task in the opening phase of a war would be to support a NATO landing on the Northern Flank. Such a landing would have some points of similarity to the operation in Falkland Sound: the ships would have to operate close to land with degraded radar performance, and against very stiff air opposition."[69]

The other mission of the V/STOL carrier force, that of antisubmarine warfare (ASW), was conceived at the time when the Soviet Bear-D targeting aircraft was considered a menacing threat. However, with the Backfires, which can confirm their own targets, now operational, the credibility and efficacy of the ASW mission is highly questionable. One lesson of the war suggests that the current British fleet is ill designed for countering raids of twenty or more Backfires, which are very much within Soviet capabilities.[70] The fundamental point remains that that aspect of British defense policy did not pay serious attention to strategic developments in the external environment.

The Falklands War demonstrated that surface ships have great versatility and usefulness in modern warfare, provided they have certain capabilities. They remain "essential to the power projection mission," and one of the key lessons of the war remains "that surface ships must become more survivable platforms."[71] The Falklands War also demonstrated that the utility of an asset configured for a particular mission may not extend to other situations. If the mission environment in which the asset will operate is undergoing changes, then the asset must adapt to those changes. In short, the Royal Navy should not be circumscribed to only a NATO role. Threats to British interests are more real in extra–NATO waters. Moreover, the strategic assets and capabilities that make up the hardware aspects of the threat from potential enemies are undergoing rapid changes. Hence British defense policymakers ought to pay more attention to the political and strategic changes taking place in the international environment.

## Importance of Logistics

The Falklands War reinforced the old adage that good logistics are a necessary condition for success on the battlefield. While amateurs and armchair strategists pontificate on strategy, the professional soldier, whose task it is to fight the battle, preoccupies himself with the concerns of logistics. Although this topic was dealt with at some length in Chapter 2, it is necessary at this juncture to make a few linkages in the context of our central argument.

For the British, the task of retaking the Falkland Islands was formidable. The scope of the operation was tremendous because of Britain's distance from the Islands and because the Argentines were already entrenched.[72] To cope with these problems, Britain employed a particularly ingenious solution—it called on civilian assets, which were rapidly converted for military use. The success of Operation Corporate hinged heavily on the efficient maintenance of this long logistics pipeline. The lesson is unambiguously clear: any state contemplating operations at remote distances must pay heed to the demands of logistics if its forces are not to wither on the battlefield "for want of a bullet."[73] The government's white paper reaffirmed the need for such a level of logistic support to be maintained for "out-of-area" operations.[74]

Britain's logistical operation, with its attendant high cost considerations, underscored a strategic imperative of the war. The government's financial and political commitment to an undertaking of this scale would seem to strengthen the argument that when vital interests are at stake, economic considerations will be pushed aside. Moreover, the urgent call on, and the extensive use of, civilian assets for the logistics campaign indicated not only the strategic gravity of the crisis, but also the insufficiency of the necessary military hardware. The transportation of troops and war materiel to the battle zone required the extensive use of civilian naval assets.

The logistics campaign, though spectacular and ingenious, was part of the larger combined operations. The comparative absence "of military corrosive inter-service bickering" facilitated the entrance and continued operation of these civilian assets.[75] The Falklands War was the sort of conflict that required individual and unit initiative, as well as joint service integration.

## *Technology—Smart Weapons*

The Falklands War was not a high technology war like the 1982 conflict in Lebanon or the more recent Gulf War. Nevertheless, some high technology was used by both sides. Both combatants used high technology missiles to shoot at their targets. The British, in particular, employed a variety of electronic communications equipment, as well as specialized equipment for the SAS and SBS, both of which fall within the class of high technology. In the Falklands conflict, there was not an overreliance on computers and technology. The microchip was definitely not the deciding factor in this war.

Technology is a double-edged sword. A reliance on it brings the edge of triumph or disaster much closer. An overreliance on it can turn out to be very paralyzing, as an example from the Vietnam War illustrates: "In late 1972 when 'The Computers' at Headquarters, 7th Air Force, Saigon, broke down for a few days, the air war over North Vietnam came to a halt. So dependent was the Air Force on its big computer that ... the human brain and verbally transmitted orders to strike were deemed inadequate."[76]

By contrast, the Falklands War reinforced the supremacy of the human machine in conflict and gave a further shot in the arm to the Clausewitzian dictum. Having said that, we must hasten to point out that the war in the South Atlantic was also fought at the technological level—behind cockpits and radar screens—and not a few of the weapons used could be classified as "smart weapons." Many, if not all, of these smart weapons were missiles. Ever since the British lost HMS *Sheffield* to an Exocet missile, public attention has focused on the apparent vulnerability of the surface ship to the modern antishipping missile (ASM). Moreover, it seemed that the "smart" Exocet missile had revolutionized naval warfare. A single $200,000 weapon had sunk a $40 million ship. This was not, however, the first recorded incident of its kind.

In 1967 the Israeli destroyer *Eliat* was sunk by Soviet SS-N-Z Styx missiles fired from Egyptian patrol boats. Western military analysts were alarmed. That incident, revolutionary in character and stupendous in technological mastery, spawned the development of the French Exocet, the Franco-Italian Otomat, the American Harpoon, and the Israeli Gabriel ASMs between 1968 and 1970. The revolutionary impact and threat of ASM technology was not fully grasped until 1982, however, when the "British Royal Navy lost a modern warship to Argentina, a nation of modest military proportions."[77] That incident confirmed the offensive advantage of ASMs over the defensive abilities of surface ships. The belief that the sinking of the Israeli *Eliat* was no flash in the pan and the realization that almost any nation can purchase a weapon system to threaten even the most formidable naval combatant has brought about redoubled interest in defensive technology efforts, and a rethinking of naval strategy.[78]

Apart from the much publicized and feared Exocet missile, many other smart weapons were employed in the South Atlantic war—in naval engagements, as well as in air and ground encounters. But what makes a weapon "smart"? According to a retired U.S. Navy captain, William Ruhe, "the term 'smart' weapon seems to be synonymous with the frequently used term 'precision-guided' weapon."[79] In other words, a smart weapon is one that has built-in electronic features which allow it to carry out many functions by itself, for example, a weapon that has a built-in capability able to guide it to a specific target. At the more sophisticated end of the spectrum of "smartness" are missiles which are totally divorced from the firing platform after launching and have "programmed trajectories" enabling them to carry out several tasks like shifting radar frequencies while in flight or distinguishing between decoys and target.

Many smart missiles were used in the Falklands War. These ranged from the sea-skimming Exocet to the long-range Sea Darts. In the air war, the effect of "smartness" in weapons was most dramatically demonstrated. The British Harriers which used the AIM-9L Sidewinder missiles, a fire-and-forget weapon, killed twenty-four Argentine aircraft with only twenty-seven missiles.[80] The Argentines, on the other hand, used the French-built Matra R. 530 missiles which failed to down any Harrier. At the lower end of the scale, weapons like the shoulder-launched Blowpipe and Stinger were also used. But so too was the Mark VIII torpedo, a World War II vintage, that sank the Argentine cruiser *General Belgrano*.

The use of high technology weaponry gave a decided advantage to the British. It has been estimated that more than a billion dollars worth of high technology equipment was expended by both sides.[81] The war did seem to show that future combats will be characterized by further levels of sophistication in smart weaponry. If one side is to dominate, there must be a marked disparity between the technologies of the combatants. Moreover, the war underscored the truly revolutionary nature of the changes that are taking place, particularly with respect to the implements of war. Military strategy and defense policymaking cannot remain static. For Britain to face the potential threats in a changing international environment in which high technology weapons can be readily acquired or are already in the possession of an aggressor, more attention should be paid to strategic concerns. Securing the state and its interests is the fundamental responsibility of governments.

The lessons of the Falklands War must be viewed in the context of the changing nature of the international system and in light of the prospects for crisis and conflict in the 1980s and beyond. Contrary to cherished beliefs, strongly encouraging a total Continentalist orientation of British defense policy, the war demonstrated that "the enemy is not always a Soviet proxy, even in a low-intensity war."[82] Moreover, the threat to British interest is not circumscribed to only one theater, but can conceivably arise from the most unexpected of places. One of the many lessons which the war underlined, apart from those few discussed above, relates to the questions of warning and intelligence. Was the Falklands War preventable? This is a difficult question, but much can be said about the predictability of the conflict.

There seems to be little or no doubt that warning signals preceded the Argentine invasion. The attack on 2 April 1982 was the culmination of several weeks of tension. Although the immediate precrisis period spanned only the preceding month, Argentina had demonstrated consistently since 1945 both the seriousness of its purpose and its willingness to consider resorting to force. In late 1977 there was a serious threat of invasion. British ships had been fired upon, and fuel supplies to the Falkland Islands had been cut off. Relations between Argentina and Britain at that time were strained, but it was not until after 26 February 1982 that things really went wrong. After Argentina virtually repudiated its negotiations following the February talks in New York, war fever intensified in the local press. There was no shortage of intelligence data about these activities in Buenos Aires reaching London. London was swamped with intelligence data, but the receipt of more and more data did nothing to alter the belief already formed in London. Herein lies the fundamental problem on both the Argentinean and the British sides. Both parties relied on certain reassuring but very misleading political and strategic assumptions. These assumptions which relate to "facts" about one's own capabilities and the opponent's capabilities, intentions, and calculations formed an interlocking intellectual syndrome that reinforced certain already held beliefs.

Perhaps the most dramatic recent illustration of the disastrous impact of such strategic assumptions was the Israeli belief in 1973 that Egypt would not attack until it had attained superiority.[83] Hopple made this point:

> This central premise, the master belief in the Israeli strategic calculus, was accompanied by a secondary belief: Syria would not attack unless Egypt did. These two assumptions ... formed the Israeli "conception." Together, the two core assumptions operated as a strategic conceptual straitjacket, suppressing, shaping and biasing the interpretation of an incoming stream of contrary tactical indications.[84]

In the Falklands crisis, strategic assumptions played a key role on both sides.[85] The British assumed that Argentina would not try to take by force what it could not achieve by negotiations. According to Hopple, "this assumption was reinforced by the length of the dispute, the earlier false alarms, and the consistently strident Argentinean rhetoric."[86] The Argentines, on the other hand, believed that the British would not react with force. This assumption was reinforced by their lack of concern about Britain's ability to react. For example, the junta could have delayed the timing of the invasion or could have moved some of its vital strategic air assets to the Islands. Their signal failure to take those rational steps underlines the plausibility of the argument that the junta assumed—that Britain would not go to war.

The fundamental point in this exercise relating to warning and intelligence is a simple yet complex one. Strategic assumptions played a significant role in the prewar analysis and decision-making processes. The

British in particular tried to substitute bluffing for a credible commitment, and had ended up with the very commitment they had consistently avoided.[87] Argentina tried to seize what it thought rightfully belonged to it and ended up paying a heavy price.

Intelligence analysis is not only about the collection, storage, and retrieval of information. What is done with the information collected is the essence of good intelligence. That task involves painstaking work of evaluation, analysis, and synthesis that leads to conclusions and recommendations.

Far from being a "one-off" event, the Falklands War also demonstrated the changing milieu of the international environment. The diffusion of the power process is continuing, and the world is becoming increasingly complex. The Third World not only remains a central arena for conflict, crisis, and war, but undoubtedly has become a more dangerous and volatile environment in the 1990s. Defense policymaking in Whitehall ought to reflect these changing political and strategic realities.

# Effects on British Defense Policy

The question of whether the Falklands War should have fundamentally altered Britain's military priorities "has breathed new life into the general discussion and argument about future defence policy."[88] The central theme which characterized that debate has changed very little, however, from that which preceded the war. That debate, which was triggered by the announcement of the government's defense review in June 1981, was centered on the restructuring of force dispositions. It gained momentum in the aftermath of the Falklands War, but the essence of those arguments carried over from 1981 was not new. According to Nailor, those arguments can be traced to the "East of Suez" policy:

> Since the middle of the 1960's at least, when the United Kingdom began to bring home its military forces and to redefine its security priorities to concentrate, almost entirely upon N.W. Europe, the defence policy of successive governments has striven to provide the best and most appropriate military structure at a cost that does not intrude too severely upon our national economic and budgetary position.[89]

While economic arguments were seen as the perennial underpinning factor that determined British defense policy, the point needs to be emphasized that strategic considerations nearer home were critically important.

151

The economics behind British military dispositions was never in a state of equilibrium. The national economy, characterized by irregular and constant shifts, dictated "what the best and most appropriate military structures should be."[90] That assessment in part is historically correct. What is missing from the defense policy equation, however, is the external dimension. My point is that it was the strategic environment with the perceived Soviet threat that helped to shape British military dispositions during the Cold War. If force structures are dictated solely on the basis of economics, then strategy and military doctrine do not assume sufficient importance. It is strategy which determines the structure and the composition of military forces. Strategy in turn is shaped by both domestic economic and political factors and by the international environment.

The Falklands War did not bring about any radical restructuring of British defense policy. To have carried out such restructuring purely on the basis of that war would have been a futile and strategically myopic exercise. Having said that, let me hasten to add that the war did have some effects on British defense policy, however marginal. It reinforced certain lessons and at the same time spotlighted a few gaps in the strategic dimension of British defense policy. These gaps related to force structures and international politicostrategic analyses. The war demonstrated the need for better political and strategic analyses of the developments taking place in the international environment. We live in a complex and increasingly interdependent global system which shows every sign of becoming even more complex and interdependent. Therefore analysis and strategic warning of secondary crises and conflicts will become even more vital in the future. In the context of the South Atlantic crisis, Martin Richards made the forceful point that "the U.K. intelligence service and Foreign Office operations need to come under scrutiny and review."[91]

The Falklands War also brought into sharp focus the need for advanced preparations to handle Third World conflicts. A failure to prepare for such a contingency revealed the extent to which Whitehall has preoccupied itself with one scenario for which a structure of deterrence is firmly in place. Ironically, the absence of certain capabilities such as shipboard missile defenses, long-range, high-speed interceptors, and early warning aircraft nearly cost Britain the war. A restructuring of British armed forces to make their capabilities consonant with the changing threat will definitely enhance their ability to deal with Third World contingencies. To some extent, this exercise has already taken place—since the South Atlantic war.

I shall attempt to examine the effects the Falklands War has had on British defense policy in three areas: economics, power projection capability, and politicostrategic impact. These areas are not mutually exclusive, but are separated out only for analytical purposes. It will be shown that all three factors had a positive effect on British defense policy and that contrary to the official line, the Falklands War did affect British defense policy. The extent to which it was affected is another matter, however, and one that also shall be explored.

## Economic Effects

The United Kingdom mounts a comprehensive and balanced defense effort for the fulfillment of both its obligations as a member of NATO and certain exclusively national security responsibilities.[92] To fulfill these obligations which are viewed as a public good, the government allocates each year funds from its public expenditure budget. The defense allocation has been rising steadily each year. According to Greenwood,

> between 1978/79 and 1983/84 military spending in volume terms rose by 20 per cent. The bill has also been taking progressively larger slices of both central government outlays and total public expenditure. The Ministry of Defence (MOD) budget for 1984/85 represents almost 19 per cent of the former, about 13.5 per cent of the latter; the corresponding proportions in 1978/79 were approximately 16.5 per cent and 11.5 per cent.[93]

Nott's 1981 defense review, *The Way Forward*, refers to five roles—four major and one minor—that defense dispositions have to fulfill. Prior to April 1982, the official perception was that the minor role was of low priority, indeed residual, and budgetary allocations reflected that posture. The Falklands War forced a change, however, in official perception, which triggered a stronger commitment to out-of-area interests. Official pronouncements since the Falklands War have given greater weight to those interests. The defense budget for the fiscal year 1984-85 showed an allocation of one billion pounds to non–NATO commitments. When compared with pre–Falklands allocations, this figure was indeed impressive. It represented nearly 6 percent of the defense budget and a full 27 percent of what was earmarked for the defense of the home base.

David Greenwood argued that the limited funds allocated to that "part of the defense effort devoted to extra–European interests and responsibilities" resulted from the "mismatch between resources and commitments."[94] That ubiquitous explanation, centering on dwindling resources and rising commitment costs, has been peddled for years. It fails to consider the view that defense appropriation is an allocative exercise, predicated not exclusively on the availability of resources, but on developments taking place in the international environment at the time. A hostile environment with an imminent threat to security will dictate the choices made by governments. Granted that resources for defense are always going to be constrained in a democracy, the fact remains that such constraints boil down to the question of choice. And the choice made will inevitably reflect the strategic assumptions underlining the country's defense policy.

The economic effects on post–Falklands British defense policy are traceable to a wide range of areas and include budgetary appropriations. Since the war, the defense budget has risen appreciably. In 1981–82, total defense expenditure was £12.6 billion.[95] By the fiscal year 1984–85, it had risen to over £17 billion. This increase in total defense outlays reflected the rising real costs of equipment to which nearly half the budget was devoted. While the Falklands factor did not dramatically inflate the defense budget, it has nonetheless imposed a lingering effect on the overall budgetary dispositions. The costs of the war, replacing combat losses, and creating the "fortress" were not met from the MOD's budget, but from the Treasury. Maintenance costs of the "garrison" will come out of the defense budget.

The out-of-area commitment dramatized the economic effects the war has had on British defense policy. That commitment not only mirrored a change in official perception, but also strongly underscored the strategic rationale of that policy. It also provided "extra weight to the arguments for a strong Royal Navy," which, according to Grove, "has to rest on a firm foundation of British strategic interests, as perceived at the end of the twentieth century."[96] Those interests, to be sure, may not be limited wholly to the European theater. While the government claimed prior to 1990 that the main threat to the nation's security came from the Soviet Union and its Warsaw Pact allies, thereby devoting a virtually exclusive attention to that threat, its Fortress Falklands policy and subsequent out-of-area budgetary allocations did not square with that view. Moreover, the strongest criticism of the government's claim "is that preparation for the main threat does not automatically provide the right sort of capabilities for lesser contingencies, especially from the point of view of deterrence."[97]

Following the Falklands War, there has been a change of plans with respect to some aspects of the economic geography of defense. Dockyards (such as, Chatham) that had been earmarked for closure or a scaling-down of activities have been given a new lease of life. The net economic effect of this move has been a retention of jobs for thousands of workers in many locations and a boost to the gross domestic product.

154

The economic effects on British defense policy are viewed more appropriately in the interface role. Economics interface with and affect every defense activity. But at the end of the day, it is political will that prevails. The commitment of extra economic resources to the defense effort after the Falklands War was a demonstration of political judgment grounded in strategic realities. Projected defense allocations prior to the Falklands War did not reflect the actual results. In this respect, the war was significant.

## Effects on Power Projection Capability

British defense policy prior to April 1982 can be seen as following NATO orthodoxy by concentrating on land and air forces, forces that would be backed up by a nuclear deterrent, capable of blocking a conventional invasion of West Germany.[98] This orientation brings into sharp focus the significance of the Falklands War. It was a war fought well outside NATO waters and with the Royal Navy in the lead. "It was," according to Freedman, "precisely the war for which Britain was planning least."[99] Had the Nott review been put into immediate effect by the time of the Falklands campaign, "the run down in amphibious capabilities, and the very limited ground and air capabilities envisaged in *The Way Forward* for overseas operations would have meant that the task of retaking the islands would have been even more difficult than it was."[100] The lesson for defense policy was clear: token intervention forces are not useful in an emergency. That lesson was not lost on defense planners and Nott. Moreover, it became clear that the war would have important consequences for defense policy, particularly in the area of a stronger power projection capability.

Prior to April 1982, there appears to have been no strategic rationale for the nominal size of the surface fleet. One British naval analyst made the point that "Mr. Nott had to come up with more 'economic' criteria to determine its size."[101] However, the Falklands War gave a powerful strategic argument, not only for the relevance of having a balanced surface fleet, but also for one of an acceptable size, equipped and available for out-of-area tasks. The Royal Navy, which suffered its worst warship losses in the post–1945 period, scored "its greatest success in projecting power over many thousands of miles to the other side of the world."[102] In short, the Falklands campaign was a showcase for an extraordinary and timely demonstration of British sea power. The First Sea Lord could not have wished for a better show.

A naval power projection capability had already taken root in Nott's

1981 defense review, when reference was made to the preservation of a "balanced fleet." It was not, however, too readily transparent at that time. The role of the Royal Navy in the Falklands War gave substance and meaning to the concept. The consolidation and improvement of the out-of-area capabilities implied a formidable strengthening of naval power projection capacity. Admiral Sir John Fieldhouse, who became the First Sea Lord and Chief of Naval staff after leading the Fleet Command to its Falklands victory, made numerous public statements that emphasized operations outside the NATO area as a major reason why Britain possessed a balanced fleet.[103]

Moreover, the 1984 defense white paper, unlike it predecessors, duly gave a major heading to "Beyond the NATO area." It referred to events in the Middle East, both the Iran-Iraq War and the imbroglio in Lebanon. The Royal Navy had played a significant part in both areas. It also drew attention to the purchase of the oil rig support ship *Stena Inspector* "to provide afloat support for naval vessels operating a great distance from their bases" and to give "a considerable enhancement to the out-of-area capability of the destroyer/frigate force, and of conventional submarines."[104]

The enhancement of the out-of-area capability also involved a significant increase in naval and maritime assets. Expenditures earmarked for the "garrison" and for replacements were also used by the MOD to purchase additional equipment that could be employed for a variety of alternative purposes. The December 1982 announcement included the purchase of at least 12 Phantom F-4 J aircraft, wide-bodied tanker transports, 24 additional Rapier units, 8 Chinook medium-lift helicopters, an increase in the number of frontline destroyers and frigates, and a £10 million boost to the stockpile of stores and ammunition.[105]

More significant in the listing was the decision to keep HMS *Invincible*, along with its two sister ships, the recently completed HMS *Illustrious* and HMS *Ark Royal*. These undertakings not only accentuated Britain's power projection capability, but also had a direct effect on defense policy. Freedman argues that they involve "a substantial change of policy."[106] Instead of a fleet with two carriers, the Royal Navy now has a complement of three. It should be recalled that the role of the carriers was central to the whole debate in Nott's 1981 defense review. In the aftermath of the war, therefore, Britain has acquired a larger and more modern navy than had been envisioned. Both factors of larger size and modernity have increased substantially power projection capabilities and the capacity for rapid out-of-area interventions.

The out-of-area capability has also been accentuated by the government's decision to enhance the flexibility and mobility of the 5th Infantry Brigade. According to the official line, "These enhancements," which included stockpiles of weapons, equipment and stores, "represent a major improvement to our capability for airborne operations out-of-area."[107] Some of the equipment purchased for the Falklands garrison will add to the capacity to intervene in conflicts outside the NATO area.

Thus, while the government insisted that its main focus for defense policy remained the Soviet threat to Europe, the aftermath of the Falklands War and the need to protect the reconquered islands had resulted not in a radical restructuring, but in a significant shift in defense policy. The shift was manifested in the enhancement of power projection capabilities and a rekindling of interest in beefing up the resources for out-of-area tasks. In short, rather than weakening the armed forces, the Falklands War has made possible a significant expansion. The thinking behind the exercise reflected to a large extent the realities of appropriate strategic assumptions.

## Effects on Strategy

The defense of the realm is intertwined with the defense of Western Europe. However, British defense strategy, while remaining in the main Eurocentric, also has other dimensions. For forty years, the Soviet Union has been regarded as the greatest threat to British vital interests. Britain's answer, as that of the rest of Western Europe, to this perceived threat has been to engage the other superpower, the United States, in its defense arrangements. NATO has sought to influence the force structures of its constituent members, but not to impose structures upon them.[108] Britain's defense effort, while operating within the parameters of NATO's requirements, also has an international dimension.

After the Falklands War, the Conservative government appeared eager for Britain to play a major role in the defense of Western and national interests outside the NATO area. In an interview with the *Financial Times*, the prime minister's message was clear about Britain's defense efforts worldwide. "We are a global power, and we do our bit."[109] Within six months of the war, the government's policy statement underscored that posture: "Following the Falklands Campaign, we shall now be devoting substantially more resources to defence than had been previously planned. In allocating these, we shall be taking measures which will strengthen our general defence capability by increasing the flexibility, mobility and readiness of all three Services for operations in support of NATO and elsewhere."[110]

The intellectual debate over a maritime, as opposed to a Continentalist, strategy for British defense policy, was sharpened right after the Falklands conflict. Nott's white paper, *The Way Forward*, strongly emphasized a continentalist strategy which reflected historical precedents and argued that Britain's vital interests are intertwined with those of Western Europe. Proponents of the maritime strategy have also used history to buttress their arguments. Lord Hill-Norton, Admiral Sir Henry Leach, and supporters of the naval lobby like John Wilkinson and Michael Chichester believe that Britain should continue to give priority to its traditional expertise at sea.[111]

A true reading of history would seem to suggest a maintenance of both roles. Given Britain's international position and its continuing commitment to alliance obligations, a judicious balance between the two roles appears to be the preferred policy. The Falklands War, while demonstrating the need for balanced forces in maritime terms, did not undermine the Eurocentric orientation of British defense policy. If anything, it pointed towards a balanced role. Baylis makes the important point that when "faced with the legacy of the Falklands War and the public and private disagreements between the Service Chiefs since the early 1980's, the Government has struggled to avoid the kind of clear decision made by John Nott in 1981, and instead has attempted to balance the continentalist and maritime lobbies."[112]

Moreover, the changes announced in the December 1982 document did not amount to a fundamental reordering of priorities, but as Greenwood asserts: "They were significant enough to indicate that a somewhat different view might be taken in future for the 'proper' balance between NATO and non–NATO commitments in defence planning, and of the 'proper' place of naval power in the national force structure."[113]

In a *Daily Telegraph* article published three weeks before the Argentine defeat, Lord Chalfont suggested not only the need for "an improved maritime capacity," but for "an effective and flexible military establishment."[114]

The urgent need for a strategic reassessment of Britain's defense policy after the Falklands War was given prominence in a series of articles appearing in the *Times* between November 2 and November 5, 1982. Arguments were put forward for a strategic revision of British defense policy based on complementarity and not competition between the Continentalist and maritime concepts. Moreover, one of the articles made the point that the most important strategic assumption which should underlie the post–Falklands review was that Britain's forces should be deployed in such a way as to give Britain, and its allies the greatest freedom of action.[115]

The Falklands War demonstrated the need for a more balanced approach to British defense policy. The fact that Britain is militarily part of Europe does not mean that there ought to be a conflict between a maritime and Continentalist view of strategy. Further, there need not continue to be an overcommitment to NATO at the expense of depriving the country of any independent strategic flexibility. Judgments about Britain's post–Falklands defence role should not be driven by short-term politicoeconomic expediency but by "long-term strategic sense."[116]

The connection between the state of the economy and defense capabilities and commitments as indicated by several white papers would seem to suggest that there is a direct relationship between the two. Archer puts it well when he says that "as the state of the British economy has deteriorated, so expenditure on defense has to be reined in."[117] While this argument appears plausible and does command the high ground of the intellectual debate in British defense policy, it is nonetheless predicated on a faulty assumption. The argument that a healthy British economy would automatically make room for increased defense capabilities and commitments is a tenuous one. The major argument against this notion holds that defense capabilities and commitments should match the external threat, rather than respond to economic buoyancy.

British defense policy after the Falklands War would seem to support the argument that defense considerations ought to respond more to the threat (external developments) than to domestic economic constraints. The idea of cutting the defense cloth to suit diminished economic circumstances no longer holds in an environment in which there is a perceived threat.

# Conclusion

It is extremely difficult to summarize in one chapter the many lessons and implications of a war, the results of which continue to be studied in great detail. Perhaps the most important lesson was one alluded to earlier— that of the danger which arises when planners focus on only one scenario, however demanding it might be. Such an emphasis tends to overlook the importance of flexibility, the sine qua non for coping with crises not foreseen by planners.[118] The need for flexibility in both policy and force structure was not, however, lost on Whitehall after June 1982. The economics of British defense policy after the Falklands War, as demonstrated by "Fortress Falklands" and increased power projection capabilities, underlined a change in orientation.

That change, which was foisted on Whitehall by the Falklands War, manifested itself in several areas of British defense policy. Apart from structural changes relating to power projection capabilities and commitments, there were also changes of a politicostrategic nature. The war, while demonstrating the need for a better and a more effective political analytic capability, also highlighted the salience of strong political will. The potency of the British government's will was equal to the recalcitrance of the junta's attitude. In such a climate, a clash of arms appeared unavoidable.

While the war did not bring about a reordering or a radical restructuring of British defense policy, it nonetheless spotlighted a few weak links in that policy. The move towards a more flexible military capability in the context of a weakened economy would seem to suggest that wider strategic considerations lay behind it. In maintaining its role as a major economic and military power with global interests, Britain could ill-afford not to have certain diplomatic and military capabilities. Those capabilities, especially the military ones, were sharply accentuated after the contretemps with Argentina from April to June 1982. The crucial factor underlining the decision to make those changes in capabilities was clearly strategic.

The Falklands War was definitely not a bolt out of the blue. Neither was it as unique as the official line stated.[119] It was a war that highlighted the precarious and volatile nature of the international system. In a system where sovereign entities prosecute their own interests, collisions and conflicts are inevitable. The watch words are preparation and flexibility. Both of these concepts were strengthened for Britain after the Falklands War. And that strength was derived in part from a healthy appreciation of the changes that characterized the international environment. It was also a war with a near-zero economic entry cost for Britain. However, the consequential costs of the war because of Britain's victory were indeed burdensome.[120] But the burden was not so much predicated on economic considerations of affordability and opportunity costs as it was on perceived political and security imperatives. And these imperatives remained the anchor of post–Falklands British defense policy.

# *Five*

# Conclusion

The Falklands War was an important watershed event that influenced subsequent British defense policy. Although its impact was not earth shattering, it nevertheless constituted a potent catalyst for change in some important aspects of the structure and emphasis in the nation's defense policymaking. During the Cold War, British defense effort was heavily concentrated on the defense of the Central Front and the containment of Communism. This proclivity in posture was determined largely by perceptions of a preponderant external threat and strategic imperatives. But after the conflict in the South Atlantic, changes reflecting strategic mobility in defense strategy began to take place. Thus in a number of ways, the Falklands War served a useful purpose for the seismic events that would unfold less than eight years later. In this chapter, we shall look at four major issues, all of which have an important relation to the analysis presented in this book. These are the political nature of the Falklands question, the time frame of the British decision to recapture the Islands, the recalcitrant issue of economic constraints on the formulation of British defense policy, and finally, the salience of strategic realism in British defense policymaking after the Falklands War.

## The Political Nature of the Falklands Issue in Britain

The end of 1968 marked the complete turnaround of official British policy towards the Falklands. The object of British diplomacy prior to December 1968 was to induce the unwilling (the Falklanders) to accept what some considered to be the unavoidable (Argentinian jurisdiction). However, that objective of British diplomacy was overturned by a Parliament hostile to the idea not only of a transfer of territorial sovereignty but also a transfer of people to a foreign power. In 1968, when Michael Stewart, the "reincarnated" foreign secretary, informed the House of Commons that "the Government of the United Kingdom would recognize Argentina's sovereignty from a date to be agreed," the response from MPs was dramatic and instantaneous. The opposition from both sides of the House was overwhelming. Robin Edmonds, the head of the Latin American Department of the Foreign Office in the 1960s, gave an accurate assessment of the scenario: "He [Stewart] was howled down on the floor of the House, this gentle, kind, humane man. Howled down by members and nobody, no member of Parliament in any party, and above all, not in his own party ever forgot that."[1]

The impasse reached in the House of Commons that year revolved around the entrenchment of the Islanders' wishes and, above all, the promise that those wishes were paramount. From now on, no settlement of the Falklands question can be reached with Argentina without the explicit consent of the Islanders. In short, "the population of the Islands now had the right of veto."[2] But in the context of British diplomacy, the end of 1968 also heightened the nature of the Falklands issue. According to Edmonds,

> December 1968 [was] an absolute watershed. From then on, in my view, in this country the Falkland Islands issue became primarily an issue of domestic politics. Previously, we have regarded it, rightly or wrongly, as largely a foreign policy issue with, of course, like every *foreign policy* issue, some overtones of domestic politics.... From then on it was exactly the other way round—a domestic policy with foreign policy overtones.[3]

Herein lies the quintessential nature of the Falklands issue. It came to the fore as a domestic political issue, no different from issues in Aberdeen or in Kent. This recognition transformed completely official British attitudes towards the Falkland Islands and the Islanders. They were fellow British citizens living on British sovereign territory located 8,000 miles from the homeland. And it was this recognition which was put to the test in April 1982. On this occasion, the House of Commons remained unwavering in its stance. Once again, the Islands were treated more or less like any village in England. The Falklands invasion was seen as a national crisis.

# The Time Frame of the British
# Decision to Recapture the Islands

The time element in the British decision has given rise to much speculation, and many of these conjectures were not unfounded. Some were based on statements adumbrated in the House of Commons, while others flowed from the assumptions inherent in the rational-actor model of decision making. These speculations had one common denominator with respect to the War Cabinet's decision: the decision was taken incrementally and was quite separate from the decision to launch the Task Force. Indeed, the latter decision was regarded widely as one that served to buttress diplomacy, not to lead to war.

The government's purpose, it would seem, was well served through the ventilation of such a view. London was not to appear to the international community to be preparing for war from the outset. Diplomacy had to be seen as being given a chance to work. While it is true that Thatcher never believed for a moment that diplomatic means would bring about the withdrawal of Argentine forces from the Islands, she nevertheless was not hostile or averse to those types of initiatives being pursued. Those initiatives painted a very favorable image of the British government by showing it to be somewhat pacific and not sabre-rattling. Hence the three-pronged tactic was characterized by diplomacy, economic sanctions, and the launching of the Task Force. The latter was seen as an instrument of military pressure and not as a decision for war.

While such a view appeared reasonable, it nonetheless did not reveal the whole picture of the War Cabinet's decision. That decision, as explained by Lord Lewin, told a different story. Lord Lewin, chief of the Defence Staff (1979–82), was a member of the Falklands War Cabinet (see Appendix for the full composition of the War Cabinet) and one of the architects of the government's military posture. The other one was Admiral Henry Leach, First Sea Lord. At the time of Argentina's seizure of the Falklands, Lord Lewin was in New Zealand on official business. He confided to this researcher that during the course of his long return journey to London, the Suez debacle occupied much of his thinking. In his own words: "I was determined that we should not make the mistakes of Suez. The military must have a clear operational directive from ministers as to what they expected us to do, and we would carry it out."[4]

Before Lewin arrived for the first War Cabinet meeting, he had a concise and clear objective typed out. It read in part, "to cause the withdrawal of the Argentinian forces and to restore British administration." "This military objective," according to Lewin, "was in fact an execution of U.N. Resolution 502."[5] But what is very revealing now was the sense of "hopelessness" that Lewin detected when he arrived for that first meeting. He recalls: "The mood was sombre and I perceived a sense of drifting. A firm direction was needed and I provided it with my statement of objective."[6] The statement was not only well received, but according to Lewin, "We stuck to it for the next seventy days—and we achieved it."[7]

At that first War Cabinet meeting, it was firmly understood that if negotiations failed, the Task Force would have to be used. Lord Lewin made it abundantly clear to this researcher that no special or separate decision was taken afterwards for war. "There was," according to him, "a tacit understanding from the inception."[8] In other words, the decision to launch the Task Force which was widely perceived at the time to be supportive of diplomacy, was, in fact, a decision for war, should negotiations fail. Thus, the decision was conditional, and it was this conditionality factor which apparently obfuscated the picture relating to it. Francis Pym, foreign secretary at the time, confirmed that "if we did not manage to get a settlement, we would go to war."[9]

Interestingly, the question of economic cost was never addressed, nor was it a consideration. The higher objectives of national interest made achieving the goal a strategic necessity.

# The Issue of Economic Constraints on British Defense Policy

It is wrong to assume that changes in British defense policy over the past two decades have been associated with purely economic factors. Greenwood holds the view that "economic constraints have compelled successive British governments to take a hard look at the defence effort. But this is not the same thing when one says that economic factors have impelled those changes to defence policy."[10] Any exercise in defense involves a balancing of resources in relation to commitments. This balancing is central in economics. And in the context of the British defense effort, this act of balancing is crucial. But the need to balance resources in relation to commitments does not stem from purely economic considerations, but also from external strategic developments and priorities. If Britain had a permissive economy—one with a high and sustained level of growth—it would be reasonable to assume that Britain would still have forces in Asia and the Middle East. But such an assumption would be highly misleading. Apart from the Far East, economic factors did not influence British withdrawal from its empire. "It was," according to Lord Carver, "the political difficulties of staying in those locations that prompted the decision to withdraw."[11] Thus the crucial decision to withdraw from its empire emerged not from economic factors but from the changing political and strategic developments taking place in the international environment.

While it appears that the British withdrawal from the Far East (1967–68) can be attributed to economic reasons, such a view does not reveal a very accurate picture. The British government clearly experienced economic difficulties in sustaining the "Confrontation," but its decision to pull out came only when the strategic circumstances changed. Thus the force of economic pressures came to bear with a change in politicostrategic circumstances. On the other hand, British military activities in the Middle East were economically feasible. They were getting good value for money. So why leave a good thing? The withdrawal policy that went into operation stemmed from political considerations and not just from economic hardships.

The Falklands War was pursued by the Thatcher government in the face of serious domestic economic constraints. A defense review which was widely regarded as one impelled more by budgetary considerations than by the imperatives of strategy had only just been completed when the South Atlantic erupted. Nonetheless, in the face of all these constraints, the government plunged Britain into a costly war with Argentina. Before that war, economic constraints were perceived to be very important in the formulation of British defense policy. The war demonstrated, however, that economic constraints can be pushed aside for higher national goals. It demonstrated also that the imperatives which economic circumstances have imposed can be overturned by wider political and strategic developments. According to Professor Freedman, "the Falklands did not generate an economic crisis but it was pursued in the face of one."[12] And Gavin Kennedy added, "There never has been a 'golden age' in defence budgeting where resources matched demands upon them and were sufficient to provide what professionals consider to be a 'safe level' of defence preparedness."[13]

# The Salience of Wider Politicostrategic Developments on British Defense Policy

It is abundantly clear that the major influence behind Britain's withdrawal from its empire and its subsequent military contraction has been Europe. The story of British defense policy over the past twenty years eloquently portrays the centrality of the European dimension. The emphasis on Europe arose out of a politicostrategic necessity and not from the dictates of economic permissiveness or constraints. While it is conceded that budgetary considerations allowed certain defense roles to be undertaken, they have not dictated which of those roles ought to be pursued when and how. The matter of sorting out priorities is based on politicostrategic considerations. The decision to sustain and strengthen commitments to NATO flows from these considerations. So too did the British response in the Falklands War.

The war demonstrated in an unambiguous way the impact of external politicostrategic developments in the formulation of British defense policy. Those developments have exercised a profound influence on defense. And apart from the discernible hardware changes which resulted after the war, there was also a return to strategic mobility in defense posture and military orientation. The Gulf Flotilla was a case in point. Moreover, the Falklands War demonstrated the unexpectedness of events and underscored the crucial need of "being prepared."

British defense policy in the post–Falklands era will continue to reflect the imperatives of the external environment. Dramatic and unprecedented political developments in the former Soviet Union and in Eastern Europe have brought about fundamental changes to NATO and to the British defense effort. Cuts and recommended changes in defense expenditures were assessed very carefully in the light of those developments. While it remains inevitable that a thorough review of British defense policy must be undertaken, such an exercise will necessarily depend on the state of the politicostrategic environment at the time. It would have been foolhardy to undertake a defense review in 1989 or 1990, so soon after the fall of Communism and the diminution of the former Soviet threat. But with the dense fog of German reunification and other complex and thorny issues having been lifted, the time has come for a fundamental review of British defense policy to take place.

Whitehall has lost no time in initiating a number of drastic changes in British defense policy. Guided by the notion of "options for change" in the 1990s in the post–Cold War era, the Ministry of Defence in its "Frontline First" defense costs study announced a wholesale review of all the support services. The need to "meet Treasury demands for savings of £750 million a year from 1996–97" lay behind this exercise.[14] But while this series of actions would cut deeply into the support services for the three armed forces, Malcolm Rifkind, the new defense secretary, made it abundantly clear that he would reject any recommendation to cut a support area if it affected frontline capability.[15] Exercise "Frontline First" was deemed a big success from a cost-saving standpoint. Moreover, the Options for Change defense study culminated in a smaller but better equipped armed forces. Behind these notions and exercises lay the guiding posture of strategic mobility. Britain was responding in a very meaningful way to the fundamental changes that were transforming the external political and security environment.

Now that the Cold War has finally ended, Whitehall took the "big decision" in 1995 to cut the armed forces. More than 11,000 Royal Navy, Army, and Royal Air Force personnel were made redundant. With this reduction in place, the armed forces manpower strength will be down to 231,500—48,000 in the Navy, 117,000 in the Army, and 66,500 in the Royal Air Force. These figures represented a considerable reduction in the estimates in the previous year's white paper, when it was stated that the armed forces strength would be 241,000 personnel. But according to the government's 1995 white paper, *Stable Forces in a Strong Britain*, "there will be no cuts to our frontline, even if our commitments reduce." And "with the promise of a period of stability for the three forces, the Government is ready to offer the services of what Malcolm Rifkind, the Defence Secretary, described yesterday [3 May 1995] as Britain's 'world-class Armed Forces' to tackle the peacekeeping commitments that are expected to proliferate during the next few years."[16] The 1995 white paper also warned that even though the era of ideological confrontation with the former Soviet Union had ended, "it would be imprudent to write off entirely the possibility that a strategic threat could re-emerge."[17]

## Conclusion

This work does not constitute a definitive study on British defense policy. Neither is it a historical treatise on the Falklands War. Rather, it involves the use of a case study to support a fundamental thesis. And in the execution of that undertaking, it attempts to paint a broad, as against a very detailed, picture of both the Falklands War and the recent history of British defense policy.

It is hoped that this work will interest students of international relations in general and the community of British defense policy analysts in particular. Moreover, this undertaking is a first attempt to challenge in a broad, comprehensive way the conventional view that economic factors have been the major determinants in shaping British defense policy over the past three decades. This work advances the view that the importance of wider politicostrategic developments taking place in the international environment has been equal to or greater than that of economic factors in the formulation of post-war British defense policy. In short, this analysis attempts to bring balance to the debate on British defense policy. The aim of this book has been to stay on the high ground and examine the broader strands in the analytic process in order to present a comprehensive picture of British defense policy. However, assumptions about world politics profoundly affect what one sees and how one constructs theories to explain events, and it is abundantly clear that the model imposed on the world affects directly the policies prescribed.

# Notes

## Introduction

1. James Roherty, "Policy Implications and Applications of International Relations Research for Defence and Security," in *A Design for International Relations: Scope, Theory, Methods and Relevance*, ed. Norman Palmer (American Academy of Political and Social Science, 1970), p. 184.

2. Michael Banks, "The Evolution of International Relations Theory," in *Conflict in World Society: A New Perspective on International Relations*, ed. Michael Banks (Brighton, England: Wheatsheaf, 1984), p. 4.

3. John Vasquez, *The Power of Power Politics: A Critique* (London: Francis Pinter, 1983), p. 17.

4. Julius Goebel, *The Struggle for the Falkland Islands* (Princeton, N.J.: Princeton University Press, 1982), p. 468.

5. Lord Terrence Lewin, interview with author, London, House of Lords, 21 March 1990.

6. The Rattenbach Report, Article 890. Quoted in A. Gavson and D. Rice, *The Sinking of the Belgrano* (London: Secker and Warburg, 1984), p. 176.

7. Lord Lewin interview.

8. Lord Michael Carver interview with author, London, House of Lords, 20 March 1990.

## Chapter One

1. Hazel Fox, "Legal Issues in the Falkland Islands Confrontation 1982," *International Relations* (November 1983): 2456.

2. See Raphael Perle, *The Falkland Islands Dispute in International Law and Politics: A Documentary Source Book* (London: Oceana, 1983), p. 539.

3. Lario H. Destefani, *The Malvinas, the South Georgia and the South Sandwich Islands: The Conflict with Britain* (Buenos Aires: Edipress, 1982), p. 30.

4. F. S. Northedge, "The Falkland Islands: Origins of the British Involvement," *International Relations* (November 1982): 2170–71.

5. Ian F. Strange, *The Falkland Islands* (London: David and Charles, 1983), p. 25.

6. Ibid., p. 20.

7. Destefani, *Malvinas*, p. 25.

8. Perle, *Falkland Islands Dispute*, p. 540.

9. Ibid.

10. Strange, *Falkland Islands*, p. 18.

11. Taken from Perle, *Falkland Islands Dispute*, p. 540.

12. Fox, "Legal Issues," p. 2464.

13. Sn. Aguirre Lanari, Argentine minister for foreign affairs, Provisional Record of the 51st Meeting, 37th Session of the U.N. Security Council of 2 November, pp. 7–36.

14. Fox, "Legal Issues," p. 2464.

15. Martin Honeywell and Jenny Pearce, *Falklands/Malvinas: Whose Crisis?* (London: Latin American Bureau, 1982), p. 2.

16. Allen Gerlach, "The Falkland Islands," *Contemporary Review*, 240 (June 1982): 287.

17. For a detailed presentation, see *The Disputed Islands—The Falkland Crisis: A History and Background* (London: HMSO, 1982).

18. Honeywell and Pearce, *Falklands/Malvinas*, p. 6.

19. See the *Shackleton Report*, 1976.

20. Richard Johnson, "The Future of the Falkland Islands," *World Today* 33, no. 6 (June 1977): 226.

21. *Economic Survey of the Falkland Islands*, vol. 2 (Economist Intelligence Unit, 1976), p. 104.

22. Peter Beck, "History Goes Public," *Times Higher Education Supplement*, 21 January 1983, p. 13.

23. Josef Goldblat and Victor Milan, *The Falklands/Malvinas Conflict: A Spur to Arms Build-ups* (Stockholm: SIPRI, 1983), p. 3.

24. Letter of 18 October 1982 from the permanent representative of Argentina to the United Nations, addressed to the secretary general, Annex I.

25. Julius Goebel, *The Struggle for the Falkland Islands* (London: Yale University Press, 1982), pp. 1–46. First published in 1927, this book is quite an authoritative work on the history of the Falklands.

26. Destefani, *Malvinas*, p. 50.

27. Ibid., p. 41.

28. David Cross, *Times*, 15 April 1982.

29. Northedge, "Falkland Islands," p. 2175.

30. Ibid., p. 2176.

31. J. C. Metford, "Falklands or Malvinas? The Background to the Dispute," *International Affairs* 44, no. 3 (July 1968): 469.

32. James Gravelle, "The Falkland (Malvinas) Islands: An International Law Analysis of the Dispute Between Argentina and Great Britain," *Military Law Review* 107 (Winter 1985): 12.

33. See Goebel, *Struggle for the Falkland Islands*, pp. 230–40, especially p. 238.

34. Northedge, "Falkland Islands," p. 2177.

35. Taken from Goebel, *Struggle for the Falkland Islands*, p. 410.

36. Gerlach, "Falkland Islands," p. 289.

37. Ove Bring, "The Falklands Crisis and International Law," *Nordisk Tidskrift for Int'l Ret.* (1983), 136.

38. Peter Calvert, "Sovereignty and the Falklands Crisis," *International Affairs* 59, no. 3 (Summer 1983): 406.

39. See V. F. Boyson, *The Falkland Islands* (Oxford: Clarendon Press, 1924), p. 12.

40. Bring, "Falklands Crisis," p. 133.

41. Gerlach, "Falkland Islands," p. 289.

42. Northedge, "Falkland Islands," p. 2184.

43. Strange, *Falkland Islands*, p. 56.

44. Perle, *Falkland Islands Dispute*, p. 12.

45. See M. Gamboa, *A Dictionary of International Law and Diplomacy*, p. 244, and M. Korowicz, "Some Present Aspects of Sovereignty in International Law," quoted in Perle, "Falkland Islands Dispute," p. 13.

46. Michael Akehurst, *A Modern Introduction to International Law* (London: Oxford University Press, 1982).

47. H. V. Hodson, "Sovereignty Demoted," *Round Table* 290 (April 1984): 132.

48. 23 House of Commons Debates (1982), 6th series, col. 25.

49. Peter J. Beck, "Britain's Falklands Future—The Need to Look Back," *Round Table* 290 (April 1984): 141.

50. Roy Jennings, *The Acquisition of Territorial Sovereignty in International Law* (Manchester: Manchester University Press, 1963), pp. 6–7.

51. Perle, *Falkland Islands Dispute*, p. 14.

52. Ibid., p. 15.

53. L. Oppenheim, in *International Law*, ed. H. Lauterpacht (ed.), (London: University Press, 1955), p. 546.

54. Malcolm N. Shaw, *International Law* (London: Hodder and Stoughton, 1977), pp. 220–21.

55. Ibid., pp. 221–22.

56. John Hanessian, *Polar Area Studies*, vol. 2, no. 5, as quoted in *Millenium* (Spring 1983): 26.

57. Gravelle, "Falkland (Malvinas) Islands," p. 22.

58. "Legal Status of Greenland (Denmark v. Norway)," *P.C.I.J.*, serial A/B, no. 53 (1933): 46.

59. Alfred Rubin, "Historical and Legal Background to the Falkland/Malvinas Dispute," in *The Falklands War*, ed. Alberto Coll and Anthony Arend (Boston: George Allen and Unwin, 1985), p. 16.

60. Ibid., p. 17.

61. "The Clipperton Island Arbitration," 2 R. International Arbitration Awards, 1931, p. 1107.

62. Rubin, "Historical and Legal Background," p. 17.

63. Bring, "Falkland Crisis," p. 136.

64. J. C. Metford, "Falklands or Malvinas?" pp. 469–70.

65. Rubin, "Historical and Legal Background," p. 16.

66. Ibid.

67. Moreno Quintana, *Toatado de Derecho Internacional*, vol. 2 (Buenos Aires: Editorial Sudamerican, 1963), p. 148.

68. Quoted in Alfredo Bologna's article, "Argentinian Claims to the Malvinas Under International Law," *Journal of International Studies* 12, no. 1 (Spring 1983): p. 42.

**171**

69. Ibid., p. 43.
70. Rubin, "Historical and Legal Background," pp. 11–12.
71. Bologna, "Argentinian Claims to the Malvinas," pp. 46–47.
72. Bring, "Falklands Crisis," p. 139.
73. Second United Nations Reports of International Arbitral Awards, p. 829.
74. See *The Falkland Islands and Dependencies*, British Central Office of Information (London: HMSO, 1982).
75. See Byron Farwell, "Falklands: Myth and History," *Marine Corps Gazette* (October 1982): 47.
76. Gravelle, "Falkland (Malvinas) Islands," p. 29.
77. David Cross, "History of Sovereignty Claim," *Times*, 15 April 1982, p. 7.
78. Bring, "Falklands Crisis," p. 135.
79. Ibid.
80. Rosalyn Higgins, "Falklands and the Law," *Observer*, 2 May 1982.
81. See *The Falkland Islands: The Facts* (London: HMSO, 1982).
82. *Daily Telegraph*, editorial, 27 April 1982.
83. See *Times*, 12 November 1982.
84. James Fawcett, "Legal Aspects in the Falkland Islands Dispute: International Dimensions," *Royal Institute of International Affairs Journal* (1982): 6.
85. See International Commission of Jurists, "The Argentine Claim to the Falkland Islands," *Review*, No. 28 (1982), 31–32.
86. Beck, "Britain's Falklands Future," p. 143.
87. See House of Commons Foreign Affairs Committee, minutes of the proceedings, *Hansard* (1982–83): XXIII.
88. Gravelle, "Falkland (Malvinas) Islands," p. 32.
89. Beck, "Britain's Falklands Future," p. 144.
90. Peter J. Beck, "Britain's Antarctic Dimension," *International Affairs* 59, no. 3 (Summer 1983): 429.
91. David Stephen, "The South Atlantic Triangle," *Contemporary Review* 242 (February 1983): 89.
92. Peter J. Beck, "Cooperative Confrontation in the Falkland Islands Dispute: the Anglo-Argentine Search for a Way Forward, 1968–1981," *Journal of International Studies and World Affairs* 24, no. 1 (February 1982): 41.
93. Stephen, "South Atlantic Triangle," p. 92.
94. See the four-page special in the *Guardian*, 19 June 1982.
95. Keith Speed, *Sea Changes: The Battle for the Falklands and the Future of Britain's Navy* (Bath: Ashgrove, 1982), p. 117.
96. See, for example, E. G. Irving, *Times*, 26 October 1981, and Lesley Garner, *Sunday Times*, 1 November 1981.
97. See the *Shackleton Report*.
98. See *Hansard* (Commons), vol. 925, cols. 550–552, 2 February 1977.
99. Beck, "Britain's Antarctic Dimension," p. 430.
100. Beck, "Cooperative Confrontation," p. 50.
101. Beck, "Britain's Antarctic Dimension," pp. 430–431.
102. See *Hansard* (Commons), vol. 925, cols. 550–52, February 1977.
103. Stephen, "South Atlantic Triangle," p. 94.
104. See *Hansard* (Commons), vol. 925, cols. 200, 2 December 1980.

105. Beck, "Cooperative Confrontation," p. 51.
106. Beck, "Britain's Antarctic Dimension," p. 432.
107. See *Hansard* (House of Lords), Official Report, col. 185, 30 June 1981.
108. See the *Franks Report*, 1983, para. 115.
109. See *Hansard* (House of Commons ), Official Report, col. 856, 9 February 1982.
110. See the *Franks Report*, 1983, para. 114.
111. Beck, "Britain's Antarctic Dimension," p. 433.
112. See *Hansard* (House of Lords), vol. 426, col. 211, 16 December 1981.
113. Ibid.
114. See the *Franks Report*, 1983, para. 116, p. 34.
115. Beck, "Britain's Antarctic Dimension," p. 433.
116. Lawrence Freedman, "The War of the Falkland Islands, 1982," *Foreign Affairs* 61, no. 1 (Fall 1982): 198.
117. Bernard Crick, "The Curse of Sovereignty," *New Statesman*, 14 May 1982, p. 7.
118. Sir Rex Hunt, "The Falkland Islands: The Political and Economic Aspects," *RUSI Journal* (December 1985): 11.

## Chapter Two

1. Lawrence Freedman, *Britain and the Falklands War* (Oxford: Basil Blackwell, 1988), p. 1.
2. See for example, Max Hastings and Simon Jenkins, *Battle for the Falklands* (London: Michael Joseph, 1983), p. vii.
3. John Maurer, "Sea Power and Crisis Diplomacy," *Orbis* 26, no. 3 (Fall 1982): 570.
4 Thomas C. Schelling, *Arms and Influence* (London: Yale University Press, 1976), p. 2.
5. Captain A. Brent Merrill, "The Causes of War," *Military Review* 62, no. 7 (July 1982): 45.
6 Quoted from David Dunn, "War and Social Change," in *The Use of Force in International Relations*, ed. F. S. Northedge (London: Faber and Faber, 1974), p. 224.
7. Quincy Wright, *A Study of War* (Chicago: University of Chicago Press, 1964), p. 110.
8. See Karl von Clausewitz, *On War* (London: Routledge and Kegan Paul, 1966), pp. 10–40.
9. See John Garnett's "Strategic Studies and Its Assumptions," in *Contemporary Strategy: Theories and Policies*, John Baylis et al. (London: Croom Helm, 1976), p. 5.
10. Mao Tse-Tung, *Quotations from Mao Tse-Tung* (Peking: Peking Foreign Language Press, 1966), p. 58.
11. See Lord Carver's paper in *Symposium on Global Security for the Twenty-First Century* (New York: UN Publications, 1987), p. 71.
12. Merrill, "Causes of War," p. 46.
13. See C. R. Mitchell, "Conflict and War," in *International Relations The-*

*ory: A Bibliography*, ed. A.J.R. Groom and C. R. Mitchell (London: Frances Pinter, 1978), pp. 86–92.

14. The leading proponents of the structural arguments of war are Hans Morgenthau, *Politics Among Nations*, 4th ed. (New York, Knopf, 1967), and Kenneth Waltz, *Theory of International Politics* (Reading, Mass.: Addison-Wesley, 1979).

15. Jack Levy, "The Diversionary Theory of War: A Critique," in *Handbook of War Studies*, ed. Manus Midlarsky (London: Unwin-Hyman, 1989), pp. 259–88.

16. F. S. Northedge, "The Resort to Arms," in *The Use of Force in International Relations*, ed. F.S. Northedge (London: Faber and Faber, 1974), p. 11.

17. Ibid., pp. 12–13.

18. Ibid., p. 13.

19. Barry Blechman and Stephen Kaplan, eds., *Force Without War: U.S. Armed Forces as a Political Instrument* (Washington, D.C.: Brookings Institution, 1978), p. 517.

20. Robert L. Scheina, "The Malvinas Campaign," *U.S. Naval Proceedings* (May 1983): 98.

21. See Martin Honeywell and Jenny Pearce, *Falklands/Malvinas: Whose Crisis?* (London: Latin American Bureau, 1982), pp. 64–65.

22. Ibid., p. 65.

23. Donald C. Hodges, *Argentina's Dirty War: An Intellectual Biography* (Austin: University of Texas Press, 1991), p. 7.

24. Juan E. Corradi, "Argentina: A Story Behind a War," *Dissent* 29 (Summer 1982): 285. This is a very incisive article by an Argentine scholar.

25. Richard Ned Lebow, "Miscalculations in the South Atlantic: The Origins of the Falklands War," *Journal of Strategic Studies* 6, no. 1 (March 1983): 11.

26. See Honeywell and Pearce, *Falklands/Malvinas*, p. 69.

27. Corradi, "Argentina," p. 290.

28. Quoted in Honeywell and Pearce, *Falklands/Malvinas: Whose Crisis?* (London: Latin American Bureau, 1982), p. 67.

29. Corradi, "Argentina," p. 290.

30. Honeywell and Pearce, *Falklands/Malvinas*, p. 69.

31. Hodges, *Argentina's Dirty War*, p. 7.

32. Corradi, "Argentina," p. 291.

33. Roland Dallas, "Which Way for Argentina," *Contemporary Review* (September 1982): 88.

34. Honeywell and Pearce, *Falklands/Malvinas*, p. 74.

35. Ibid., p. 80.

36. See Commander Marshall Van Sant Hall, "Argentina Policy Motivations in the Falklands War and the Aftermath," *Naval War Review* 36, no. 6 (Nov-Dec 1983): 28.

37. Ibid.

38. George Phillip, "Argentine Politics and the Falklands Issue," *RUSI and Brassey's Defence Yearbook 1984* (London: Brassey Defence, 1984), p. 155.

39. Van Sant Hall, "Argentine Policy Motivations," p. 34.

40. Richard Ned Lebow, "Miscalculations in the South Atlantic: The Origins of the Falklands War," *Journal of Strategic Studies* 6, no. 1 (March 1983): 10.

41. E. W. Hunter Christie, *The Antarctic Problem* (London: Allen and Unwin, 1951), p. 265.

42. Van Sant Hall, "Argentine Policy Motivations," p. 24.

43. Lebow, "Miscalculations," p. 20.

44. Phillip, "Argentine Politics," p. 156.

45. Honeywell and Pearce, *Falklands/Malvinas*, p. 81.

46. See Lebow, "Miscalculations," p. 23.

47. J. Nef and F. Hallman, "Britain and Argentina Alike Under the Skin: Reflections of the Anglo-Argentine War," *International Perspectives* (September–October 1982): 6.

48. Ibid.

49. Barry Buzan, *An Introduction to Strategic Studies* (London: Macmillan, 1987), p. 6.

50. See Nef and Hallman, "Britain and Argentina," p. 7.

51. *Guardian*, 3 April 1982, p. 17.

52. David Stephens, "Why the Junta Took the Glory Trail," *New Society*, 6 May 1982, p. 210.

53. The *Economist*, 10 April 1982, p. 23.

54. Lebow, "Miscalculations," p. 5.

55. Scheina, "Malvinas Campaign," p. 117.

56. Lawrence Freedman, "The War of the Falkland Islands, 1982," *Foreign Affairs* 61, no. 1 (Fall 1982): 198.

57. Peter J. Beck, "Britain's Antarctic Dimension," *International Affairs* 59, no. 3 (Summer 1983): 435.

58. See Adrian English, "Argentina's Military Potential," *Navy International* (May 1982): 1046–50.

59. Ibid., p. 1046.

60. Ibid., p. 1047.

61. Freedman, *Britain and the Falklands War*, p. 34.

62. F. L. Hoffmann and Olga Hoffmann, *Sovereignty in Dispute: The Falklands/Malvinas 1493–1982* (Boulder, Colo.: Westview Press, 1984), p. 160.

63. Ibid., p. 152.

64. Martin Middlebrook, *Operation Corporate: The Story of the Falklands War, 1982* (London: Viking/Penguin, 1985), p. 40.

65. Charles W. Korburger, *Sea Power in the Falklands* (New York: Praeger, 1983), p. 23.

66. Middlebrook, *Operation Corporate*, p. 24.

67. "The Falklands Crisis," *Armed Forces Journal* (July 1982): 207.

68. See Mark Hewish, "The Falklands Conflict Part 3: Naval Operations," *International Defence Review* 15, no. 10 (1982): 1340.

69. See Middlebrook, *Operation Corporate*, p. 68.

70. Ibid.

71. John Nott, "The Falklands Campaign," *U.S. Naval Proceedings* (May 1983): 120.

72. See Lieutenant J. V. Goldrick, "Reflections on the Falklands," *U.S. Naval Proceedings* (June 1983): 103.

73. Freedman, "War of the Falkland Islands," p. 201.

74. G. M. Dillon, *The Falklands: Politics and War* (London: Macmillan, 1989), p. 133.

75. See "The Falkland Islands: Background, Political Considerations and Military Operations," *Navy International* 87, no. 5 (May 1982): 1033.

76. Peter Norman, "EEC supported Britain with dramatic speed," *Times*, 14 April 1982, p. 4.

77. See Peter Norman, "Britain urges EEC to impose more sanctions on Argentina," *Times*, 12 April 1982, p. 4.

78. Freedman, "War of the Falkland Islands," p. 201.

79. Dillon, *Falklands*, p. 170.

80. Ibid., p. 176.

81. See Appendix One for a complete list of naval vessels and STUFT involved in the South Atlantic.

82. Hewish, "Falklands Conflict," p. 1341.

83. See Valerie Adams, "Logistics Support for the Falklands Campaign," *RUSI Journal* 29 (September 1984): 43.

84. Charles Koburger, *Sea Power in the Falklands* (New York: Praeger, 1983), p. 91. An entire chapter of this book is devoted to logistics.

85. Captain David Kenney, "The Fascinating Falklands Campaign," *U.S. Naval Proceedings* (June 1983): 100.

86. Neville Trotter, "The Falklands Campaign Command and Logistics," *Armed Forces Journal International* (June 1983): 38.

87. Valerie Adams, "Logistics Support," p. 46.

88. Trotter, "Falklands Campaign," p. 40.

89. See Major W. J. Tustin, "The Logistics of the Falklands War—Part 1," *Army Quarterly and Defence Journal* 11, no. 3 (July 1984): 298.

90. Ibid.

91. Adams, "Logistics Support," p. 46.

92. Major W. J. Tustin, "The Logistics of the Falklands War—Part II," *Army Quarterly and Defence Journal* 114, no. 4 (October 1984): 408.

93. Admiral Sir John Woodward, "The Falklands Experience," *RUSI Journal* 128 (March 1983): 25.

94. Thomas M. Franck, "The Strategic Role of Legal Principles," in *The Falklands War: Lessons for Strategy, Diplomacy and International Law*, ed. Alberto Coll and Anthony Arend (London: George Unwin, 1985): 24.

95. Ibid., p. 31.

96. See Alberto Coll, "Philosophical and Legal Dimensions of the Use of Force in the Falklands War," in *The Falklands War: Lessons for Strategy, Diplomacy, and International Law*, ed. Alberto Coll and Anthony Arend (London: George Unwin, 1985), p. 39.

97. Ibid., p. 43.

98. Ibid.

99. Leslie Green, "The Falklands, the Law and the War," in *The Yearbook of World Affairs 1984* (London: Stevens and Sons, 1984), p. 112.

100. Coll, "Philosophical and Legal Dimensions," p. 45.

101. James Fawcett, "The Falklands and the Law," *World Today* 38, no. 6 (June 1992): 205.

102. See letter by Professor Rosalyn Higgins, *Times*, 30 April 1982.

103. See Alejandro Dabat, *Argentina: The Malvinas and the End of Military Rule* (London: Verso Editions, 1984), p. 75.

104. David Rock, *Argentina 1516–1987: From Spanish Colonization to the Falklands War and Alfonsin* (London: I. B. Tauris, 1987): 374.

105. Phil Williams, "Miscalculation, Crisis Management and the Falklands Conflict," *World Today* 39, no. 4 (April 1983): 144.

## Chapter Three

1. Douglas McCallum, "What Is Politics," in *The Pieces of Politics*, ed. Richard Incy (Melbourne: Macmillan, 1983), p. 428.

2. A. Anichkin, "The Britain-Argentina Crisis," *New Times*, 16 April 1982, p. 8.

3. Dmitry Volsky, "The Mainsprings of the Conflict," *New Times*, 20 May 1982, p. 8.

4. Vitaly Korionov, "Crime in the South Atlantic," *Pravda*, 24 May 1982, p. 5.

5. Alexander Haig, *Caveat: Realism, Reagan and Foreign Policy* (London: Weidenfeld and Nicolson, 1984), pp. 267–268.

6. Ibid., p. 268.

7. Johan Galtung, "Battle for the Falklands: What Kind of Conflict?" *Trinidad Guardian*, 6 June 1982, p. 2.

8. Ibid.

9. See Anthony Barnett, "Iron Britannia," *New Left Review*, no. 134 (July-August 1982): 1–96.

10. Ibid., p. 67.

11. See Michael Banks, "The Inter-Paradigm Debate," in *International Relations Theory: A Handbook of Current Theory*, ed. A. J. R. Groom and M. Light (London: Pinter, 1985), p. 17.

12. Ibid., p. 18.

13. Editorial, *Times of India*, 20 May 1982, p. 5.

14. Haig, *Caveat*, p. 281.

15. Ove E. Bring, "The Falklands Crisis and International Law," *Nordisk Tidskrift for Int'l Ret.* 51 (1982): 144.

16. See Chapter Three for an extensive treatment of this dispute.

17. Interview with Dr. Victor Millan, a research fellow at SIPRI, May 1984.

18. John Ball et al., *War in the Falklands* (New York: Harper and Row, 1982), p. 119.

19. Editorial, "Fallout from the Falklands: a Preliminary Assessment," *International Defence Review* 15, no. 6 (1982).

20. Lord Shackleton, *Falkland Islands Economic Study 1982* (London: HMSO, 1982), p. 25.

21. A Reuter report, published in major newspapers around the world, expressed in dollar terms the annual receipts from the granting of fishing licenses to Japanese, Russian, and Polish trawlers. In 1986 the Falklands GDP per capita was the highest in the world.

22. Shackleton, *Falkland Islands Economic Study 1982*, p. 95.

23. Ibid.

24. See Alejander Dabat, *Argentina: The Malvinas and the End of Military Rule* (London: Verson, 1984), p. 47.

25. Ibid., p. 48.

26. Bruce Russett, "Security and the Resources Scramble: Will 1984 Be Like 1914?" *International Affairs* 58, no. 1 (1981–82): 42.

27. Peter J. Beck, "Antarctica Since the Falklands Conflict: The Continent's Emerging Role in International Politics," paper delivered at BISA Conference, University of Durham, December 1984, p. 23.

28. Shackleton, *Falkland Islands Economic Study,* p. 69.

29. Ibid., p. 78.

30. John Ezard, "Foreign Fleets Depleting Falklands Fish Stocks," *Guardian,* 10 December 1984, p. 28.

31. See the *1976 Shackleton Report,* p. 6.

32. J. Goldblat and V. Millan, *The Falklands/Malvinas Conflict: A Spur to Arms Build-ups* (Stockholm: SIPRI, 1983), p. 3.

33. Sir Donald Logan, "Resources of the Falkland Islands" in *Falklands Islands Dispute: International Dimensions* (London: RIIA, 1982), p. 10.

34. David Brown, *The Royal Navy and the Falklands War* (Leo Cooper, 1987), p. 22.

35. Captain Joquin Stella, "Stabilizing the Uneasy South Atlantic," *U.S. Naval Proceedings* (March 1989): 59.

36. Ibid.

37. Peter J. Beck, *The Falkland Islands as an International Problem* (London: Routledge, Chapman, and Hall, 1985), p. 145.

38. Louis Peltier and Etzel Pearcy, *Military Geography* (Princeton: Van Nostrand, 1966), p. 138.

39. Andrew Thompson, "Who Controls the South Atlantic?" *New Statesman,* 7 May 1982, p. 5.

40. Ibid.

41. Stewart Menaul, "British Defence Perspectives After the Falklands War," *Strategic Review* 12, no. 1 (Winter 1984): 48.

42. See "Panama Canal No Longer Vital to the United States," *Gleaner,* 19 December 1989, p. 38. The article quotes the views of Michael Kozak, principal deputy assistant secretary in the United States Bureau for Inter-American Affairs.

43. Ibid.

44. Shackleton, *Falkland Islands Economic Study 1982,* p. 3.

45. Goldblat and Millan, *Falklands/Malvinas Conflict,* p. 3.

46. Haig, *Caveat,* p. 267.

47. Ajit Singh, "Full Employment Capitalism," *Socialist Register* (December 1981): 12.

48. Rupert Pennant-Rea, "Three Years of Hard Thatcher," *Economist,* 1 May 1982, p. 42.

49. Barnett, "Iron Britannia," p. 51.

50. *Economist,* 1 May 1982, p. 41.

51. Lord Carrington, in a letter to author, 1 February 1990.

52. Haig, *Caveat,* p. 265.

53. See *The Falklands Campaign: A Digest of Debates in the House of Commons, April to June 1982* (London: HMSO, 1982), p. 5.

54. *Nairobi Daily Nation,* 16 June 1982, p. 10.

55. *La Repubblica* (Rome), 6 May 1982, p. 7.

56. *Background Brief: Falkland Islands—Self-Determination* (London: FCO, 1982), p. 3.

57. Ibid., p. 1.

58. Quoted in *Falkland Islands Dispute: International Dimensions* (London: RIIA, 1982), p. 8.

59. Ibid.

60. Quoted James Cable, *Diplomacy at Sea* (London: Macmillan, 1985), p. 104.

61. Ibid.

62. Christopher Dobson et al., *The Falklands Conflict* (London: Coronet, 1982), p. 53.

63. See Cable, *Diplomacy at Sea*, p. 103.

64. Ibid., p. 104.

65. Ibid.

66. Quoted in John Laffin, *Fight for the Falklands* (London: Sphere, 1982), p. 19.

67. See *Falklands Campaign: Digest of Debates*, p. 17.

68. David Watt, *Falkland Islands Dispute* (London: RIIA, 1982), p. 24.

69. Lord Peter Carrington, *Reflect on Things Past* (London: Collins, 1988), p. 340.

70. Dov Zakheim, "The South Atlantic Conflict: Strategic, Military and Technological Lessons," in *The Falklands War*, ed. Alberto Coll and Anthony Arend (Boston: George Allen and Unwin, 1985), p. 170.

71. *Daily Express*, 26 July 1982, p. 8.

72. Denzil Dunnet, "Self-determination and the Falklands," *International Affairs* 59, no. 3 (Summer 1983): 415.

73. See *A Digest of Debates in the House of Commons, 2 April to 15 June 1982*, p. 77.

74. Ibid, p. 277.

75. See *Britain and the Falklands Crisis: A Documentary Record*, pamphlet no. 176 (London: HMSO, 1982), p. 5.

76. Ibid.

77. Max Hastings and Simon Jenkins, *The Battle for the Falklands* (New York: W. W. Norton, 1983), p. 335.

78. Laffin, *Fight for the Falklands*, p. 156.

79. *Illustrated Weekly of India*, Bombay, 9 May 1982, p. 5.

80. *Times of Zambia*, 24 May 1982, p. 3.

81. *Philadelphia Enquirer*, 16 June 1982, p. 7.

82. *Estado de São Paulo* (Brazil), 16 June 1982, p. 4.

83. *Dominion* (Wellington, New Zealand), 16 June 1982, p. 5.

84. James D. Hessman, "The Lessons of the Falklands," *Sea Power* (July 1982): 18.

85. See Nigel Williamson, "Fate of the Ilois People," *Tribune*, 25 June 1982, pp. 7–8.

86. Peter Kellner, "Mrs. Thatcher's War of Bogus Principles," *New Statesman*, 21 May 1982, p. 5.

87. Barnett, "Iron Britannia," p. 52.

88. See Bruce L. Berg, *Qualitative Research Methods for the Social Sciences* (Newton, Mass.: Allyn and Bacon, 1989), p. 15.

89. Admiral Stansfield Turner, "The Unobvious Lessons of the Falklands War," *U.S. Naval Proceedings* (April 1983): 53.

90. Haig, *Caveat*, pp. 297–8.
91. See the Terry Coleman interview, *Guardian*, 12 June 1982.
92. Haig, *Caveat*, pp. 273–74.
93. Douglas Kinney, *National Interest/National Honour: The Diplomacy of the Falklands Crisis* (New York: Praeger, 1989), p. 114.
94. The *Times*, 29 April 1982, p. 10.
95. Turner, "Unobvious Lessons," p. 53.
96. Lord Pym, letter to author, 26 January 1990.
97. Carrington, letter, 1 February 1990.
98. Sir Nicholas Henderson, "America and the Falklands," *Economist*, 12 November 1983, p. 49.
99. See *Strategic Survey*, 1982–83, p. 119.
100. Ibid.
101. Kinney, *National Interest/National Honour*, p. 4.
102. Ibid., p. 6.
103. Lord Lewin, interview with author, 21 March 1990.

## Chapter Four

1. Walter Little, "Anglo-Argentine Relations and the Management of the Falklands Question," in *British Foreign Policy Under Thatcher*, ed. Peter Byrd (Oxford: Phillip Allan, 1988), p. 152.
2. Peter Calvert, "Britain, Argentina, and the Falklands," *Contemporary Review* 224 (February 1984): 66.
3. Lawrence Freedman, "British Defence Policy After the Falklands," in *Alternative Approaches to British Defence Policy*, ed. John Baylis (London: Macmillan, 1983), p. 62.
4. See Bruce Watson and Peter Dunn, eds., *Military Lessons of the Falkland Islands War: Views from the United States* (Boulder, Colo.: Westview, 1984), p. 3.
5. G. M. Dillon, ed., *Defence Policy Making: A Comparative Analysis* (Leicester: Leicester University Press, 1988), pp. 18–19.
6. Michael Chichester and J. Wilkinson, *The Uncertain Ally: British Defence Policy 1960–1990* (London: Gower, 1982), p. 51.
7. See Francis Pym, *The Politics of Consent* (London: Sphere Books, 1985), pp. 24–26.
8. *Statement on the Defence Estimates 1980*, Cmnd. 7826 (London: HMSO, 1980).
9. Chichester and Wilkinson, *Uncertain Ally*, p. 67.
10. David Greenwood *Reshaping Britain's Defences: An Evaluation of Mr. Nott's Way Forward for the United Kingdom*, ASIDES No. 19 (Aberdeen: Centre for Defence Studies, 1981), p. 15.
11. David Greenwood, "Setting Defence Priorities," *ADIU Report* 3, no. 3 (May-June 1981).
12. Greenwood, *Reshaping Britain's Defences*, p. 16.
13. See *The United Kingdom Defence Programme: The Way Forward*, Cmnd. 8288 (London: HMSO, 1981).
14. Greenwood, *Reshaping Britain's Defences*, pp. 11–13.

15. David Greenwood "The Fleet, the Falklands and the Future," in *The Yearbook of World Affairs 1984* (London: Stevens and Sons, 1984), p. 61.

16. *The Way Forward*, p. 4.

17. T. D. Bridges, "U.K. Defense: The Next Ten Years," *The Army Quarterly and Defense Journal* 3, no. 3 (1981): 268.

18. Greenwood, "The Fleet, the Falklands and the Future," p. 63.

19. James Wyllie, *The Influence of British Arms* (London: Allen and Unwin, 1984), p. 90.

20. See Bridges, "U.K. Defence," p. 275.

21. John Nott, "After the Falklands, Let's Not Go Overboard on Navy Spending," the *Times*, 27 July 1982.

22. *The Falklands Campaign: A Digest of Debates in the House of Commons, 2 April to 15 June 1982* (London, HMSO, 1982), p. 70.

23. For example, the Israeli operation during the Six-Days War in 1967 cost much more.

24. See Third Report from the Defense Committee, session 1982–83, *The Future Defense of the Falklands* (London: HMSO, 1983), p. xiv.

25. Bridget Bloom, "Nott Announces £1 Million Orders as Result of Falklands Conflict," *Financial Times*, 15 December 1982.

26. G. M. Dillon, *The Falklands, Politics and War* (London: Macmillan, 1989), p. 239.

27. Ibid., p. 241.

28. Report by the comptroller and audit general, *Property Service Agency: Defense Works in the Falklands Islands* (London: HMSO, 13 November 1984), p. 6.

29. Stewart Menaul, "British Defense Perspectives After the Falklands War," *Strategic Review* 12, no. 1 (Winter 1984): 48.

30. Ibid.

31. *The Falklands Campaign: A Digest of Debates, 2 April–15 June 1982*, p. 354.

32. See Appendix 2 for losses of ships and aircraft.

33. See *The Falklands Campaign: The Lessons* (London: HMSO, 1982), p. 46.

34. Peter Smithers, "Lessons of the Falklands Episode," *Contemporary Review* 242 (May 1983): 243.

35. See Brenda Ralph Lewis, "Fortress Falklands," *U.S. Naval Proceedings* (March 1984): 151.

36. Ibid.

37. Keith Speed, *Sea Change: The Battle for the Falklands and the Future of Britain's Navy* (Bath: Ashgrove, 1982), p. 173.

38. Menaul, "British Defence Perspectives," p. 44.

39. Ezio Bonsignore, "Hard Lessons from the South Atlantic, *Military Technology* 6 (August 1982): 31.

40. Anthony Cordesman, "The Falklands Crisis: Emerging Lessons for Power Projection and Force Planning," *Armed Forces Journal International* (September 1982): 29.

41. See Norman Friedman, "The Falklands War: Lessons Learned and Unlearned," *Orbis* 26, no. 4 (Winter 1983): 907.

42. Jeffrey Record, "The Falklands War," the *Washington Quarterly* 5, no. 4 (Autumn 1982): 46.

43. Watson and Dunn, *Military Lessons* (Boulder, Colo.: Westview, 1984), p. 1.

**181**

44. Ibid.
45. Ibid., p. 74.
46. Sir James Cable, "The Falklands Conflict," *U.S. Naval Proceedings* 107 (September 1982): 74.
47. Ibid.
48. Record, "Falklands War," p. 48.
49. David Greenwood argues that "the invasion was indisputably a failure of deterrence." See "The Fleet, the Falklands, and the Future," p. 66.
50. James Hessman, "The Lessons of the Falklands," *Sea Power* (July 1982): 16.
51. See Dov S. Zakheim, "The South Atlantic Conflict: Strategic, Military, and Technological Lessons," in *The Falklands War*, ed. Alberto Coll and Anthony Arend (London: George Allen and Unwin, 1985), pp. 167–68.
52. Ibid., p. 167.
53. John F. Lehman, Jr., *Command of the Seas* (New York: Macmillan, 1988), p. 273.
54. Ibid., p. 273.
55. Zakheim, "South Atlantic Conflict," p. 168.
56. Ray Braybrook, "V/STOL in the South Atlantic: Employment and Lessons," *Military Technology*, no. 4 (April 1983): 82.
57. Zakheim, "South Atlantic Conflict," p. 168.
58. Ibid.
59. Andrew J. Pierre, *The Global Politics of Arms Sales* (Princeton: Princeton University Press, 1982), p. 73.
60. Ibid., p. 102.
61. *Parliamentary Debates*, British House of Commons, 11 May 1966, col. 404.
62. Cordesman, "Falklands Crisis," p. 38.
63. Norman Friedman, "Surface Combatant Lessons," in Watson and Dunn, *Military Lessons*, p. 33.
64. James L. George, "Large versus Small Carriers," in Watson and Dunn, *Military Lessons*, p. 13.
65. See Lehman, *Command of the Seas*, Chapter 8, "The Falklands War."
66. George, "Little Versus Small Carriers," p. 32.
67. Zakheim, "South Atlantic Conflict," p. 172.
68. For example, John Nott.
69. Friedman, "Falklands War," p. 919.
70. Ibid., p. 920.
71. Capt. Roland Brandquist, "Falklands Fallout: Strengthen the Surface Navy!" *U.S. Navy Proceedings* (July 1984): 134.
72. See Earl Tilford, Jr., "Air Power Lessons," in Watson and Dunn, *Military Lessons*, p. 39.
73. See Zakheim, "South Atlantic Conflict," p. 178.
74. See *The Falklands Campaign: The Lessons* (London: HMSO, 1982), p. 25.
75. Record, "Falklands War," p. 44.
76. Peter M. Dunn, "Lessons Learned and Unlearned," in Watson and Dunn, *Military Lessons*, p. 127.
77. Dan Smuckler, "Sea-Skimming Missiles Creating Waves in Conventional Navies," *Journal of Defense and Diplomacy* 6, no. 12 (December 1988): 44.

78. Ibid.

79. William J. Ruhe, "Smart Weapons," in Watson and Dunn, *Military Lessons*, p. 83.

80. Ibid., pp. 92–93.

81. Ibid., p. 93.

82. Friedman, "Falklands War," p. 926.

83. Janice Stein, "'Intelligence' and 'Stupidity' Reconsidered: Estimation and Decision in Israel, 1973," *Journal of Strategic Studies* 3 (September 1980): 155.

84. General Hopple, "Intelligence and Warning Lessons," in Watson and Dunn, *Military Lessons*, p. 98.

85. See "Falklands Islands: The Origins of a War," in the *Economist*, 26 June 1982, p. 41.

86. Hopple, "Intelligence and Warning Lessons," p. 104.

87. Ibid., p. 111.

88. Peter Foot, "British Defence: The Falklands and After," *AIDU Report* 4, no. 4 (July-August 1982): 1.

89. Peter Nailor, "Lessons of the Falklands Crisis?" *International Relations* (November 1982): 2163.

90. Ibid.

91. Martin Richards, "Current Knowledge, Present Responsibility, Immediately Relevant Experience," *The Army Quarterly and Defense Journal* 112, no. 3 (July 1982): 263.

92. See David Greenwood, "Defense," in *Public Expenditure Policy 1984–85*, ed. Paul Cockle (London: Macmillan, 1984), p. 172.

93. Ibid.

94. Ibid., p. 182.

95. See *Statement on the Defense Estimates 1987, Cmnd. 101–II* (London: HMSO, 1987), p. 9.

96. Eric J. Grove, "After the Falklands," *U.S. Naval Proceedings* (March 1986): 124.

97. David Greenwood, "Revising the Blueprint: British Defense Policy After the Falklands," *Defense Attaché*, no. 4 (1982): 19.

98. See Lawrence Freedman, "British Defense Policy After the Falklands," in *Alternative Approaches to British Defense Policy*, ed. John Baylis (London: Macmillan, 1983), p. 64.

99. Ibid.

100. John Baylis, *British Defense Policy: Striking the Right Balance* (London: Macmillan, 1989), p. 136.

101. Eric J. Grove, *Vanguard to Trident: British Naval Policy since World War II* (London: Bodley Head, 1987), p. 351.

102. Ibid., p. 357.

103. Ibid., p. 386.

104. *Statement on the Defense Estimates 1984, Cmnd. 9227-I* (London: HMSO, 1984), p. 29.

105. See *The Falklands Campaign: The Lessons* (London: HMSO, 1982), pp. 34–35, for a complete listing.

106. Freedman, "British Defense Policy After the Falklands," p. 67.

107. *The Falklands Campaign: The Lessons*, p. 32.

108. Admiral J. R. Hill, *The Future Size and Role of the Royal Navy's Surface Fleet*, Defense Committee Sixth Report, session 1987–88 (London: HMSO, 1988), p. 11.

109. See the *Financial Times*, 23 November 1987, p. 12.

110. *Falklands Campaign: The Lessons*, p. 35.

111. See Baylis, *British Defense Policy*, pp. 26–28, for an account of the arguments.

112. Ibid., p. 28.

113. See Greenwood, "The Fleet, the Falklands and the Future," p. 68.

114. Lord Chalfont, "Defence After the Falklands," *Daily Telegraph*, 25 May 1982, p. 14.

115. "No End of Lesson: IV," *Times*, editorial, 5 November 1982.

116. Admiral Sir Henry Leach, lecture given to RUSI, June 1981, quoted in Desmond Wettern, "First Sea Lord and Nott Clash on Post-Falkland Cuts for Navy," *Daily Telegraph*, 15 November 1982.

117. Clive Archer, "The Royal Navy's Surface Fleet: Relative Priorities in a National and Alliance Context," in *The Future Size and Role of the Royal Navy's Surface Fleet*, Defense Committee Sixth Report, session 1987–88 (London: HMSO, 1988), p. 177.

118. See Zakheim, "South Atlantic Conflict," pp. 183 and 186.

119. See *The Falklands Campaign: The Lesson* , p. 15.

120. See Gavin Kennedy, "War Economics," in *The Lessons of Recent Wars in the Third World*, vol. 2, ed. S. Neuman and R. Harkavy (Boston, Mass.: Lexington Books, 1987), p. 99.

## Chapter Five

1. Quoted in Michael Charlton, *The Little Platoon: Diplomacy and the Falklands Dispute* (Oxford: Basil Blackwell, 1989), p. 27.

2. Ibid., pp. 27–28.

3. Ibid.

4. Ibid., p. 193.

5. Lord Lewin, interview with author, 21 March 1990.

6. Ibid.

7. Quoted in Charlton, *Little Platoon*, p. 191.

8. Lewin, interview, 21 March 1990.

9. Charlton, *Little Platoon*, p. 191.

10. David Greenwood, interview with author, 16 March 1990.

11. Lord Carver, interview with author, 20 March 1990.

12. Professor Lawrence Freedman, interview with author, 19 March 1990.

13. Gavin Kennedy, "Managing the Defense Budget," *The Royal Bank of Scotland Review* (Summer 182): pp. 18–19.

14. Michael Evans, "Rifkind Vows to Defend 'Formidable' Forces," the *Times*, 27 April 1994, p. 8.

15. Ibid.

16. Evans, "Government Rules Out Further Cuts in Armed Forces," the *Times*, 4 May 1995, p. 4.

17. See *Statement on the Defence Estimates* (London: HMSO, 1995).

# *Appendix A*

# British Naval Vessels Involved in the South Atlantic During the Falklands War

*Covering approximately the period through August 1982*

**Warships**
HMS *Active* (Type 21 frigate)
HMS *Alacrity* (Type 21 frigate)
HMS *Amazon* (Type 21 frigate)
HMS *Ambuscade* (Type 21 frigate)
HMS *Andromeda* (Leander-class frigate)
HMS *Antelope* (Type 21 frigate)
HMS *Antrim* (country-class destroyer)
HMS *Apollo* (Leander-class frigate)
HMS *Ardent* (Type 21 frigate)
HMS *Arethusa* (Leander-class frigate)
HMS *Argonaut* (Leander-class frigate)
HMS *Ariadne* (Leander-class frigate)
HMS *Arrow* (Type 21 frigate)
HMS *Avenger* (Type 21 frigate)
HMS *Bacchante* (Leander-class frigate)
HMS *Battleaxe* (Type 22 frigate)
HMS *Birmingham* (Type 42 destroyer)
HMS *Brazen* (Type 22 frigate)
HMS *Bristol* (Type 82 cruiser)
HMS *Broadsword* (Type 22 frigate)
HMS *Brilliant* (Type 22 frigate)
HMS *Cardiff* (Type 42 destroyer)
HMS *Coventry* (Type 42 destroyer)
HMS *Danae* (Leander-class frigate)
HMS *Diomede* (Leander-class frigate)
HMS *Exeter* (Type 42 destroyer)

HMS *Fearless* (assault ship)
HMS *Glamorgan* (country-class destroyer)
HMS *Glasgow* (Type 42 destroyer)
HMS *Hermes* (V/STOL carrier)
HMS *Intrepid* (assault ship)
HMS *Invincible* (V/STOL carrier)
HMS *Illustrious* (V/STOL carrier)
HMS *Liverpool* (Type 42 destroyer)
HMS *Minerva* (Leander-class frigate)
HMS *Penelope* (Leander-class frigate)
HMS *Plymouth* (Type 12 frigate)
HMS *Sheffield* (Type 42 destroyer)
HMS *Southampton* (Type 42 destroyer)
HMS *Yarmouth* (Type 12 frigate)
Plus several submarines

**Auxiliary Vessels**
RFA *Appleleaf* (large fleet tanker)
RFA *Bayleaf* (large fleet tanker)
RFA *Blue Rover* (small fleet tanker)
RFA *Brambleleaf* (large fleet tanker)
RFA *Engadine* (helicopter support ship)
RFA *Fort Austin* (fleet replenishment ship)
RFA *Fort Grange* (fleet replenishment ship)

RMAS *Goosander* (mooring, salvage, and boom vessel)
RFA *Olmeda* (large fleet tanker)
RFA *Olina* (large fleet tanker)
RFA *Olwen* (large fleet tanker)
RFA *Pearleaf* (support tanker)
RFA *Plumleaf* (support tanker)
RFA *Regent* (fleet replenishment ship)
RFA *Resource* (fleet replenishment ship)
RFA *Sir Bedivere* (logistic landing ship)
RFA *Sir Galahad* (logistic landing ship)
RFA *Sir Geraint* (logistic landing ship)
RFA *Sir Lancelot* (logistic landing ship)
RFA *Sir Percivale* (logistic landing ship)

RFA *Sir Tristram* (logistic landing ship)
RFA *Stromness* (stores support ship)
RFA *Tidepool* (large fleet tanker)
RFA *Tidespring* (large fleet tanker)
RMAS *Typhoon* (ocean-going tug)

**RN Non-Combatants**
HMS *Brecon* (minehunter)
HMS *Dumbarton* Castle (OPV Mk2)
HMS *Endurance* (ice patrol ship)
HMS *Hecate* (survey ship)
HMS *Hecla* (survey ship)
HMS *Herald* (survey ship)
HMS *Hydra* (survey ship)
HMS *Ledbury* (minehunter)
HMS *Leeds Castle* (OPV Mk2)

*Source:* International Defense Review 1982

# *Appendix B*

# British Ship and Aircraft Losses

## Ships

| Serial | Date | Ship |
|---|---|---|
| 1. | 4 May | HMS *Sheffield* |
| 2. | 21 May | HMS *Ardent* |
| 3. | 23 May | HMS *Antelope* |
| 4. | 25 May | HMS *Coventry* |
| 5. | 25 May | *Atlantic Conveyor* |
| 6. | 6 June | RFA *Sir Galahad* |

## Aircraft

| *Lost to Enemy Fire* | | | | *Other Losses* | | | |
|---|---|---|---|---|---|---|---|
| Serial | Date | Aircraft Type | Parent Service | Serial | Date | Aircraft Type | Parent Service |
| 1. | 4 May | Sea Harrier | RN | 1. | 22 April | 2 x Wessex 5 | RN |
| 2. | 21 May | Lynx[a] | RN | 2. | 23 April | Sea King Mk 4 | RN |
| 3. | 21 May | 2 x Gazelle | RM | 3. | 6 May | 2 x Sea Harrier | RN |
| 4. | 21 May | Harrier GR 3 | RN | 4. | 12 May | Sea King Mk 5 | RN |
| 5. | 25 May | 6 x Wessex 5[b] | RN | 5. | 18 May | Sea King Mk 5 | RN |
| 6. | 25 May | Lynx[b] | RN | 6. | 19 May | Sea King Mk 4 | RN |
| 7. | 25 May | 3 x Chinook[b] | RAF | 7. | 20 May | Sea King Mk 4 | RN |
| 8. | 25 May | Lynx[c] | RN | 8. | 24 May | Sea Harrier | RN |
| 9. | 27 May | Harrier GR3 | RAF | 9. | 29 May | Sea Harrier | RN |
| 10. | 28 May | Scout | RM | 10. | 8 June | Harrier GR3 | RAF |
| 11. | 30 May | Harrier GR3 | RAF | | | | |
| 12. | 2 June | Sea Harrier | RN | | | | |
| 13. | 6 June | Gazelle | Army | | | | |
| 14. | 12 June | Wessex 3[d] | RN | | | | |

[a]*Lost in bomb attack on HMS Ardent.*   [b]*Lost in Atlantic Conveyor.*
[c]*Lost when HMS Coventry sank.*   [d]*Lost in missile attack on HMS Glamorgan.*

*Source:* The Falklands Campaign: The Lessons
London: HMSO, December 1982

# *Appendix C*

# The Falklands War Cabinet

Margaret Thatcher (Prime Minister)
William Whitelaw (Home Secretary)
Francis Pym (Foreign Secretary)
John Nott (Defense Secretary)
Cecil Parkinson (Paymaster General)

*Principal advisers*

Sir Robert Armstrong (Cabinet Secretary)
Sir Anthony Acland (Permanent Secretary, Foreign Office)
Sir Frank Cooper (Permanent Secretary, Defense)
Admiral of the Fleet, Sir Terrence Lewin (Chief of the Defense Staff)
Sir Michael Palliser (former Permanent Secretary, Foreign Office, Special
  Consultant on the Falklands)

# Bibliography

## Official Publications

*Britain and the Falkland Islands: A Documentary Record.* London: Central Office of Information, 1982.

*Britain and Its People: An Outline.* London: HMSO, February 1982.

*Falkland Islands: Economic Study 1982.* Cmnd. 8653 (Second Shackleton Report). London: HMSO, September 1982.

*Falkland Islands Review: A Report of a Committee of Privy Counselors.* Cmnd. 8787 (Chairman: The Rt. Hon. The Lord Franks). London: HMSO, January 1983.

*The Falklands Campaign: A Digest of Debates in the House of Commons, 2 April–15 June, 1982.* London: HMSO, 1982.

*The Falklands Campaign: The Lessons.* Cmnd. 8758. London: HMSO, December 1982.

*The Falklands Crisis: A History.* London: HMSO, 1982.

*The Falkland Islands: The Facts.* London: HMSO, 1982.

*The Falkland Islands and Dependencies.* London: HMSO, April 1982.

Fifth Report from the Foreign Affairs Committee, session 1983–84, *Falkland Islands.* Vols. I and II. London: HMSO, October 1984.

First Report from the Defense Committee, session 1983–84, *Statement on the Defence Estimates 1984*, HC 436. London: HMSO, May 1984.

*The Future Defence of the Falkland Islands.* Third report, session 1982–83. London: HMSO, May 1983.

Minutes of the Proceedings of the Foreign Affairs Committee, session 1982–83, HC 380. London: HMSO, May 1983.

Report from the Comptroller and Auditor-General, Property Services Agency, National Audit Office, *Defence Works in the Falkland Islands.* London: HMSO, November 1984.

Second Report from the Foreign Affairs Committee, session 1982–83, *Falkland Islands Inquiry*, HC 378. London: HMSO, May 1983.

Sixth Report from the Defense Committee, Session 1987–88, *The Future Size and Role of the Royal Navy's Surface Fleet.* London: HMSO, 1988.

*Statement on the Defence Estimates 1975*, Cmnd. 5976. London: HMSO, March 1975.

Third Report from the Defense Committee, session 1982–83, *The Future Defence of the Falkland Islands*, HC 154. London: HMSO, May 1983.

Third Report from the Defense Committee, session 1984–85, *Defence Commitments and Resources and the Defence Estimates 1985–86.* London: HMSO, May 1985.
*The United Kingdom Defence Programme: The Way Forward,* Cmnd. 8288. London: HMSO, 1981.
United States Department of State, Bureau of Public Affairs. *The South Atlantic Crisis: Background, Consequences, Documentation.* Washington, D. C.: Bureau of Public Affairs, August 1982.


## Books

Ball, John, et al. *War in the Falklands.* New York: Harper and Row, 1982.
Banmann, Carol, ed. *Europe in NATO: Deterrence, Defense and Arms Control.* New York: Praeger, 1987.
Barnett, Anthony. *Iron Britannia.* London: Allison and Busby, 1982.
Bartlett, C. J. *The Long Retreat: A Short History of British Defence Policy 1945–1970.* London: Macmillan, 1982.
Bateman, Michael, ed. *The Geography of Defense.* London: Croom Helm, 1987.
Baylis, John, ed. *Alternative Approaches to British Defense Policy.* London: Macmillan, 1983.
_____. *British Defense Policy in a Changing World.* London: Croom Helm, 1977.
_____. *British Defense Policy, Striking the Right Balance.* London: Macmillan, 1989.
Beck, Peter J. *The Falkland Islands as an International Problem.* London, Routledge, Chapman and Hall, Inc., 1988.
Boardman, R., and A.J.R. Groom, eds. *The Management of Britain's External Relations,* London: Macmillan, 1973.
Bobrow, Davis B., ed. Components of Defense Policy, Chicago, Rand McNally and Co., 1965.
Boyson, V. F., The Falkland Islands, Oxford University Press, 1924.
Braybrook, Roy. *Battle for the Falklands.* Vol. 3, *Air Forces.* London: Osprey, 1982.
Broadbent, Lucinda, et al. *War and Peace News.* Milton Keynes, Open University Press, 1985.
Brown, David. *The Royal Navy and the Falklands War.* London: Leo Cooper, 1987.
Burt, Gordon, ed. *Alternative Defence Policy.* London: Croom Helm, 1988.
Byrd, Peter, ed. *British Foreign Policy Under Thatcher.* Oxford: Phillip Allan, 1988.
Cable, James. *Diplomacy at Sea.* London: Macmillan, 1985.
Calvert, Peter. *The Falklands Crisis: The Rights and the Wrongs.* London: Francis Pinter, 1982.
Cardoso, Oscar, et al. *Falklands: The Secret Plot.* Surrey: Preston, 1987.
Carrington, Lord Peter. *Reflect on Things Past.* London: Collins and Sons, 1988.
Chalmers, Malcolm. *Paying for Defence: Military Spending and British Decline.* London: Pluto, 1985.
Charlton, Michael. *The Little Platoon: Diplomacy and the Falklands Dispute.* London: Basil Blackwell, 1989.
Chichester, Michael, and John Wilkinson. *The Uncertain Ally: British Defence Policy 1960–1990.* London: Gower, 1982.
Cimbala, Stephen. *NATO Strategy and Nuclear Escalation.* London: Pinter, 1989.

**192**

Coker, Christopher. *A Nation in Retreat? Britain's Defence Commitments.* London: Brassey's Defense Publishers, 1986.

Coll, Alberto R., and Anthony Arend, eds. *The Falklands War: Lessons for Strategy, Diplomacy and International Law.* Boston: George Allen and Unwin, 1985.

Dalyell, Tam. *One Man's Falklands.* London: Cecil Wolf, 1982.

_____. *Thatcher's Torpedo: The Sinking of the Belgrano.* London: Cecil Wolf, 1983.

Debat, Alejandro. *Argentina: The Malvinas and the End of Military Rule.* London: Verso, 1984.

Destefani, Laurio. *The Malvinas, the South Georgias and the South Sandwich Islands: The Conflict with Britain.* Buenos Aires: Edipress, 1982.

Dillon, G. Michael. *The Falklands, Politics and War.* London: Macmillan, 1989.

Dobson, Christopher, et al. *The Falklands Conflict.* London: Coronet Books, 1982.

Dockrill, Michael. *British Defence Since 1945.* Oxford: Basil Blackwell, 1988.

Eddy, P., et al. *The Falklands War.* London: Sphere, 1982.

English, Adrian, and Anthony Watts. *Battle for the Falklands. Vol. 2, Naval Forces.* London: Osprey, 1982.

Fowler, William. *Battle for the Falklands. Vol. 1, Land Forces.* London: Osprey, 1982.

Fox, Robert. *Eyewitness Falklands.* London: Methuen, 1982.

Freedman, Lawrence. *Britain and the Falklands War.* Oxford: Basil Blackwell, 1988.

_____, and Virginia Gamba-Stonehouse. *Signals of War: The Falklands Conflict of 1982.* London: Faber and Faber, 1990.

Fursdon, Maj. Gen. Edward. *The Falklands Aftermath: Picking Up the Pieces.* London: Leo Cooper, 1988.

Gamba, Virginia. *The Falklands/Malvinas War: A Model for North-South Crisis Prevention.* Boston: Allen and Unwin, 1987.

Gansler, Jacques. *Affording Defence.* Cambridge: MIT Press, 1989.

Gantz, Nanette. *Extended Deterrence and Arms Control.* Santa Monica: Rand Corporation, 1988.

Garnham, David. *The Politics of European Defense Cooperation.* Mass.: Ballinger, 1988.

Goebel, Julius. *The Struggle for the Falkland Islands: A Study in Legal and Diplomatic History.* New Haven: Yale University Press, 1982.

Goldblat, Josef, and Victor Millan. *The Falklands/Malvinas Conflict: A Spur to Arms Build-ups.* Stockholm: SIPRI, 1983.

Grove, Eric. *Vanguard to Trident: British Naval Policy Since World War II.* London: Bodley Head, 1989.

Haig, Alexander M., Jr. *Caveat: Realism, Reagan and Foreign Policy.* New York: Macmillan, 1984.

Hall, Ron, ed. *War in the Falkland.* London: Weidenfeld and Nicholson, 1982.

Hastings, M., and S. Jenkins. *The Battle for the Falklands.* New York: W. W. Norton, 1983.

Hobkirk, Michael. *The Politics of Defence Budgeting.* London: Macmillan, 1984.

Hoffman, Fritz L., and Olga M. *Sovereignty in Dispute: The Falklands/Malvinas 1493–1982.* Boulder, Colo.: Westview, 1984.

Honeywell, Martin, and J. Pearce. *The Falklands/Malvinas: Whose Crisis?* London: Latin American Bureau, 1982.

Horton, Frank, et al. *Comparative Defense Policy.* Baltimore: Johns Hopkins University Press, 1974.

Jones, Roy. *Analyzing Foreign Policy.* London: Routledge and Kegan Paul, 1970.

Kennedy, Gavin. *The Economics of Defence.* London: Faber and Faber, 1975.

Kennedy, Paul. *The Realities Behind Diplomacy.* London: Fontana, 1981.

_____. *The Rise and Fall of British Naval Mastery.* London: Allen Lane, 1976.

Kinney, Douglas. *National Interest/National Honour: The Diplomacy of the Falklands Crisis.* New York: Praeger, 1989.

Kissinger, Henry. *Nuclear Weapons and Foreign Policy.* New York: W. W. Norton, 1969.

Koburger, Charles. *Sea Power in the Falklands.* New York: Praeger, 1983.

Laffin, John. *Fight for the Falklands.* London: Sphere, 1982.

Lehman, John F., Jr. *Command of the Seas.* New York: Macmillan, 1988.

Middlebrook, Martin. *Operation Corporate: The Story of the Falklands War.* London: Viking, Penguin, 1985.

Nailor, Peter. "Defence Policy and Foreign Policy." In *The Management of Britain's External Relations,* ed. R. Boardman and A. Groom (London: Macmillan, 1973).

Neuman, S., and Robert Harkavy, eds. *The Lessons of Recent Wars in the Third World.* Vol. I. Mass.: Lexington Books, 1985.

_____, eds. *The Lessons of Recent Wars in the Third World.* Vol. II. Mass.: Lexington Books, 1987.

Northedge, F. S. *The International Political System.* London: Faber and Faber, 1976.

*Omega Report, Defence Policy.* London: Adam Smith Institute, 1984.

O'Neal, Robert, and D. M. Harner, eds. *New Directions in Strategic Thinking.* London: George Allen and Unwin, 1981.

Peltier, Louis, and Etzel Pearcy. *Military Geography.* N.J.: Van Nostrand, 1966.

Perl, Raphael. *The Falkland Islands Dispute in International Law and Politics.* London: Oceana, 1983.

Pierre, Andrew. *The Global Politics of Arms Sales.* Princeton: Princeton University Press, 1982.

Pym, Francis. *The Politics of Consent.* London: H. Hamilton, 1984.

Quester, George. *The Falklands and the Malvinas: Strategy and Arms Control.* Los Angeles: University of California Center for International Strategic Affairs, May 1984.

Rice, Desmond, and Arthur Gavsham. *The Sinking of the Belgrano.* London: Secker and Warburg, 1984.

Rock, David. *Argentina 1516–1987: From Spanish Colonization to the Falklands War and Alfonsin.* London: I. B. Tauris, 1987.

Roherty, James, ed. *Defense Policy Formation.* N.C.: Carolina Academic Press, 1980.

Roper, John, ed. *The Future of British Defence Policy.* London: Gower, 1985.

Rushbridge, James. *The Intelligence Game.* London: Bodley Head, 1989.

Scheina, Robert L. *Latin America: A Naval History 1810–1987.* Annapolis: U.S. Naval Institute Press, 1987.

Shaw, G. K. *Keynesian Economics: The Permanent Revolution.* London: Edward Elgar, 1988.

Smith, Dan. *The Defence of the Realm in the 1980's.* London: Croom Helm, 1980.

Speed, Keith. *Sea Changes: The Battle for the Falklands and the Future of Britain's Navy.* Bath: Ashgrove, 1982.

Strange, Ian. *The Falkland Islands.* Rev. ed. London: David and Charles, 1983.

Sunday Times Insight Team. *The Falklands War.* London: Sphere, 1982.

Thompson, Julian. *No Picnic.* London: Secker and Warburg, 1985.

Vasquez, John. *The Power of Power Politics: A Critique.* London: Francis Pinter, 1983.

Wallace, William. *The Foreign Policy Process in Britain.* London: George Allan and Unwin, 1977.

Watson, Bruce, and Peter Dunn, eds. *Military Lessons of the Falkland Islands War: Views from the United States.* Boulder, Colo.: Westview, 1984.

Wyllie, James H. *The Influence of British Arms.* London: Allen and Unwin, 1984.

Zakheim, Dov S. "The South Atlantic Conflict: Strategic, Military, and Technological Lessons." In *The Falklands War: Lessons for Strategy, Diplomacy and International Law,* ed. Alberto Coll and Anthony Arend. Boston: Allen and Unwin, 1985.

## Articles

Acland, Anthony. "The Relationship Between Foreign and Defence Policy." *RUSI Journal* 128 (June 1983).

Adams, Valerie. "Logistic Support for the Falklands Campaign." *RUSI Journal* 129 (September 1984).

Ambrose, A. J. "Falkland Islands: Logistics—The Involvement of the Merchant Navy." *Navy International* 87, no. 5 (May 1982).

Bailey, Jonathan. "Training for War: The Falklands 1982." *Military Review* 63, no. 9 (September 1983).

Bailly, Louis L. "The Navy and the Media." *Naval Review* 71, no. 3 (July 1983).

Baker, A. D. "Aircraft Carriers in the Falklands." *U.S. Naval Proceedings* (February 1984).

Baylis, John. "Defence Decision-Making in Britain and the Determinants of Defence Policy." *RUSI Journal* (March 1975).

_____. "What Is Britain's Defence Policy?: 'Greenwoodery' and British Defence Policy," *International Affairs* 62, no. 3 (Summer 1986).

Beck, Peter J. "The Anglo-Argentine Dispute Over Title to the Falklands: Changing British Perception on Sovereignty Since 1910." *Journal of International Studies* 12, no. 1 (Spring 1983).

_____. "Britain's Antarctic Dimension." *International Affairs* 59, no. 3 (Summer 1983).

_____. "Britain's Falklands Future—The Need to Look Back." *Round Table* 290 (April 1984).

_____. "Cooperative Confrontation in the Falkland Islands Dispute: The Anglo-American Search for a Way Forward." *Journal of International Studies and World Affairs* 24, no. 1 (February 1982).

_____. "Falklands or Malvinas? The View from Buenos Aires." *Contemporary Review* (September 1985).

_____. "The Future of the Falkland Islands: A Solution Made in Hong Kong?" *International Affairs* (Winter 1985).

_____. "History and Current Events: A Historian and the Media During the 1982 Falklands War," *Current Research on Peace and Violence,* no. 2 (March 1984).

Bologna, Alfredo. "Argentinian Claims to the Malvinas Under International Law." *Journal of International Studies* 12, no. 1 (Spring 1983).

Bonsignore, Ezio. "Hard Lessons from the South Atlantic." *Military Technology* 6 (August 1982).

Brandquist, Roland. "Falklands Fallout: Strengthen the Surface Navy!" *U.S. Naval Proceedings* (August 1984).

Braybrook, Roy. "V/STOL in the South Atlantic: Employment and Lessons." *Military Technology* (April 1983).

Brent-Merril, A. "The Causes of War." *Military Review* 62, no. 7 (July 1982).

Bridge, T. D. "Official Reports of the Falklands Campaign: An Appraisal." *Army Quarterly and Defence Journal* 113, no. 1 (January 1983).

Bring, Ove E. "The Falklands Crisis and International Law." *Nordisk Tidskrift for Int'l Ret.* 51 (1982).

"British Defence Policy 1975." *Survival* 17, no. 3 (May-June 1975).

Brownson, Col. D. "The Falklands 1982—July to December—the Beginning of Rehabilitation." *Army Quarterly and Defence Journal* 113, no. 3 (July 1983).

Cable, James. "Britain's Choice of Threat." *U.S. Naval Proceedings* (August 1982).

_____. "The Falklands Conflict." *U.S. Naval Proceedings* (September 1982).

Calvert, Peter. "The Causes of the Falklands Conflict." *Contemporary Review* 241, no. 1 (Spring 1983).

_____. "Latin America and the United States During and After the Falklands Crisis." *Journal of International Studies* 12, no. 1 (Spring 1983).

_____. "Sovereignty and the Falklands Crisis." *International Affairs* 59, no. 3 (Summer 1983).

Canopus. "A Personal View of the Falklands Campaign." *Naval Review* 71, no. 1 (January 1983).

Cary, Michael. "Britain's Armed Forces After the Defence Cuts." *RUSI Journal* (March 1976).

Centurion. "The Media in the Falklands Campaign: Friend or Foe?" *Naval Review* 71, no. 1 (January 1983).

Chan, Steve. "The Impact of Defense Spending on Economic Performance: A Survey of Evidence and Problems." *Orbis* 29, no. 2 (Summer 1985).

Collier, Simon. "The First Falklands War? Argentine Attitudes." *International Affairs* 59, no. 3 (Summer 1983).

Connell-Smith, Gordon. "The OAS and the Falklands Conflict." *World Today* 38, no. 9 (September 1982).

Cooper, Sir Frank. "The Management of Defence Expenditure," Adelphi Papers, no. 181, pt. I (Summer 1983).

Cordesman, Anthony. "The Falklands Crisis: Emerging Lessons for Power Projection and Force Planning." *Armed Forces Journal International* (September 1982).

Corradi, Juan. "Argentina: A Story Behind a War." *Dissent* 29 (Summer 1982).

Curtiss, John. "The RAF Contribution to the Falklands Campaign." *Naval Review* 71, no. 1 (January 1983).

Dallas, Roland. "Which Way for Argentina?" *Contemporary Review* 240 (June 1982).

Daoudi, M. S., and M. Dajani. "Sanctions: The Falklands Episode." *The World Today* 39, no. 4 (April 1983).

Dar, Maj. Gen. E. H. "Strategy in the Falklands War." *U.S. Naval Proceedings* (March 1983).

Davies, Gode. "Smarter Radar Can Tell Friend or Foe." *Popular Science* (July 1989).

Doxey, Margaret. "International Sanctions: Trials of Strength or Tests of Weakness?" *Journal of International Studies* 12, no. 1 (Spring 1983).

Dunnet, Denzil. "Self-Determination and the Falklands." *International Affairs* 59, no. 3 (Summer 1983).

Dyke, D. H. "Lessons from the Falklands—An Operator's View." *Naval Review* 72, no. 1 (January 1984).

Edwards, Geoffrey. "Europe and the Falklands Islands Crisis of 1982." *Journal of Common Market Studies* 22, no. 4 (June 1984).

English, Adrian. "Argentina's Military Potential." *Navy International* 87, no. 5 (May 1982).

"The Falklands Islands: Background, Political Considerations and Military Operations." *Navy International* 87, no. 5 (May 1982).

Farwell, Byron. "Falklands: Myth and History." *Marine Corps Gazette* (October 1982).

Fawcett, James. "The Falklands and the Law." *World Today* 1, no. 6 (June 1982).

Fox, Hazel. "Legal Issues in the Falklands Islands Confrontation 1982: With Particular Reference to the Right of Self-Determination." *International Relations* (November 1983).

Foxley-Norris, Christopher. "The Impact of the 1975 Defence White Paper." *Army Quarterly and Defence Journal* 105, no. 3 (July 1975).

_____. "The 1975 Defence White Paper." *Army Quarterly and Defence Journal* 105, no. 3 (July 1975).

_____. "Britain's Future Defence Policy: The 1975 Defence White Paper and Its Effects." *RUSI and Brassey's Defence Yearbook* (1975-76).

Freedman, Lawrence. "Bridgehead Revisited: The Literature of the Falklands." *International Affairs* 59, no. 3 (Summer 1983).

_____. "British Defence Policy After the Falklands." *World Today* 38, no. 9 (September 1982).

_____. "Intelligence Operations in the Falklands." *Intelligence and National Security* 1, no. 3 (September 1986).

_____. "The War of the Falklands Islands 1982." *Foreign Affairs* 61, no. 1 (Fall 1982).

Friedman, Norman. "The Falklands War: Lessons Learned and Mislearned." *Orbis* 26, no. 4 (Winter 1983).

Gerlach, Allen. "The Falkland Islands." *Contemporary Review* 240 (June 1982).

Gorman, Stephen. "Security, Influences and Nuclear Weapons: The Case for Argentina and Brazil." *Parameters—The Journal of the U.S. Army War College* 9, no. 1 (March 1979).

Gorton, Stephen. "Thoughts on the Falkland Islands War." *U.S. Naval Proceedings* (September 1982).

Gravelle, James. "The Falklands/(Malvinas) Islands: An International Law Analysis of the Dispute Between Argentina and Great Britain." *Military Law Review* 107 (Winter 1985).

Green, G. H. "British Policy for Defence Procurement." *RUSI Journal* (September 1976).

Greenwood, David. "Constraints and Choices in the Transformation of Britain's Defence Effort Since 1945." *British Journal of International Studies* 2, no. 1 (April 1976).

_____. "Defence Programme Options to 1980–81." *ASIDES*, no. 6 (1975).

_____. "The Fleet, the Falklands and the Future." *Yearbook of World Affairs 1984.* London: Stevens and Sons, 1984.

_____. "The 1974 Defence Review in Perspective." *Survival* 17, no. 5 (September-October 1975).

_____. "Reshaping Britain's Defence: An Evaluation of Mr. Nott's Way Forward for the United Kingdom." *ASIDES*, no. 19 (1981).

_____. "Revising the Blueprint: British Defence Policy After the Falklands." *Defence Attaché*, no. 4 (1984).

_____. "Setting Defence Priorities." *ADIU Report* 3, no. 3 (May-June 1981).

_____. "Why Fewer Resources for Defence?—Economics, Priorities, and Threats." *Royal Air Forces Quarterly* (December 1974).

Greenwood, David, and Julia Drake. "The United Kingdom's Current Defence Programme and Budget." *ASIDES*, no. 17 (Spring 1980).

Guertner, Gary. "The 74-Day War: New Technology and Old Tactics." *Military Review* 62, no. 11 (November 1982).

Hallman, F., and J. Nef. "Britain and Argentina Alike Under the Skin: Reflections on the Anglo-Argentinian War." *International Perspective* (September-October 1982).

Hartley, Keith, and Edward Lynk. "The Political Economy of U.K. Defence Expenditure." *RUSI Journal* (March 1980).

Haynes, Fred. "The Falklands: A Victory for Seapower." *Sea Power* (April 1983).

Healey, Denis. "British Defence Policy." *RUSI Journal* (December 1969).

Henderson, Nicholas. "America and the Falklands: Case Study in the Behaviour of an Ally." *Economist*, 12 November 1983.

Hessman, James. "The Lessons of the Falklands." *Sea Power* (July 1982).

Hewish, Mark, and D. Wood. "The Falklands Conflict Part 1: The Air War." *International Defence Review* 15, no. 8 (1982).

_____. "The Falklands Conflict Part 2: Missile Operations." *International Defence Review* 15, no. 9 (1982).

_____. "The Falklands Conflict Part 3: Naval Operations." *International Defence Review* 15, no. 10 (1982).

Higginbothan, Robert D. "Case Studies in the Law of Land Warfare II: The Campaign in the Falklands." *Military Review* 64, no. 10 (October 1984).

Hill-Norton, Lord. "An Anatomy of Defence Policy." *RUSI and Brassey's Defence Yearbook.* London, 1982.

Hodson, H. V. "Sovereignty Demoted." *Round Table* 290 (April 1984).

Huertas, Salvador. "65 Years of the Argentine's Aviacion Naval." *Defence Update International* 57 (1985).

Jones, B. A. "820 Naval Air Squadron in Operation Corporate." *Naval Review* 71, no. 3 (July 1983).

Kelsey, Robert. "Maneuver Warfare at Sea." *U.S. Naval Proceedings* (September 1982).

Kennedy, David. "The Fascinating Falklands Campaign." *U.S. Naval Proceedings* (June 1983).

Kennedy, Paul M. "British Defence Policy Part II: An Historian's View. *RUSI Journal* (December 1977).

Kirkpatrick, Jeane. "My Falklands War and Theirs." *National Interest* (Winter 1989-90).

Koburger, Capt. C. W. "Argentina in the Falklands: Glory Manque." *Navy International* (May 1983).

Korb, Lawrence. "Defence Policy Making: Constraints and Opportunities." *Naval War College Review* 37, no. 1 (January-February 1984).

Lake, Julian. "A Tactical Analysis of the South Atlantic War." *Naval Forces* 3, no. 6 (1982).

Lebow, Richard N. "Miscalculation in the South Atlantic: The Origins of the Falklands War." *Journal of Strategic Studies* 6, no. 1 (March 1983).

Lewis, Brenda. "Fortress Falklands." *U.S. Naval Proceedings* (March 1984).

Lindsay-Browne M. "Provisioning the Task Force: NAAFI in the Falklands." *Army Quarterly and Defence Journal* 112, no. 3 (July 1982).

Little, Walter. "The Falkland Affair: A Review of the Literature." *Political Studies* 32 (1984).

Lunt, Maj. Gen. J. D. "The Falklands Factor." *Army Quarterly and Defence Journal* 114, no. 2 (April 1984).

_____. "The Last Time We Fought Buenos Aires," *Army Quarterly and Defence Journal* 112, no. 2 (April 1982).

McGruther, Kenneth. "When Deterrence Fails: The Nasty Little War for the Falkland Islands." *Naval War College Review* (March-April 1983).

McKearney, T. J. "An Old-Fashioned Modern War." *U.S. Naval Proceeding* (November 1982).

Makin, Guillermo. "Argentine Approaches to the Falklands/Malvinas: Was the Resort to Violence Foreseeable?" *International Affairs* 59, no. 3 (Summer 1983).

_____. "The Military in Argentine Politics, 1880–1982." *Journal of International Studies* 12, no. 1 (Spring 1983).

Mason, Roy. "Setting British Defence Priorities." *Survival* 17, no. 5 (September-October 1975).

Matthew, John. "The South Atlantic: NATO an the Case for South Georgia." *Army Quarterly and Defence Review* 112, no. 3 (July 1982).

Maurer, John H. "Sea Power and Crisis Diplomacy." *Orbis* 26, no. 3 (Fall 1982).

Moore, Jeremy, and John Woodward. "The Falklands Experience." *RUSI Journal* 128 (March 1983).

Morrison, Samuel L. "Falklands/Malvinas Campaign: A Chronology." *U.S. Naval Proceedings* (June 1983).

Myhre, Jeffrey. "Title to the Falklands/Malvinas Under International Law." *Journal of International Studies* 12, no. 1 (Spring 1983).

Nailor, Peter. "Lessons of the Falklands Crisis." *International Relations* (November 1982).

Northedge, F. S. "The Falkland Islands: Origins of the British Involvement." *International Relations* (November 1982).

Nott, John. "The Falklands Campaign." *U.S. Naval Proceedings* (May 1983).

O'Ballance, Edgar. "Falkland Islands: The San Carlos Landing." *Marine Corps Gazette* (October 1982).

_____. "The Other Falkland Campaign." *Military Review* 63, no. 1 (January 1983).

Paget, Julian. "The Falklands Campaign." *Guards Magazine* (Summer 1982).

Perkins, Ken. "Blooded in Battle—An Assessment of British Defence Equipment in the Falklands Campaign." *RUSI and Brassey's Defence Yearbook* (1984).

Philip, George. "Argentine Politics and the Falklands Issue." *RUSI and Brassey's Defense Yearbook* (1984).

Piers. "Maritime Forces for the Future as Indicated by the Falklands Experience." *Naval Review* 72, no. 1 (January 1984).

Reed, Martin. "A Falklands Cruise." *Naval Review* 71, no. 3 (July 1983).

Richards, Martin. "Current Knowledge, Present Responsibility, Immediately Relevant Experience." *Army Quarterly and Defence Journal* 112, no. 3 (July 1982).

_____. "Falklands: The Storm Breaks." *Army Quarterly and Defence Journal* 112, no. 2 (April 1982).

_____. "Falklands Aftermath: A Matter of Morals and Mines." *Army Quarterly and Defence Journal* 112, no. 4 (October 1982).

Russett, Bruce. "Security and the Resources Scramble: Will 1984 Be Like 1914?" *International Affairs* 58, no. 1 (1981–82).

Scheina, Robert L. "The Malvinas Campaign." *U.S. Naval Proceedings* (May 1983).

Simpson, Christopher. "Computers in Combat." *Scientific Digest* (October 1982).

Smart, Ian. "British Defence Policy Part I: An International View." *RUSI Journal* (December 1977).

Smuckler, Dan. "Sea-Skimming Missiles—Creating Waves in Conventional Navies." *Journal of Defense and Diplomacy* 6, no. 12 (December 1988).

Stamp, Lord. "The Challenge of the Falklands." *Contemporary Review* 242 (January 1983).

Steele, George. "Warnings from the South Atlantic." *Orbis* 26, no. 3 (Fall 1982).

Stephen, David. "The South Atlantic Role." *Contemporary Review* 242 (February 1982).

Summers, Col. Harry. "Yomping to Port Stanley." *Military Review* 64, no. 3 (March 1984).

Taylor, Brian. "Coming of Age: A Study of the Evolution of the Ministry of Defence Headquarters 1974–82." *RUSI Journal* (September 1983).

Terry, P. D. G. "The 1975 Defence Review—One Man's View." *Royal Air Force Quarterly* 15, no. 1 (Spring 1975).

Thakur, Ramesh, and A. Wood. "The Falkland Islands Question: Conflict, Crisis, War and Peace." *New Zealand International Review* 1, no. 5 (September-October 1982).

Tremayne, Penelope. "The Falkland Islands." *RUSI and Brassey's Defence Yearbook* (1977-78).

Trotter, Neville. "The Falklands Campaign: Command and Logistics." *Armed Forces Journal International* (June 1983).

_____. "The Falklands and the Long Haul." *U.S. Naval Proceedings* (June 1983).

Turner, Admiral Stansfield. "The Unobvious Lessons of the Falklands War." *U.S. Naval Proceedings* (April 1983).

Tustin, Maj. W. J. "The Logistics of the Falklands War—Part 1." *Army Quarterly and Defence Journal* 114, no. 3 (July 1984).

_____. "The Logistics of the Falklands War—Part II." *Army Quarterly and Defence Journal* 114, no. 4 (October 1984).

Van Sant Hall, Marshall. "Argentine Policy Motivations in the Falklands War and the Aftermath." *Naval War College Review* 36 (November-December 1983).

Vego, Milan. "The Falklands: A Soviet View." *Navy International* (September 1983).

Walker, Peter. "The Opposition's View of British Defence Policy." *RUSI Journal* (June 1975).

Wallace, William. "How Frank Was Franks?" *International Affairs* 59, no. 3 (Summer 1983).

Williams, Phil. "Miscalculation, Crisis Management and the Falklands Conflict." *World Today* 39, no. 4 (April 1983).

Windsor, Philip. "Diplomatic Dimensions of the Falklands Crisis." *Journal of International Studies* 12, no. 1 (Spring 1983).

Wood, Derek, and Paul Maurice. "Fallout from the Falklands, a Preliminary Assessment." *International Defence Review* 15, no. 6 (1982).

Young, Elizabeth. "Falklands Fallout." *World Today* 38, no. 9 (Summer 1982).

Younger, George. "British Defence Policy: A Critical Analysis." *RUSI Journal* 121 (March 1976).

## Interviews and Letters

Barker, Nick, former captain of HMS *Endurance*. Interview with author, 12 March 1986.

Carrington, Lord Peter, foreign secretary at the time of the Falklands War. Resigned from that post on 5 April 1982. Letter to author, 1 February 1990.

Carver, Lord Michael, former chief of Defence Staff and a critical exponent of British defense policy. Interview with author, 20 March 1990.

Greenwood, David, head of the Centre for Higher Defence Studies, University of Aberdeen. Interview with author, 16 March 1990.

Freedman, Lawrence, head of the Department of War Studies, Kings College, London. Interview with author, 19 March 1990.

Lewin, Lord Terence, former chairman of the Chiefs of Staff Committee and a member of the Falklands War Cabinet. Interview with author, 21 March 1990.

Pym, Lord Francis, foreign secretary during the Falklands War. Letter to author, 26 January 1990.

## Journals and Newspapers

### Journals

Adelphi Papers
Armed Forces
Armed Forces Journal International
Army Quarterly and Defence Journal
British Journal of International
    Studies
Bulletin of the Atomic Scientists
Contemporary Review
Defence Attaché
Defence Monitor

Defence Update International
Dissent
Foreign Affairs
Foreign Policy
Guards Magazine
Intelligence and National Security
International Defence Review
International Perspective
International Relations
International Security

Journal of Common Market Studies
Journal of Defense and Diplomacy
Journal of Interamerican Studies and
    World Affairs
Journal of International Affairs
Journal of International Studies
Journal of Strategic Studies
Marine Corps Gazette
Military Law Review
Military Review
Military Technology
National Interest
Naval Forces
Navy International
Naval Review
Naval War College Review
Newsweek

Nordisk Tidskrift (Sweden)
Orbis
Parameters (Journal of the U.S. War
    College)
Popular Science
Proceedings (U.S. Naval Institute)
Royal Air Force Quarterly
Royal United Services Institute
    Journal
Science Digest
Sea Power
Strategic Review
Strategic Survey
Survival
Times
World Today

## Newspapers

Christian Science Monitor
Daily Telegraph
Financial Times
Gleaner (Jamaica)
Guardian (UK)
Guardian (Trinidad)
Independent
International Herald and Tribune

New York Times
Philadelphia Inquirer
Pravda
Times (UK)
Sunday Times (UK)
U.S. News and World Report
Wall Street Journal
Washington Post

# Index

207